THE

SETTING SUN:

A POEM IN SEVEN BOOKS.

JAMES HURNARD.

SECOND EDITION, CORRECTED AND ENLARGED.

LONDON :

F. B. KITTO, BISHOPSGATE WITHOUT.

1871.

PREFACE.

IT may perhaps be as well to state at the outset that
I have entitled my poem "The Setting Sun" in order
to indicate that it was written in the decline of life.
In offering to the public a poem which differs in many
respects from other modern productions, and which
attempts indeed to bring down poetry from its artificial
heights to the level of every-day existence, it is only
fair to myself to describe the principles upon which it
is written. It appears to me that one of the most
essential of these principles is truth—truth to selected
nature—truth as to opinion or doctrine—truth as to
good taste, and truth, or reality, as to the actors in
a poem. In reference to this last point I think that
the poetry which describes an author's own history,
actions, and inner life, is far more effective, excites
warmer interest, and makes a deeper impression
than the poetry which is put into the mouth of a
merely fictitious, or even so-called historical person-
age. I will illustrate my position by familiar examples
taken from the poet Cowper : "The verses supposed

to be written by Alexander Selkirk during his abode
on the island of Juan Fernandez" and the "Lines on
the receipt of my mother's picture out of Norfolk."
In the first example, while we admire the beauty of
the composition and the sentiments expressed, we
feel that Selkirk, a rough sailor, could never have
written the poem, or else we feel that if it had really
been written by him, how much more interesting it
would be.   We perceive that there is something deficient in it; in short, that it is not *true*—and the effect
is impaired.   In the second example, there is no
drawback to our admiration.   We feel its truth in
every line.   The poet is speaking from his own heart
of his own refined emotions and of real personages,
and thus the poem is confessedly one of the most
charming in our language.   At the risk, therefore, of
being called an egotist, of which most writers are so
morbidly afraid, I have in my poem spoken in my
own person of myself and my surroundings, not because I am of more importance than other people,
but because it suited my purpose better, and was most
in accordance with my views of the character and
province of poetry.   Having made poetry the favourite
study of my life, and been a writer of it for nearly
half-a-century, I have boldly assumed that I am a
poet.   To confess oneself a poet in this prosaic

age requires the moral courage of a martyr. If, however, I have assumed too much, I hope to be excused by reasonable people, because I have at the same time compared myself to sufficiently humble objects in the creation around.

The next great principle of poetry is, that it should illustrate the world of nature and of revelation, and the vast range of human interests which are about us, —not merely imaginary creations, and things remote from, and opposed to, actual life.

There are other important principles of poetry, both as regards quality and construction, but I will only add that it must be healthy, not morbid, in its tone ; and varied and interesting, not tedious, in its character; resembling, in short, a pleasant journey with cheerful society through a diversified country, where the eye and ear are delighted every moment with something beautiful, new, or interesting,—a shady lane, a sheet of water, an old ruin, a hanging wood, the carol of a lark, a cheerful homestead, or a happy group of children.

The genius of the poet consists chiefly in the power of throwing over the scenes of nature and of art, the workings of the intellect, and the incidents of life, the glow of his own feelings ; and thus by fresh combinations and arrangements of familiar ideas, creating

new ones, and embodying them in language for all
future time by his mastery over words.

With regard to "The Setting Sun" I wish to say
that it was begun hastily in the midst of deep mental
distress, occasioned by circumstances described in
the poem—the break-up of a household, and the
abandonment of an old dwelling-place. I was solitary, without a home, and without any family con-
nections. In the utter desolation of my feelings, I
found that literary occupation was absolutely necessary
to preserve the equilibrium of my mind. I began this
poem, therefore, chiefly as an amusement, indulging
sometimes in the liveliest fancies and most jocose
ideas, and catching at every straw to fortify my self-
confidence. The opening lines were suggested by the
commencement of a poem by a once favourite author,
Abraham Cowley:

> " What shall I do to be for ever known,
>   And make the age to come my own ? "

After some time, when I became happily settled
in a new home, I continued my poem, embodying in
it fragments of verse composed many years before.
My poem may appear to be written in a careless,
off-hand manner—the subjects being suggested chiefly
by passing events—yet it contains the thoughts and

observations of a long life-time. It has, in fact, cost much labour, but I have endeavoured by art to make it appear a work performed with ease. It was not written to suit the views of any sect or party. I have indulged both in praise and blame, and hit right and left as I saw occasion. And yet I hope there is so much variety in the poem that most persons may find something or other in it to please them. Many, of course, will not understand the humour which it contains, and be startled at the grotesque ideas interspersed here and there like the gargoyles of a Gothic edifice, which shock some people's sense of refinement, but which were not without a purpose in the artist's original design. When my poem comes to be critically examined, I trust that its qualities as a work of art will be recognised, and that these qualities will render it interesting to certain readers who would not otherwise be attracted to some of the topics which I have introduced, if those topics were discussed in a dry didactic discourse. I sincerely hope that the principles which are advocated in my poem may be advanced by its means.

Perhaps I may be allowed to add, for the information of any of my readers who may be interested in the auto-biographical portions of my poem, and more especially as an acknowledgment of my personal gratitude to Divine Providence, that since the first edition was printed, not only have I inherited a handsome fortune, but my domestic happiness has been crowned by the birth of a son.

J. H.

COLCHESTER,
   8th Month, 15*th,* 1871.

CONTENTS.

THE SETTING SUN.

BOOK I.

WHAT shall I do to benefit mankind?
I can both steer a ship and guide a plough,
Manage an oar and wield a farmer's flail;
But we have men enough to cross the sea,
And labouring poor to till the soil of England.
I can make malt, and I can brew good beer;
But some folks think we have too much already,
And look on water as the true elixir.
I can make soap—a very nasty thing—
And yet the very soul of cleanliness;
But there are men enough to make our soap.
I can make candles,—there! I have it now;
I wish to be the illuminator of mankind;
But candles now-a-days are going out,
And gas extracted from the coaly depths,
And oils that ooze from caverns of the earth,
Where they have slept a million million years,
Dazzle our antiquated bats and owls,
And I believe the coming grand discovery
Will be a light to dazzle all mankind.
I can make shoes—a humble occupation,
But a most useful, honourable calling,—

B

A business worthy of an earnest thinker.
The energy required to pull wax-ends
Imparts a kindred energy to the soul;
But there are men enough to make our shoes.
I can write verses—so can everybody,
But who can soar up to the heaven of genius?
Who can sun-graph the fancies of the brain?
Who can distil the quintessence of nature,
And from the contrarieties of being
Extract the harmonies of truth and beauty,
Winning from life its latent poetry?
None but the poet who is born a poet;
And if I am a poet I can do it,
And I was born a poet, and I know it.
Let me pluck up my spirit manfully,
I of this dunghill am cock, and I will crow;
I feel the power within me. I was nurtured,
Cradled, and disciplined and educated
In the great seminary of earth and ocean,
'Midst hardships, disappointments, dangers, difficulties,
Not crammed and drilled in schools and colleges,
According to an all-pervading pattern,
But taught by nature and celestial grace:
And I will use this precious gift of song
So as I may to benefit mankind.

    There! I have made a pretty good beginning!
This is the hardest part in writing letters,
And it is harder still, and far more difficult,
To make a good beginning to a poem;
'Tis easy enough to come to a conclusion.

I wonder what I next shall write about;
My thoughts rush diverse like a drove of pigs !
We judge of poems—as we do of people—
By the impression we receive at first.
My brightest thoughts spring forth spontaneously,
As unexpectedly as shooting stars
Coming from nobody can tell us where,
And going into space no one knows whither ;
Unless I catch them as they flicker past,
And note them down, they die and are forgot.
   But will mankind be benefited by me ?
If not, the fault is theirs, and I am clear.
I have some rather stinging things to say.
'Tis little one can do ; yet not a zephyr
Goes sighing softly through the forest leaves
But helps the mighty processes of nature ;
And not a wavelet curls on the sea-shore
But serves to form the bounds of earth and ocean ;
And thus the poet, dropping here and there
The seeds of truth and beauty, must do good.
   And yet how many men mistake their mission !
How many a cobbler thinks himself a Solon !
Mistaking the ambition for the power,
And, listening to the flattery of the heart,
Grows noteless to the warnings of the brain.
I have beheld a borough magistrate
Sitting in glory on the Bench of Justice
Who had been better picking plums at home.
I have beheld a preacher, bold and noisy,
With brow perspiring, hammering on a text,

Who had been better hammering on a lapstone.
I have beheld a member of Parliament,
One of the actual makers of our laws,
Who had been better sitting on a board
With thread and needle and a brother goose,
Making the breeches of the British people.
But inborn genius never is content:
It wrestles with surrounding difficulties,
And breaks away from its original groove;
Then, if it fails, men straightway call it folly,
And smother it with rancorous ridicule:
But, if it triumphs and achieves success,
Then men proclaim it to be noble greatness,
Flatter it, follow it, and at last bow down to it!
The ship "Success," clear of the rocks and shoals,
Spreads all her sails and catches every breeze.

A curious place is this old town of Yarmouth,
With alleys running through it like a gridiron,
Built on a treeless sandbank in the brine—
A lovely place in summer when the Drive
Along the shore beside the German Ocean
Is thronged with human butterfly existence,
Breathing the strengthening breezes of the sea,
And browning with the sunshine and the salt.
This passion for the pure air of the ocean
Has all grown up within my memory—
Is growing fast, and promises to grow
Beyond all limits of vain calculation.
Our railway system opens up the way
And makes it easy for our dull land-lubbers

To see and to enjoy the open ocean,
And so they flock in thousands to the coast.
And in the hot and thirsty days of summer
You see the youth and beauty of the land,
Drest in the garments proper for the occasion,
Bobbing and ducking in the nauseous waves
With infinite amusement and delight,
Their long hair sodden with the briny water.
Children with white and dainty little legs,
Holding their clothes up to avoid the foam,
Paddling about the playful water's edge,
Or finding never-wearying amusement
In dipping in the sand with wooden spades,
And forming mounds and caves, canals and bridges,
Soon to be swamped by the relentless waves—
All, while engaged in indolent amusement,
Unconsciously imbibing health and strength.

But now how widely different is the scene !
The dreary streets are clogged with dirty snow,
And the sea-beach is bare of human life,
Except a few old weather-beaten sailors
Eyeing the sky, the sea, and heaving ships.
The keen wind drifts the sand along the shore
In blinding clouds of stinging particles.
The dear old jetty is almost deserted ;
And vessels waiting for a change of wind
Lie anchored fast in famous Yarmouth Roads.

The ancient sailor gazes on the ocean
As on the sweetheart of his early days.
Playful and dancing, young and fair as ever,

And kindling memories crowd upon his mind
Of dreadful dangers, wonderful escapes,
And pleasant stories told by daring shipmates.
  I often see and sometimes talk with one
Whose name will long be treasured by his friends—
Old Brock, the marvellous swimmer of the sea,
A mariner of more than common strength,
Large bone and muscle, and a dauntless spirit,
And resolute yet placid countenance,
Tanned of a ruddy brown by sun and wind,
Who, on a moonlight night in chill October,
When he was young, some thirty years ago,
Whelmed in the waters of the German Ocean,
Wherein his shipmates all were swallowed up,
Swam for full seven interminable hours
For precious life, battling the stormy waves,
And praying for the help of Providence.
Thus drifting with the tide some fifteen miles,
At length he spied a little brig at anchor,
Towards which he steered his course with all his might,
And floating past her, though a long way off,
He hailed her with his utmost powers of voice.
The sailors heard his cries, put out a boat,
Found him amidst the waves, and hauled him in,
Half dead, and bore him safely to the land—
A man who had been tried both wet and dry!
I told him I should like to have his portrait.
He shook his head and gravely answered me,
That many gentlemen had wished to have it,
But he would never allow it to be taken.

I sought to know his reason for refusal,
And then I found his noble modesty,
Disclaimed self-merit in his wondrous rescue,
Meekly ascribing his deliverance
Unto the all-sufficient hand of God.—
Though kings in stately palaces may dwell,
A lowly cottage may enthrone a king.
   There is a fascination in the ocean
That stirs the youthful curiosity.
The boy, born inland, longs to see the sea
On which his quick imagination dwells.
He has read Crusoe's tempting narrative
Of dangers and of wonderful adventures ;
Also of voyages and of dreadful shipwrecks,
And he has seen engravings of the sea,
But hitherto has only made acquaintance
With the small village pond near by his dwelling,
Of which the navy is a brood of ducks,
And the frail paper ships which he has fashioned
And set adrift upon the perilous waves.
A charming vagueness fills his youthful mind.
Sideling at evening to his father's chair,
He whispers, " I should like to see the sea ;
I want to go upon it in a ship,
And ride along it, jumping up and down,
And hear the dreadful roaring of the waves.
It must be very wonderful to look at :
So big you cannot see the other side ;
But where you can go sailing on for years,
Because the other side keeps going on—

Where you can look and see plenty of water
To drown a thousand people all at once.
The sea is full of herrings and of whales,
And fish that can bite off a sailor's leg.
Father, as soon as ever I'm a man,
I mean to go to sea and catch a whale."
    How jealous neighbouring towns are of each other!
'Tis thus with Yarmouth and her rival, Lowestoft.
No love, I understand, is lost between them.
They are as spiteful as two rival ladies—
Neither can bear to hear the other praised.
Yarmouth lays claim to prouder ancestry,
And wealth, and consequence, above her neighbour.
Lowestoft, whose emblem is the full-blown rose,
Boldly relies upon superior beauty,
And tosses her fair head in proud defiance.
Beauty, 'tis true, may be her only fortune,
But poverty and pride oft go together.
    Affairs were in this amiable state
When an adventurer blithe, with loads of gold,
And boundless promises of benefits,
Having a handsome handle to his name,
Made suit to Yarmouth, sanguine of success.
The haughty damsel, conscious of her merits,
Thought fit to show her airs, and spurned his suit.
O! fatal blindness of high-topping dames!—
Her slighted lover turned upon his heel,
And made advances to her handsome rival.
Lowestoft received him with annoying favour.
He lavished on her many precious gifts,

Enriched her with his overflowing wealth,
And won her heart as quick as he could kiss.
Yarmouth meanwhile repented at her leisure,
And feeling wrathful at her disappointment,
And desperate at the loss of such a lover,   ·
And jealous of her rival's happiness,
'Tis said is growing indiscreetly reckless
About her character, and has given her smiles
·   To a rich brewer, whose strong beer she likes.
The affair makes endless talk amongst the gossips,
And the Law Courts, 'tis said, will hear of it;
While Lowestoft chuckles at her rival's fall.
   It was " The Shipwreck," sung by Falconer,
That first called forth my love of poetry.
Its music, and its passion, and its pathos,
Carried away my young imagination.
Where can be found a tale of love more touching
Than that of young Palemon and his Anna?
Or where a sad catastrophe more tragic
When the wrecked youth, cast bleeding on the shore,
Breathed his last accents in Arion's ear?
" Tell her, my love inviolably true,
No change, no diminution ever knew;"
And then the ship, the sea, the savage storm,
The final wreck, how vividly the poet
Engraves them all for ever on the mind !
How many a sailor can confirm the story!
   The poet has his mission upon earth,
However much the world may laugh at him,
And call him an unprofitable dreamer,

Misunderstand the workings of his mind,
And sneer, perhaps, at his peculiar ways.
His thoughts live after him, and mould the thoughts
Of other people, while his language lasts.
Is not this task a very noble one?
He may not give men brains who have no brains;
But if they happen to have brains at all
He sows the seeds of common sense in them.

How many a pebble on the ocean shore,
Washed by the briny waves, looks beautiful!
We take it home with fond enthusiasm,
But, after all, our hopes are disappointed,
It proves, when dry, to be a plain dull stone;
And then we cast it carelessly away.
So, when the dew of youth is on the soul,
The glow of boyhood dazzles every one
With prophecies of greatness and of glory,
But when the dew exhales, the shining promise
Soon fades away, and a dry dolt remains.

Which is the most propitious scene for boyhood,
The busy city or the quiet country?
The country air gives health and rosy cheeks,
But adds a sluggish dulness to the brain.
The city makes youth delicate and pale,
But gives a certain sharpness to the wits.
The country boy associates with calves,
Dogs, horses, bullocks, pigs, and clodhoppers,
And grows a tyrant over his inferiors.
The city boy mixes with boys and men,
And hears and sees the ways of human life,

And finds his level in the general throng.
The country boy's amusements are debasing,
And give a fatal hardness to his heart—
Stealing the eggs or callow young of birds,
Fishing with hooks baited with writhing worms,
Making a donkey trot with spur and cudgel,
Rat-hunting, fox-hunting, capturing hares and rabbits,
Or shooting birds—killing a few outright,
Leaving the wounded ones to starve and die.
The city boy enjoys athletic games—
Sees panoramas, exhibitions, palaces,
Shops, mansions, crowds of people, equipages—
All sights and sounds that fascinate the mind,
And stimulate the intellectual being.
Yet has the city its more glaring vices—
Its mingled squalor and depravity,
Its selfishness, its heartlessness, its falseness—
All tending to crush out the youthful virtues ;
While the fresh beauty of the cultured country—
Its lordly trees, rich groves, and smiling downs,
Its wild-flowers, song-birds, honey-bees, and hay-fields—
Seem to breathe purity into the soul.

It is a worthy and a noble mission
To make the laws that give a generous impulse
To human welfare and the world's advancement.
The statesman may have been an errand-boy,
And played at marbles with the village urchins,
Ate bread and cheese and swallowed penny beer ;
Have scared the hungry birds with noisy clapper
From off the fields throughout the livelong day,

And shed the tears of lonely bitterness;
He may have struggled through the city crowds,
Have perched upon a long-legged writing-stool,
Penned page succeeding page of dry accounts,
Longing sometimes to scare the birds once more;
Have grown with steady pains to be a merchant;
Yet looking not alone at wealth and station,
He may have set his mind to higher aims—
To store the golden grains of truth and wisdom,
Look backward from effects to hidden causes,
And forward to their ultimate results;
Weigh history in the scales of evidence,
Master the facts and figures of statistics,
Work out the problem of a reformation,
And give his life and soul to the achievement—
And such a man was Cobden.   From seclusion
Working his way through life's opposing trammels,
Outliving hatred, falsehood, and contumely—
True greatness calmly smiles at insolence,
'Tis littleness that promptly takes offence—
From greatness unto greatness ever rising,
Winning the favour of his enemies,
Accomplishing the triumphs which he aimed at,
Taking his place amongst earth's greatest statesmen,
Then dying—mourned and wept by all good men—
A single-minded, unambitious statesman,
Who, like the noble Grecian of old time,
If good were done, cared not by whom 'twas done
So it were done, regarding not himself.
    Borne to the churchyard of his native village,

The still seclusion of his early days,
His chosen resting-place after life's toils,
Better than under the cold Abbey flagstones,
Amongst perennial primroses he sleeps.
  When the sun sets of such a noble being
How joyful must the retrospection be,
That he has laboured for his country's good !
That he has borne reproach from evil men,
Falsehood, malignity and opposition,
But has not borne their poisoned shafts in vain,
Nor toiled without his full and high reward ;
But leaves his country better than he found it—
More free, more happy, wiser, richer, greater,
Her old foundations deepened, widened, strengthened,
And giving promise of long years to come
Of glory, greatness, happiness and peace.
So have I seen a crimson band of glory
Circle Ben Nevis of a summer's evening,
And as the sun declined the glory rose,
Until his lofty brow stood full in view,
Bright with a coronet of peerless splendour.
  Our life has two grand objects set before it—
Happiness here and happiness hereafter.
The first is like the earth which we inhabit,
Presenting an infinitude of aspects,
And having an attendant moon of duties
Revolving round it—old, yet still renewed.
The second may be likened to the sun,
The glorious centre of the universe,
Round which our earth, or earthly happiness,

Centrifugally rolls, carrying its moon
Of duties with it in its mystic chain,
Together with the planets in their courses,
Which, like the eternal principles of truth,
Sailing along the ebon sea of heaven,
Shine calmly in their purity and beauty.

  Be happy, is the true philosophy,
But wisely, temperately, justly, lawfully;
Not resting only in the uncertain present,
But blending with it the eternal future;
Looking beyond all sublunary things
Towards the eternal and unchangeable—
The inheritance so dearly purchased for us,
And the bright promised mansions of the blest,
That when the body shall lie deep in earth
The spirit may be soaring high in heaven.

  Here in this lower world we are surrounded
On every side by hidden mysteries—
The strange and tempting mysteries of nature,
And mysteries of our spiritual being.
The extinction of one elemental gas
Would revolutionize the natural world;
So the destruction of one human passion
Would change the habits of the human race.
Which way soever we may strive to track
The winding path of this world's labyrinth,
We come at last unto an iron door,
With locks and bolts of sternest adamant.
No skill, no strength of ours, can help us further.
All, all that lies beyond it is conjecture,

Sealed up by nature's great Artificer,
Till man's inquiring spirit shall be disrobed
Of its incumbering garment of mortality;
And entering on a new and higher existence,
And gifted with new faculties of vision,
The iron door shall be a door of glass,
And secret things shall clearly be revealed.
　　Nothing annoys a great philosopher
So much as being baffled by a mystery,
And driven to that extremity, " Don't know."
How will he wriggle like a twisting eel
To avoid the painful mortifying confession,
Or, like a Polar bear within a cage,
Moving monotonously to and fro,
Vainly make head against the iron door!
What fancies, subterfuges, and gross delusions
The gravest of philosophers resort to !
The flimsiest thread of floating gossamer
Is not too weak to form his arguments;
The skilfully-constructed spider's web
Is not too fragile to sustain his theories.
What is the end and aim of all his logic ?
To unthrone the living, all-creative God—
To save, forsooth, the Great First Cause the trouble
Of supervising what his hands have made,
Who upholds all things by the word of his power,
And prove that he who formed and rules the world,
And constantly renews the face of the earth,
Cannot work miracles as once he did—
Deducing all things from that phantom, Nature.

Miracles have not ceased.   It is a miracle
When one of these hardened sinners is converted.
    There never was a doctrine so absurd
As not to find disciples to adopt it;
There never was a theory so Utopian,
So shallow, crass, jejune, and contradictory,
As not to find shrewd men to swallow it,
Write for it, fight for it, and at last go mad for it.
One fool draws other fools into his net;
This is the law of Natural Selection.
What an achievement for a man of reason,
To prove himself descended from a monkey!
The monkey seems degenerated man!
The Holy Book of heavenly inspiration,
Which is the exhaustless comfort of the humble,
To these acute and learned cogitators
Seems a peculiar and perpetual teazer.
They use a microscope to view the sun,
And find a mass of glaring contradictions,
The retroflection merely of themselves.
These merchantmen, who only sell us doubts,
And take hard cash, not paper, for their pay—
These builders who are always pulling down,
And build up nothing better than themselves,—
Who try to measure the immeasurable,
In their presumption, with a two-foot rule—
Nothing they prove, and disprove everything,
Unless it be their own incompetence
To judge of light who are themselves in darkness,
In things divine enough has heaven revealed

For man's instruction, comfort, and salvation ;
But secret things belong alone to God.
  Tell me, thou learned, wise philosopher,
With such a world of knowledge in thy head,
That thou art wiser than Almighty God,
And canst correct the errors of the Bible—
Tell me the reason of one simple thing,
And I will pin my faith upon thy sleeve :
Tell me the reason why the hops in Kent
Curl round the poles always in one direction,
The same in which the sun his circuit makes,
While the convolvulus and scarlet-runner
Twist always in the contrary direction?
A fact which I found out and oft have noticed :
And wherefore do the tails of sucking-pigs
Curl, some of them to the right and some to the left?
And why art thou, O man, without a tail?
  But there are fields open and wide enough,
For man's commendable examination,
And none more fruitful than the field of science.
As Science slowly lifts the ancient veil
From Nature's face what beauties are disclosed !
What glories of the interstellar realms !
What marvels of the abysses of the sea !
What wonders of the strata of the earth—
Of perished and of still existent life !
What new-found elements of vital power !
Each mystery solved revealing other mysteries
In constant and interminable progression !
I wonder very much how old the world is.

C

Its flowery mantle is a fond deception,
New every spring and fading in the autumn;
Like a smart wig upon a hoary head,
It only half conceals the proofs of age;
The closer that we look into its wrinkles
The clearer are the ravages of time.
I take into my hand this common pebble
And scan it carefully.   It is misshapen,
And plainly has at some past time been melted,
When earth itself was one vast crucible;
But when that period was who shall declare,
Or who can tell this pebble's history?
The sailor who surveys the chalky cliffs
Of England, after an adventurous voyage,
And glows with rapture at the thought of home,
Dreams not that, long before men lived, those cliffs
Were formed of tiny shells beneath the sea,
Slowly accumulating through countless ages,
And hardening by the tedious lapse of time,
Till winds within the stomach of the earth,
Or feverish heat, convulsed the frame of nature,
And heaved them high above the raging ocean,
A joy and terror to the mariner.
    The name of ocean hurries me away.
Some people call the sea monotonous;
Perhaps they are monotonous themselves.
The ocean always is a glorious object:
For ever changing, never twice alike,
Varied by all the different tints of heaven,
And moved diversely by each wind that blows:

Now like a kitten playing with its tail,
Now lashing like contending angry lions.
Yes! how it roars and bellows in its wrath,
When furious winds race wildly over it!
It is a power, a beauty, and a mystery;
Its solitude, its depth, its boundlessness
Operate ever as a fascination.
What unknown treasures sleep beneath its waves!
What swarms of living creatures traverse it!
Each drop of it is redolent of life;
How faithfully its heaving bosom swells
In constant love to the retreating moon;
By night how full of phosphorescent fire,
Raging and hissing like a molten sea.
And what a scene it is of daring courage,
Patient endurance, unrecorded hardship,
While the good ship alone upon the deep—
Now plunging down the precipice of waves,
Now springing forward like a mountain roe—
Holds steadily its earnest, onward course;
While every rope and brace throughout the rigging,
Taut as a bowstring, or Æolean harp,
Sings cheerily a music all its own,
More thrilling than the proudest orchestra.

All nature is replete with varied music;
Each kind of tree has its peculiar voice;
Each kind of bird its separate minstrelsy;
Each rivulet its pleasant gurgling sound—
All carrying to the soul a sentiment,
Either a discord or a harmony.

Few turn away from music's talisman :
The little infant loves it wonderingly,
And beats its little fingers to the time.
It soothes the evil temper of the felon,
The young, the old, the ignorant, the learned—
All ages and all classes love it passionately.
Some people love it merely for its sound,
Some people love it for its sentiment,
Some for the difficulty of playing it ;—
A joy as sensible as walking backwards,
Or dancing gracefully on lanky stilts.
It is when sound and sentiment unite,
When song and sense go hand in hand together,
That ear and soul in sympathy are charmed.
'Tis pitiful to see a pale-faced creature,
To whom the breezy morn and youthful play
Would give health, beauty, bloom, and symmetry,
Beating the ivory keys in vain disgust,
And wasting precious days for years together,
To accomplish nothing but a worthless difficulty;
But Fashion's word is law, and fools obey.

Driven from my anchorage in Yarmouth Roads,
By stress of weather from the German Ocean,
I have brought up at good old Colchester.
The bells of Colchester, from many a tower,
Are jangling forth their independent tones,
Forming familiar inharmonious music.
I love to hear the well-known bells again,
For my affections cling around old places,
Although sad memories stab me to the heart.

For forty years I here possessed a home,
And now I am a temporary lodger.
All whom I used to love are dead and gone.
I roam about the neighbouring Barrack-field,
Sheltering myself from the cold wintry blasts
As best I may under the lengthened walls,
Without a path through life, without a plan,
Writing this song for lack of other aim.
 This is the third of March, the anniversary
Of quite a great event in my career,
When, like a kitten mewing plaintively,
I came a poor intruder into life,
The last of four, unwanted and unloved,
Save by a mother's gentle, yearning heart.
No doubt, my first remark might be interpreted,
"What a cold world is this to come into!"
An observation which I often make
When I behold the dear young new-dropt lambs
Stand shivering on the frosty grass in spring,
And bleating at the first sharp taste of life.
This day I enter on my sixtieth year!
My time of life is now the "setting sun,"
Apt title of my desultory song;
Too late to re-commence one's course again
And shun the various errors of the past:
Too late to hope for dear domestic joys,
Fond clinging arms and soft warm-breathing kisses,
Youth's passionate love and happy laughing children
(Of course, not always laughing—sometimes crying);
Too late to toil for wealth and lofty station,

The objects that allure the youthful heart :
Too late to look for fame, which Milton calls
"The last infirmity of noble minds ——"
Say, rather, that strong instinct of the soul
Which prompts the will to struggle for success.
Davenant was born upon the third of March,
Waller was born upon the third of March,
Otway was born upon the third of March,
And I was born upon the third of March ;
But this affords no proof I am a poet,
Thousands of blockheads, in the lapse of time,
Were also born upon the third of March.
Milton was born in Sixteen Hundred and Eight,
And I was born in Eighteen Hundred and Eight ;
But what a mighty interval divides us,
Besides the simple interval of time !
Milton I look on as our greatest poet,
Greater than Shakespeare, great as were his gifts.
Shakespeare was master of the minds of men,
In all their subtle workings and revealings.
Beggars and kings, poor maids and stately queens,
Were puppets in his hands to practise with.
He knew how minds would work upon events,
And how events would operate on minds.
All nature, and the mystic world of fancy,
Were open to him as a spelling-book ;
And he possessed the dainty art of wording,
In happiest phrase, the promptings of his brain ;
Thus speaking to all hearts intelligibly :
But Milton was a mightier child of song,

His genius bore him to profounder depths,
And wafted him to far sublimer heights;
Yet never did his marvellous spirit quail,
Even in Pandemonium, or on earth,
In Paradise with Eden innocency,
Or midst the immortals on the plains of heaven.
A master of the art of composition—
With all the aids that learning could bestow,
Armour which yet encumbered not his limbs—
His verse is instinct with unequalled strength,
Crowded with full emphatic syllables;
His wondrous cadences delight the sense
With music caught from the melodious spheres,
The lines commencing with accented words.
But Milton never has had justice done him.
The sycophants of arbitrary power,
And those who profit much by Prelacy,
"Of whom to be dispraised is no small praise,"
Have looked with knitted brows upon a poet
Who dared to speak unpalatable truth,
And so have hushed the voice of admiration,
And set a mark of enmity upon him.
But he cared nothing for their praise or blame,
Who only sought "fit audience, though few."
    This is the sixth of March; the glorious sun
Just now is undergoing an eclipse;
His beamy shield is darkened in mid heaven;
The moon, his big and rather forward daughter,
Threatens ere long to get the upper hand,
And elbow him civilly into the shade.

His radiant disk, too bright to look upon,
Will soon seem nothing but a silver ring
To those who view him from a southern clime.
Men like to look on greatness under a cloud,
Brought down as to the level of themselves;
And crowds who take no notice of the sun
When shining at noon-day in all his glory,
Are quizzing at him now his state is dimmed :
A commentary on the ways of men.

   Time strides much faster than he used to do :—
I write with haste, my time perhaps is short.
Being no slave to literary dogmas,
I would be bold rather than too fastidious,
Leaving a host of careless blemishes
For learned critics with their microscopes
And clever forceps to lay hold upon,
And thereby for their wives and clamorous children
Earn honest bread and cheese and twopenny.
It is too late in life to enjoy renown,
For those are dead whom I most wished to please ;
Yet dear to me, and ever has been dear,
The hope still is of an undying name—
A name to be beloved and fondly cherished
When I am mouldering in my dull cold grave:
Not a proud name that stirs no sympathies,
But one that is allied to loves and tears.
It is the instinct of immortal being,
The evidence of an eternity :
The boy who carves his name upon a tree
Reveals the undying principle within him,
And proves himself an heir of endless life.

Fame is a matter of mere accident—
Those who deserve it most obtain it least.
Millions of noble actions are performed
Which only the All-seeing eye beholds ;
Good actions, which the world knows nothing of,
Yet are recorded in the Book of Life.
Fame sometimes is developed suddenly,
Wide spread and beautiful to look upon,
Springing up in a night as doth a mushroom,
But fading quickly in the glare of day.
Fame sometimes, like an acorn in the earth,
Lies latent long, and slowly shoots at last,
Growing by slow degrees from a small grain
Up into vastness and enduring strength.
Justice avenges the awards of fame.
The more applause is thrust into men's faces
The briefer is its durability.
The impassioned actor and the orator
Drink overflowing goblets of applause
Whose effervescence ends as it begins.
The statesman who enjoys the gifts of power—
Whose influence guides the progress of events,
Whom all men cringe to as a demigod,
Whom plaudits welcome when he deigns to speak,
Dies, and bequeaths an unregarded name ;
His eloquence, employed on fleeting topics,
And power withdrawn, his name is soon forgotten,
Although a coronet may surround his brows ;
While the starved author in his cobwebbed garret,
Unknown to all the passers in the street,

Sitting upon an antiquated chair
Beside his rickety worm-eaten table,
With smudgy paper, pen, and bottle of ink,
Writes words which glow with more than mortal fire;
And which shall glow more and more bright with time,
And mould and make the destiny of nations—
Circling his brows with never-ending fame!
  I am a lonely man—no wife, no child,
No brother, and no sister, nephew or niece
To cheer me with the pleasing sense of home:
And yet I have a very loving heart.
Within my breast I feel in every fibre
Boundless capacity for endless joy:
And what should I be worth to anybody
Without this fiery mind that burns within?
My aching heart beats hard at heaven's gate;
My weary days and lonely sleepless nights·
Roll like the billows of an angry sea
Over my wretched and defenceless head.
Nor have I friends to tell my fancies to;
And what is the use of being a bachelor
Unless one can indulge one's harmless fancies?
I see a plenty of familiar faces
About the streets, but no familiar friend,—
I am shut up within my lonely self:
All know my face, but no one knows my heart.
How oft I think how charming it would be
To call on Goldsmith over Breakneck Stairs—
Good-natured man! whom every reader loves:
Whose pen performed whate'er he wished it to,

But who himself could not do anything—
And talk with him of gentle Doctor Primrose,
And ask the fate of those green spectacles
Which have called up so many million smiles ;
Or listen to the thunder of old Johnson
Sitting in all his glory at the Club,
And arguing stoutly on the weaker side
To show the vigour of his reasoning powers ;
Or hear what Burke with fervid eloquence
Would pour into our ears on State affairs ;
How pleasant also of a summer's evening
To walk with Cowper in his Wilderness,
And listen to his sweet refined discourse ;
Or sit with Burns beside his plough to rest,
And hear the fiery breathings of his heart
Telling some tale of witchcraft or of love.
Thus do I dream of sweet congenial talk
With kindred spirits that have passed away,
But am myself condemned to dwell in silence.
    There is in poetry one singularity—
The manufacture never has improved.
" Practice makes perfect " is the common rule,
But it has not held good in poetry,
For Poetry can now scarce spread her wings,
Since our ingenious and precise grammarians
Have put our free-born and magnificent language,
By their pedantic laws and rigid rules
And nice refinements, into a strait-waistcoat.
Science and arts advance with onward time,
But poetry grows sickly, weak and shallow,

Can the old world be made brand new again
By science and the spread of useful knowledge,
By endless enginery impelled by steam,
By railroads, telegraphs, and photographs,
And must our poetry be stale and flat,
Faint echoes of the past, quaint and unreal,
With nothing of the instinct of the times—
Its freshness and rapidity of motion?
Homer, who sang the first, is still the first.
Our greatest poets—Milton, Shakespeare, Spenser—
With all their genius never over-passed him.
We have had Young and Cowper, Burns and Byron,
Great in their way, captains of tens of thousands,
But only second to the highest order.
In these degenerate days of poetry
We seldom get beyond a weak dilution
Of what has been far better sung before,
Which people only buy for Fashion's sake,
Or read, to mystify themselves to sleep ;
Poems, whose authors should have writ in prose,
Full of obscure inane philosophy,
Flat as their lakes and barren as their mountains.
True poetry is philosophical,
The mineral veins pass through it vigorously ;
But never should philosophy itself
Become the sum and substance of the song,
Else will its leaden weight soon sink it down.
Poets must write as other people talk—
At least must write as other people feel,
Simply, forcibly, truthfully, and naturally.

Not puzzle us with dark and dull enigmas,
Scarce worth the cloud of words that wrap them round.
Genius is ever its own lawgiver;
Every great poet has his own vocabulary,
His armoury of language and of thought,
As every kind of tree has its own drapery
Of leaves that flutter in the passing breeze,
And sing a song exclusively its own.
How grandly and with what unequalled strength
Milton discourses in his wondrous song,
Sitting stone blind but having light within;
While Shakespeare, sailing like a silver sea-gull,
Now glances upward on the boisterous wind.
Now boldly darts through the tumultuous waves,—
Alike at home in either element.
As birds may be distinguished by their plumage
So may each poet by his separate style:
A fragment taken from a genuine poet,
Like an unearthed disjointed fossil-bone,
At once reveals the source from whence it came.
  The characters of nations may be known
According to the way men hold their heads.
An Englishman's is carried stifly straight;
He walks right on and boldly looks before him.
A Scotchman lifts his elongated chin
And speers his metaphysical abstractions.
The Irish have no heads, or else they carry them
With such a strange perverse obliquity
One never knows exactly where to find them;
Their very faces have a lateral twist.

The Frenchman's head keeps bobbing up and down,
Bobbing and bowing like a mere machine
Under a patent form of government.
The Spaniard hides his chin within his breast,
And looks askance, suspicious of his friend.
The great American nation loll their heads
From side to side, and talk about themselves
As the only really free enlightened people,
Deeming themselves quite equal to us English,
If not, in fact, a trifle in advance—
An innocent bit of rational rivalry ;
But yet a physical impossibility :
The sun himself decides the little question,
They being inevitably five hours behind us.
   A peerless country is Columbia,
A world new risen from the ocean's foam.
I know the ground, for I have trodden it
In my young days with naked bleeding feet ;
Unbounded in its habitable extent,
And matchless in its products for man's use,
Possessing every climate in the world,
And channelled by innumerable rivers,
At once the great highways throughout the land,
The sources of untold mechanic power,
And swarmed by fish, the tasteful food of man.
All metals valuable for civil life
Lie hidden in its rich exhaustless mines,
With fuel for a hundred thousand years.
It is a land of corn, and wine, and oil,
And flocks and herds, and roving buffaloes,

All fruits of sweetest, exquisitest flavour—
Apples, pears, peaches, melons, grapes and oranges :
A country hid throughout the historic ages,
Now rising like its emblematic eagle,
Full fledged and soaring upwards in its strength.
  May never crazy knaves across the sea,
Or selfish demons on this side the ocean,
Madly rush headlong with the torch of war,
And fire each other's standing corn and haystacks ;
May never the infuriated mother
Forget the instincts of maternity,
And clutch her daughter's throat with deadly grip ;
And never may the exasperated daughter,
Hating the breast she sucked in infancy,
Plunge her keen dagger in her mother's heart.
Let them remember that they both are one
In kinship, language, creed, and lofty mission,
Destined to spread their empire o'er the world !
  Winter has come again—the third this season ;
Snowdrops are dead, but snow once more has fallen :
All things are folded in a crystal mantle,
Dazzlingly white and feathery, soft and pure :
All objects, whether graceful or ungraceful,
Are garmented as with a heavenly beauty :
The trees are silver trees, their pendant branches
Are glittering softly in the morning sunshine ;
They seem transplanted from some holier sphere—
From the bright pure eternal world above us—
More pure than the blanched snow that from it falls.
Each little spray supports its little burden ;

It seems as if the sanctity of heaven
Had suddenly descended upon earth,
Causing the better part of man, the spirit,
To pant for the unsullied realms above.
But while I write, the ardour of the sun
Begins to melt the fairy-scene away;
The eaves begin to drip, the snow to vanish,
And in its stead the pathway and the road
Are now encumbered with a loathsome slush,
Trodden by anybody's dirty feet.
How horrible is purity defiled!
I love the chaste white snow when it is coming;
I loathe it soiled and foul when it is going.

    Most precious are the symptoms of the spring—
The unfolding buds, the rapture-twittering birds,
The genial sunshine and the softened breezes;
Thrice precious to the sailor from afar,
Who, leaving lands of tedious frost and snow,
Barren and cheerless, bleak and comfortless,
After a voyage across the watery waste,
Suddenly finds himself in sight of fields,
Green flowering pastures, blossoming apple-trees,
And leafy hedgerows, fresh as emerald,
And hears the melody of countless birds,
Singing in concert to his rapturous feelings,
Home! home! home! home! old England! home
      once more!

    An Englishman may well be proud of England,
And love it better than all other lands.
All the most rich and useful gifts of nature

Are showered upon her lap abundantly :
The treasures of the fields and of the seas,
The treasures of the mines and of the rocks,
And, better still, a mingled race of men—
Bold, energetic, hardy, laborious,
Blessed with a language vigorous as themselves,
Who, bending art and science to their service,
And favoured by the approving smiles of Heaven,
Have raised themselves alike to power and glory,
And placed Old England at the head of nations.
I have seen many countries in my time,
And lived long years away from mother England,
And know the bitter feeling of home sickness,
Which none can tell but those who go abroad,
And bear the hardships of a foreign region.
Long absence feeds enthusiastic love,
And a strong man will fall upon his knees
And offer worship to a bunch of daisies
That comes across the sea from his old home.
I give it as my strong and fixed opinion,
That not a country in the outstretched world
Can be compared—no, not for a single moment—
To England, our loved country, dear old England !
    The happy isolation of our island,
Cut off from meddlesome hot-headed neighbours,
By a convenient moat of cool salt water,
Gives concentration to our love of country.
We all are proud of her: we prize her honour ;
We feel it, if we do not talk of it ;
We take for granted hers is the highest place.

D

The nations round admit her power and greatness,
Implore her help in every time of trouble,
Accept her refuge as an ark of safety,
And then abuse her out of jealousy.
She makes a home for Europe's discrowned monarchs,
Where they may keep a shadowy regal Court,
Indulge their hopes, enjoy their mimic pomp,
Blame false mankind and justify themselves.
Old England is the world's palladium.
   But Englishmen are never satisfied,
And would be miserable without a grievance
To whet their daily combativeness on.
The frequent changes in our fickle climate
Afford the readiest subject for complaint.
The weather is Old England's safety-valve,
Through which we let off our superfluous wrath
From the hot boiler of our discontent ;
And yet we have the very best of climates,
A little variable, like a woman's temper,
But charming at all seasons of the year,
So that a man may daily walk abroad
And see what other people are about;
Not melting hot like France and Germany,
Nor yet intolerably cold like Russia,
Nor yet both hot and cold like North America ;
Not burning to a cinder like the tropics,
With all their floods of devastating rain,
Their pestilential fevers, loathsome reptiles,
Their noxious insects and their beasts of prey;
Nor freezing into stone like arctic realms,

Where men are muffled up something like owls,
So that you only see their blinking eyes,
And live on blubber, fish, and tough raw flesh.
But England has a pleasant temperate climate,
That gives a matchless bloom to British faces,
By which they are recognised all round the world.
  We English have another standing grievance
To shake our fists at, and to storm against—
The way in which our rulers govern us.
Our laws somehow are always going wrong,
Yet we, meanwhile, are always going right,
Becoming year by year more rich and powerful.
Our Constitution, like a pigeon-house,
Is full of holes to aim our arrows at,
And yet it does its duty pretty well;
But Englishmen contend it might do better.
Our old State-coach goes rumbling on its way,
Slow, very slow, but also very sure;
Roads may be rough, but nothing overturns it,
It bends but does not break; horses may kick,
But try in vain to run away with it.
Some folks would like to pull it all to pieces,
And build another of improved materials,
And a more modern elegant construction.
'Tis true it needs at times some reparation,
And wants a little oiling of the wheels;
But what is good may sometimes be exchanged
For that which is not better, but far worse.
Our neighbours on the other side the channel
Are sadly fond of building new State-coaches,

Contrived on philosophic principles,
And very smart and gay with paint and gilding,
But each one in its turn soon comes to grief,
While our old English coach outlasts them all.
　When I was young our English coaching system
Was rising to its state of high perfection—
I saw its culmination and its fall.
Macadam, the first Adam who made roads,
Began the work by mending our highways.
Before his time the turnpike roads were made
By spreading gravel deep along the centre;
No carriage could be jolted through this gravel;
The wheels sank in and wore the horses out;
The coachmen drove on either side the road,
Wearing in time the bank of gravel down;
Slow was the pace and dangerous was the way.
Macadam put an end to this old plan
By sprinkling gravel sparsely on the road,
Which, being quickly trodden in by traffic,
Made the highways at once smooth, hard, and good;
Then first stage-coaches went full speed to London,
And people lost their meals to save their time.
Instead of breakfasting at some old inn
Along the road, and dining at another,
And finding time perhaps to smoke a pipe,
Thus getting in a leisure way to town,
Through rain or dust, weary and cramped and spent,
As they were wont to do in days of old—
For nobody was in a hurry then—
.They now sped on full gallop all the way,

Every ten miles with hurry changing horses,
And hastening as if life depended on it,
Soon brought the travellers to their journey's end.
A killing time it was for those fine horses;
But so uncertain was the accommodation
That those who wished to take a distant journey
Were fain, some days before, to book their places,
Whether the weather might prove fair or foul.
   The coachman was an English character—
The world did not contain his parallel—
Handsome, polite, and graceful in his movements,
With cheeks as ruddy as a rosy apple,
Dressed in the stylish fashion of the day,
Looked up to by young beardless gentlemen,
Who sometimes by his favour took the reins,
Proud of the task of driving four-in-hand;
The friend of all the gentry on the road;
Oft with a noble on the box beside him;
Aware who lived at every handsome mansion,
With something of their history to tell;
Lifting at times the handle of his whip
In salutation to a passing coachman;
Learned in horses, dogs, and country sports;
Knowing where all the prettiest girls resided,
And smiling at them as he rattled by—
(They mostly happened to be near the windows,
Remembering when the punctual coach would pass)—
A cheerful and a consequential life,
The thirsty, jovial, English coachman led;
And when the journey of each day was done
He asked no fee, but proudly looked for it.

Upon a bright and cheerful summer's morning,
When bean-fields scented the delicious air,
And trees and hedgerows wore their greenest beauty,
A most exhilarating treat it was,
Perched on the outside of the lofty coach,
Though crushed a bit by fellow passengers,
Perhaps between two lively, laughing school-girls,
Cramping at first but easier afterwards,
To bowl along at such a swinging pace,
And view the fair and ever-changing landscape,
And hear the clatter of the horses' hoofs.
The pace indeed was something terrible,
Up hill and down hill it was all the same,
And even on the darkest winter's night
The mail, with flaring lamps, would gallop on
Through open turnpike gates, and not draw bit,
Escaping gateposts as by miracle ;
But many a fatal accident occurred.
And what a sight it was at Christmas time,
When all the coaches laden with Christmas gifts—
Nice things perchance from good old Norwich
        market—
Hampers, boxes, baskets, hares and turkeys,
Clustering about both coach and passengers,
Like bees around a hive ready to swarm,
Went toiling up to London with their loads—
London whose appetite is always good :—
Hard times were they for poor coach horses then.
    A fine exciting thing it was to see
On summer days the hot and panting steeds
Pull up before the village "Angel Inn,"

While the red-coated guard, playing his bugle,
Roused all the village with his cheery music.
There other harnessed horses waiting stood,
Warm from their stables, with their horse-cloths on.
A group of villagers mostly stood around ;
Decrepit age and curly-headed youth
Shewing their crutches or their rustic rags,
And waiting wishfully for welcome halfpence
Bestowed sometimes by generous passengers.
The coachman copped his whip down to the ostler,
Who ready stood to catch it as it fell ;
Unbuckling then the ribbons in his hands,
He let them fall, and gracefully dismounting,
Retreated to the bar of the hotel,
Having some business with the landlady.
Meanwhile the ostlers loosed the panting steeds,
That slowly staggered off with steaming sides.
Soon the fresh horses, with their horse-cloths on,
Were cleverly put to—one minute's work—
The coachman, taking then his whip and ribbons,
And climbing like a monkey to his seat,
Chirrupped, and touched his horses with his whip :
They, rearing and curveting, bounded off,
While on each side the ostlers seized the horse-cloths
And pulled them from each dappled creature's back,
Leaving them free to take their glorious run.
 These things of only yesterday have passed
From our experience suddenly away,
Like the bright pageant of a village fair,
But never, never to return again.

A shrewd young working man named Stephenson,
Enlisting fire and water to his aid,
Devised a quicker way to get to London.
We now are fastened in a noisy box,
And, seeing little of the lovely country,
And hearing little if we try to talk,
A puff of steam propels us like an arrow
Along an iron road, through dismal cuttings
And dreadful tunnels, to our journey's end.
A glorious victory of engineering,
By which we shorten time and travel cheaply,
So that where one used formerly to ride
A hundred now can go and see their friends :
We lose the beauty of the scenery,
But quickly reach our wished-for destination.

    In the still evening air I hear a sound,
A roaring like a distant cataract ;
It dies and dies away, and wholly ceases ;
Suddenly and louder still it roars again
Along the valley and the wooded hill.
If my good, gentle, timid grandmother
Could waken up, and sit in her old chair,
Plying once more her rapid knitting-needles,
With what blank wonderment her eyes would open
To hear this crashing, most unwonted sound.
Is it an earthquake gathering up its strength ?
Again it dies away, yet keeps on muttering,
Till on a sudden, bursting from the hills,
And thundering like an alpine avalanche,
The railway train dashes along the line—

A fiery centipede, terribly beautiful,
More wonderful than any fabled dragon,
Disgorging sulphurous smoke and clouds of steam—
The embodiment of swiftness and of power.
  Strange that a merry singing tea-kettle
Should be the sire of such a prodigy !
Poker and tongs rattle in rivalry !
Frying-pan and gridiron clash with jealousy !
To think the tea-kettle should get above you,
And make so great a figure in the world !
  The railway system is an innovator,
A revolutionary propagandist,
Able to turn the whole world upside down ;
While telegraphy brings the ends together.
It is the greatest leveller of the age,
It breaks down many an ancient barrier,
Removes old landmarks that were once held sacred,
Serves to unite the family of nations,
And makes us better acquainted with our neighbours ;
Its energy gives energy to men,
Forcing them to be prompt and punctual ;
It stimulates the commerce of the world ;
It is a thing of boundless powers of growth ;
The " Bean-stalk " of our youth was nothing to it.
Magnanimously profitless itself,
It is the source of wealth to tens of thousands :
Like a broad river flowing through the land,
Without increasing its original wealth
It spreads fertility on every side ;
It is a forward movement in existence,

A stride once taken never to be retraced,
A grand advance from whence there's no return.
    Why were these great and marvellous discoveries
Hidden so many ages from man's use?
Why did our fathers with such needless labour
Travel on foot, slowly and wearily,
And ride rough roads in still more costly wise,
Or have to stay at home in dull seclusion?
The Assyrians and Egyptians, who could build
Colossal pyramids and tombs and temples ;
The Greeks and Romans, who had arts and letters,
Who sang the wondrous story of old Troy,
Cut out the living statue from the marble,
And taught the highest type of architecture—
These giants of primeval intellect
Never so much as dreamed of such inventions.
Had Euclid solved this problem of our day,
And old Lycurgus passed a Railway Bill,
How altered would have been the course of history,
And what a different world should we inhabit!
    'Tis well to keep the chain of friendship bright
By frequent and familiar intercourse,
For friendship adds a precious charm to life.
Our railways therefore are a public boon,
For friendship opens up the path to love,
And love leads on the way direct to marriage,
And marriage needs must be life's best estate,
Crowned with embodied cherubs, loves, and joys.
I wish I had been married in my youth,
But duty, fortune, fate alike forbade.

Perhaps if I had married and been happy,
I never should have written this long poem.
If I had gained, the world would then have lost ;
For, like a lonely bullfinch in a cage,
I sing to chase unhappiness away.
But though the married state in theory,
Also in poetry, is very charming,
Yet it involves some rather serious drawbacks :
Rents, rates, and taxes, doctor's bills and school bills,
Eatables, drinkables, and also wearables,
Enough to make a merry man look grave.
Avaunt with this cold calculating creed !
Is not a loving wife herself a fortune,
A mine of inexhaustible contentment,
The kindest and the carefullest of friends,
The first of earthly counsellors in trouble,
The best of earthly comforters in sorrow ?
Is she not like the ballast to a ship,
The pediment to manhood's stately column :
Part of himself, the mother of his offspring ?
(I speak of things of which I know but little,
Mostly from hearsay and from taking notice :
Much may be said on both sides of the question.)
The summer sea is fair to look upon,
It seems a pleasant thing to sail across it,
And yet how many wrecks, alas ! take place,
How many a pretty gallant craft goes down !
So fares it on the sea of matrimony :
The ship of love can outride many a storm
If she is kept with care in sailing trim,

And wisely steered by Heaven's appointed compass;
. But sometimes love is hustled overboard
When poverty climbs through the open port-holes,
And those on board come down to short allowance;
Sickness breaks out, a sail is blown away,
Perhaps a leak is sprung, a topmast lost,
Sometimes the ballast of the ship gets shifted,
And then she heels abeam, and will not sail;
Sometimes there is a mutiny aboard,
And all the saucepans rattle round their ears;
Sometimes the foolish captain takes to drinking,
Goes staring mad, and upsets everything;
Sometimes the mate aspires to be the captain,
Then every thing of course gets topsy turvy.

Amongst the advertisements on various subjects
Which fill the columns of the daily papers,
I read of medicines that will cure all ailments,
But none that will protect us against trouble.
There is no Insurance-office in the world
To guarantee us against every evil.
Our life indeed appears a lottery,
With blanks and prizes shuffled up together;
But if we look into the subject closely,
We find that nearly all our knocks and bruises
Are self-inflicted and preventible—
This might have been, and that need not have been.

When I look back upon my path of life
It makes me somewhat sad and melancholy.
Dead friends, changed scenes, missed opportunities,
Losses and crosses chequer all the road,

With spots of brightness gleaming here and there,
That half relieve it of its gloominess.
Life has its joys, though joys may have their wings;
Let me not dwell too much upon the past,
For what is yesterday but a lost world?
Wiser it is to look upon the future;
'Tis better to look forward than look backward;
The future is the time that most concerns us.
We rake amongst the ashes of the past
To find the fuel for our melancholy;
The present dances best with our frivolity,
But to the soul that seeks for happiness
The future is the all-important good.
We never cast aside a worn-out coat
Without a momentary pang at parting.
Oh for the robe of the Redeemer's righteousness:
The only garment to escape from life in!
Why should we tremble at the fear of death?
'Tis but the instinct of self-preservation
To bear us up under the stress of trouble.
To die can be no worse than to be born,
A passing pang of which we are unconscious.
We must be loosened from this dear old world,
This vain, deluding, transitory scene,
Whose vintage is so pleasant to our taste:
Its sourness sometimes sets our teeth on edge,
And yet the smack and flavour seldom tire.
Life's plain seems wide to cross and wearisome,
With one inevitable gate of exit;
But we must pass it and be seen no more.

Beyond it to the upright and the just,
The washed and the redeemed and purified,
Nothing but brightness gilds the onward view :
Fields of unfading flowers, and endless summer,
Trees whose immortal leaves are full of healing,
And the pure river of the water of life.

Here endeth Book the First of this my Poem.
After the freshening breezes of the day
The evening closes in, and the wide west,
With all its pomp of armies of thick clouds
Marching to battle, hurrying grandly by,
Glows with an upward stream of burning glory,
Yet broken here and there by overthrown
And ruined baggage trains and equipages,
And wreaths of smoke from some deserted camp :
So fancy solves the evanescent vision.

BOOK II.

BOOK II.

I SEEM to have broached at last the proper barrel;
The tap runs freely and the draught is pleasant—
Sound if not strong, and sparkling if not heady,
Bitter but not too bitter to be wholesome,
Wholesome and suited to a healthy palate.

Cheer up! the wind has changed, the sun is warm;
March, that came in upon us like a lion,
Tossing and brindling up his snowy mane,
Is skipping out like a meek innocent lamb.
How strange the change!   For several weary weeks
Wind, rain and snow, snow, rain and wind prevailed.
'Twas piteous but a day or two ago
To see the sparrows grouped upon the trees,
Holding a council on the state of things,
While the thick drifting snow pelted them sore.
How out of place were dreams of nest-building
And sitting warmly upon speckled eggs!
They seemed like helpless shipwrecked mariners
Clinging half frozen in the sailless rigging,
Dumb and resigned, waiting the dreadful end:
Now all the air is ringing with their gladness,
And hopes parental swell their little breasts.

Philosophers! I love to see you puzzled—
These birds that never built a nest before
Know how to set to work like journeymen

E

Duly apprenticed to the building business.
Tell me, what is the principle called instinct?
Instinct, you cleverly reply, is instinct.
I know it is, but tell me what it is?
You say it is below the gift of reason.
Truly, I did not ask you where it is;
No doubt sometimes it is as much above it.
You say it is a special kind of reason.
Indeed I see small reason in your answer;
I fear we are no nearer than at first.
Will you believe me if I tell you it?
It is the mystic indefinable gift
Of the Creator, just as reason is,
And even the graspless thing called life itself;
Beyond the powers of mind to comprehend,
Lest man should deem himself more wise than God.
If reason scales the stars that roll above us,
Explores the depths of wisdom and of knowledge,
And regulates the complex mechanism
Of national and individual life,
Instinct is just as various in its powers;
Each kind of living creature in existence
Has its own special range and kind of instinct
Adapted to its nature and abode,
Supplying thus their multitudinous wants.
The spider spins its complicated web
To catch the roving insects on the wing,
A web no barrister on earth could spin.
Their sophistries are clumsy nets to it.
No lawyer is more cunning than a rat;

No miser hides his treasure like a fox ;
The dappled deer is said to see the wind—
Your statesman only sees which way it blows ;
The dog can scent and follow up its prey
Better than your policemen can a thief ;
The carrier-pigeon through the pathless air
Can take its rapid flight straight to its nest,
Which some men cannot do who dine from home ;
And then the bees, those merry highwaymen
That bring home so much plunder to their cells,
They have more architectural skill and knowledge
Than half your great professors of the art.
They never pull their edifices down
To build them up again some better way :
There's more geometry in their small heads
Than in the heads of all our colleges.
    Our colleges are noble seats of learning,
A little narrowed by old strait-laced laws,
A little crusted with the rust of time,
But full of skulls as full of curious knowledge
As eggs are full of chicken pabulum,
And intellects by dint of constant grinding
As sharp or sharper than a Sheffield razor.
I was at Oxford ; but I took more there
Than many other youngsters bring away.
Though short my term I took a high degree
In abstract studies—sitting upon the coach
While it changed horses at the old Star Inn.
I was at Cambridge also—at the Station,
And walked along the road into the town,

And saw the outside of the Colleges;
And from the town I walked back to the Station,
Wiser and better doubtless for my walk.
I met the portly Whewell in the street,
Striding along, an intellectual giant.
I looked at him; he likewise looked at me:
In sooth I had the weather-gage of him,
For I knew him, but me he did not know:
Thus passing ships upon the lonely sea
Sail proudly by each other without speaking,
Unconscious of a bond of sympathy.

   One morning, on a steamboat's quarter-deck,
Bound but from Westminister to London Bridge,
I came in contact with a famous man,
Daniel O'Connell—Ireland's demigod.
A nobler presence few have ever owned,
Wrapt in his ample blue and tasselled mantle,
And with his hat tossed over on one side;
I knew his broad, good-humoured, manly face,
Like the bronzed visage of an old sea-captain.
His forehead was the grandest I e'er saw—
A living buttress of enormous brain.
His luscious accents trickled from his lips
With a sweet fascinating little lisp,
And deepened into solemn organ tones.
He talked with me as though we were old friends,
Conversing like the affable archangel:
He said he was the best abused of men.
His was a name that was a word of power—
A talisman to loving myriads,

Feared, flattered, envied, idolised, and trusted ;
Then it collapsed in weakness and contempt.
He was the fearless, eloquent defender
Of liberty for every race and nation,
The stern denouncer of mean tyranny,
The advocate of every patriot cause.
How did his matchless tongue move multitudes,
And sway them as the winds drive the sea waves !
The first great champion of moral force,
He brought about a mighty revolution,
Not by the suicidal gage of war,
But by the peaceful triumph of opinion.
He loved his little Emerald Isle too well—
A patriot passion which at last betrayed him.
He sought to raise her into independence,
Not seeing that two little sister islands
Must live united to be great and happy.
The bubble of his darling project burst,
And, broken-hearted, the great patriot died.
Doubtless his memory will soon rise again
In honour foremost of his age and race,
Who freed his country from a galling yoke.
      Little and great, we all have darling projects—
Our various hobbies which we love to ride.
Few people are content to go on foot ;
Some ride on elephants and trample over us ;
Some ride on camels which go stalking on
Across the arid sands of their ideas ;
Others ride mettlesome highflying hunters,
And get at last a pitch into a ditch,

Breaking their precious necks for a fox's brush ;
Some ride on obstinate, dull, kicking donkeys,
And make themselves the general laughing-stock.
'Tis very well to ride our various hobbies;
The worst of it is that men will ride too fast,
Or ride too far,—which is about as bad.
Extreme opinions end in fallacies ;
Truth pushed too far degenerates into error :
Crime does less harm sometimes than indiscretion,
Good, overstrained, is worse than actual evil.
These are but samples of a paradox,
But paradoxes often speak the truth.
What can be prettier than a paradox ?
It is a species of backhanded argument
That boldly carries everything before it.
Solomon bids men not be over righteous ;
The conscience may be too much cultivated,
And so at length may come to be diseased,
Weakening the character with erroneous crotchets,
And making men neglect great principles,
And rest their hopes of heaven on petty scruples.
We view life through the prism of our feelings,
Which give false colours to the world around us.
Truth is the glorious centre of creation,
The happy medium 'twixt the poles of being.
Beyond the compass of that glorious centre
Error and truth are dovetailed in each other,
A broad, debatable and trackless region,
Where many clever people lose themselves.
    When a man gets on horseback of a theory,

Twenty to one it runs away with him!
Some people take the saddle so unskilfully,
They gallop over everybody else.
Preserve me from the men who din their crotchets
Into the wearied ears of other people,—
Most wearisome because most aimless crotchets ;
Yet truth itself is sometimes wearisome,
And thus great principles are made to triumph,
And that which seemed sheer madness at the first
Comes to be owned the very loftiest wisdom.
So England's old restrictive laws were conquered,
The galling chains of trade were stricken off,
And the great blessing, plenty, brought to our doors.
Let every man pursue some worthy object ;
It gives him healthy exercise of mind ;
In one department of the range of knowledge
It probably makes him wiser than his neighbours.
I knew a man who sought perpetual motion—
A vain attempt, as everybody knows.
Long years he wasted in the fond pursuit ;
Yet even that was better than inaction.
It fed his brains at least with pleasing hopes ;
Ever upon the threshold of success,
He used to tell his friends " all that was wanted
Was only one more wheel" to crown his triumph.
　　My favourite pursuit is poetry,
But little counted of in modern times,
When every thought is given to business ! business !
And the great struggle is to outshine others.
Now poetry is either good or bad,

Though what the fashion of to-day calls good
The fashion of to-morrow may call bad ;
If genuine, it is inestimable,
True diamond from nature's laboratory.
If spurious, it is even worse than worthless—
It is a troublesome impertinence,
A bit of glass whose dazzling sheen deceives us,
But being found out we throw it in the fire.
The common rhymester is esteemed a fool,
True poets being birds but rarely seen,
When they are seen are rarely recognised :
Only the well-instructed eye can see.
Thus few but amorous boys write poetry,
And some old men turning to second childhood ;
Yet true it is some of our noblest poems
Were written in the calm decline of life
By poets having minds well stored with wisdom,
And knowing what to choose and what reject.
Poetry is the noblest of the arts,
The loveliest, loftiest attribute of mind ;
The medium through which the prophets spoke.
Painting is Poetry's sweet maid of honour,
Winning sometimes the smiles due to her mistress.
Painting, indeed, can speak all languages,
And has a glorious beauty of its own,
But only has a narrow local triumph.
A picture's fame may spread throughout the world,
And yet the picture hang upon a nail
In some lone corner of a gallery,
Receiving now and then a passing glance

From accidental roving visitors,
But be unknown and unenjoyed by millions,
And as its beauty is ethereal,
So is it subject to a sure decay,
And injury from officious ignorance.
Sculpture is also local in its sphere,
And subject to the accidents of time,
But grand and beautiful to look upon ;
Yes, even in its melancholy fragments ;
Witness the relics of the Parthenon !
Such also is the lot of architecture,
Amenable to countless casualties—
War, earthquakes, wind and rain, and men's caprices ;
But poetry is indestructible :
Age gives it but a richer, fuller flavour.
We carry it in our brain and in our pocket,
Alike the luxury of rich and poor.
The labourer can enjoy it in his cottage
As well as England's Queen in Windsor Castle.
It sways insensibly the minds of men,
And educates the moral sentiment,
Teaching the maxims of exalted truth,
The harmonies betwixt incongruous things ;
It quickens with a sense of heavenly beauty
The plastic soul, and elevates its aims,
Governing mankind above all parliaments !
  This is the first of April ! All Fools' day ;
A pretty fancy of our ancestors.
Suppose I turn it into Old Fool's day ;
I am a lonely, desolate old man ;

What doubts, what fears, what dreadful perturbations
Distract my mind, and steal away my sleep;
Yet Hope, man's faithful friend, not quite forsakes me.
Could I be worse off if I were to wed?
Perhaps I might be better off than ever
If I had one to take an interest in me,
And speak a few kind loving words to me;
That would be better than this loneliness.
Suppose I should fall ill, and groan with pain,
Shut up a prisoner in my own small castle,
No longer able to explore the meadows,
Or ramble on the sands of the sea-shore,
Who then will charm the physic to my palate,
And bring sweet rest to my uneasy head?
Sometimes I fancy that the gales of life
Have broken all the cordage of my heart;
I trust, though sorely battered, it is sound.
The longer that I live I love men less;
I hate their coldness and their selfishness;
But I love women better and better still.
Reliance on the faith of men fails often,
But on a woman's love, seldom or never.
I have been most unfortunate with women.
In early life death stole away, untasted,
The ripened fruit I waited for so long.
Perhaps my fond ideal was too bright,
And so I missed the good attainable.
Either I loved and was too old or poor,
And was requited only with disdain;
Or I was loved and might not love in turn;

Or duty drove me far from love astray.
But, now I am the master of my fate,
Shall I plunge headlong into matrimony?
There are no fools like old fools, it is said.
I must! I will!—why shiver on the brink?
Kind heaven, protect me in this trying hour!

    To spend my little fortune on myself,
And live a lonely crabbed life is miserable;
To leave it to some sycophant relation
Affords small consolation to the mind.
The meanest of pursuits is hoarding money,
The most condemned by general consent.
It seems to turn the inner man to stone;
And yet the miser has as great a pleasure,
Mingled of course with a few aches and pains,
In gathering solid gold into his coffers,
As the gay spendthrift who comes after him
In melting it like butter in the sun.
Could people when they die take their wealth with them,
The world, I fear, would come to poverty.
Now, when a rich old uncle quits the scene,
His heirs can hardly help respecting him,
And say a good word to his memory,
Laying the money down to buy a hatband
With a meek sentiment of satisfaction.

    To die, and have an end of all one's troubles,
And find admittance to a better world,
May soothe the pillow of a sinking man;
But to have eager, prying relatives
Ransack out all one's precious drawers and boxes,

Read one's most valued, sacred, secret letters,
Laugh at one's little tear be-sprinkled keepsakes,
. Disarrange all one's chosen books and papers,
And have one's treasures cast aside as rubbish;
To have one's old apartments desecrated
By an unfeeling, prying auction-crowd—
To have a flippant, callous auctioneer
Make jokes upon one's dear familiar chairs,
Selling one's loved inanimate old friends,
The furniture that we have used from childhood,
Fondly associated with our daily life;
To have one's very garments chaffered for,
By our relations, with a clothes'-dealer—
This seems to me one of the saddest pictures
A poor old dying bachelor can ponder.
   A sad fatality has dogged my steps
Throughout my long and varied pilgrimage—
The loss of those most near and dear to me,
The kith and kin of my own age in life—
All my own family, except my father,
Who clung to life with strong tenacity,
And to whose apron-strings I seemed fast tied
Till the decline of life came over me.
A man may see his friends struck down around him,
Until he thinks himself almost invulnerable.
Three Alfreds were my most especial friends:
Singly, and dying in exact succession,
Each friendship ending ere the next began.
In London dwelt my darling cousin Jane,
A widow with two girls on whom she doted;

She was inveterate as a London sightseer;
She knew the streets just like a hackney coachman,
And knew the history of all the streets ;
She knew the churches and the public buildings,
The arcades, the bridges, and the exhibitions ;
She was a scholar and knew everything :
Loved pictures, poetry, and statuary,
And botany, mythology, and history.
She was for years my friend and correspondent,—
Indeed almost the only one I had.
Fine fun it was to visit London then.
This might not last.   At length her daughters died,
One died in Paris, one in London died,
And she who seemed the strongest of the strong
Faded and died like them.   Her heart was broken.
There are no tears like those a mother sheds ;
And as she fell into the sleep of death,
For the last time she lifted up her eyelids
And whispered, " What a glorious company ! "
Catching, no doubt, a glimpse from her calm death-bed
Of the bright angels she was soon to join.
What a strange volume of psychology
Might be composed of dying utterances,
And from the lispings of young children's lips !
She died—and London now is changed to me,
As well as also changed within itself,
Turned upside down with railways underground,
Enormous railway-stations, Thames' embankments,
And piles of pompous modern architecture.
What would my cousin Jane have said to it ?

She knitted me a handsome green silk purse,
Every fair stitch of which she wrought with care
Beneath the glass roof of the Crystal Palace.
I kept it sacredly until her death,
And then I wore it in remembrance of her.
    To be an Englishman was always felt
A glory and a noble privilege,
But never such a privilege as now,
When all things are provided to his hand
That modern art and science can accomplish.
Not the least luxury of London life
Is the possession of the Crystal Palace,
A beautiful resort for old and young,
For wearied spirits and for ardent hearts,
So light, so airy, so exhilarating,
Ample in space for any company,
And inexhaustible in interest ;
Full of choice objects for all sorts of tastes ;
Art, science, nature, here hold festival.
Beneath this wondrous roof of dazzling glass,
Enriched with beauteous works of human skill,
A hundred thousand folks at once can ramble,
And twice as many roam about the grounds,
Parade the terraces and winding paths,
Wander amidst the fountains and the flowers,
Gape at the monsters of the olden world,
Or on the lawns in various games disport.
A Londoner is blessed above all others.
He quits the hubbub of the stifling streets,
The puzzling scramble of the chimney-pots,

And by a railway ride of half-an-hour
Transports himself into this fairy palace,
Breathes the invigorating country air,
And revels in a world of magic beauty,
Where he can find abundant elbow-room,
Shake off his cares, and lay aside constraint,
And feel himself a new and better man,
With happy faces everywhere around him,
With children glancing gaily in the sun,
And female beauty blent with floral sweetness.
　The natural texture of a woman's soul
In warp and woof is finer than a man's,
And, being beautiful by constitution,
She clings for ever round the beautiful.
In every woman's soul there dwells pre-eminently
A natural fond affinity for flowers.
The humblest female loves a flower-garden,
Although no bigger than a window-sill
High amidst roofs, where it can catch the sun,
A sort of half-way house 'twixt earth and heaven.
Flowers are the nearest types we have on earth
Of heavenly beauty, purity, and sweetness.
How strange that from the ground we tread upon,
And which for delicacy and cleanliness
We even shrink from touching with our fingers,
Should spring up countless flowers spontaneously,
Of texture fine beyond all imitation,
Of every beautiful and graceful form,
Of every perfect tint of colouring,
And every exquisite and pleasing odour !

All ye who love fair flowers in full perfection,
Go see a Flower-show in the Crystal Palace !
It is a scene of perfect fairy-land,
Arched over with a hemisphere of glass ;
A spectacle of transcendental beauty,
Showing the power of scientific knowledge
In supplementing the best floral gifts.
Here are displayed in wonderful profusion
A galaxy of nature's choicest works ;
Blossoms and fruits, magnificent in size,
Perfect in form and exquisite in perfume ;
The soul is surfeited with richest beauties ;
The senses faint with overpowering sweetness—
A sight once seen never to be forgotten,
A bright experience to remain through life.
　　Like to some gipsy tinker with his cart
Wandering at will amidst our English lanes,
I now have found my way to Kelvedon,
The favourite scene of my young blooming days,
And pitched my traps beside the public road ;
But not like him, with a long-black-haired wife
And dirty children tumbling on the grass,
And a rough cur to frighten folks away :
I am a sad and lonely bachelor.
　　How pleasant are the meads of Kelvedon,
Where in my youthful days I played at will,
And which I now revisit in my age !
How sweetly winds its little humble river,
Known by its sounding name, the Blackwater—
Through the green level meadows it refreshes,

Where lowing heifers indolently graze,
And sheep repose or idly chew the cud.
This river, when I was the miller's son,
To me was a perpetual dear delight ;
But not for any beauty it possessed
That my philosophy was conscious of.
How eagerly I used to bathe in it
When sultry summer days made the earth pant !
But that which most of all delighted me
Were the small fish that glanced within its
    waters.
How many pleasant hours have I expended
Angling for gudgeons in the pebbly stream—
Myself a happy gudgeon all the while,
The patient votary of distant hope !
But my ambition rose to nobler fish ;
To catch an eel was then my loftiest aim,
And I succeeded and secured my prize.
I even dared to bait my line for pike,
But tempted Fortune then deserted me.
How do the memories of those early days
Come over me with freshness and delight !
But while the scene remains almost the same,
What a new world it is in which I dwell !
The living figures which then filled the scene
Are gone and vanished utterly away,
And are well-nigh forgotten, like a dream—
Faint shadows of departed human beings
That haunt the silent courts of memory.
Another generation has sprung up,

F

With new surroundings, sympathies, and tastes,
To whom my past is all a shapeless blank.
Such is this ever-changing human life;
And I must be forgotten in my turn.
A pensive sadness overspreads my feelings,
Teaching those lessons we are prone to shrink from:
There oft are golden sands in sorrow's stream.

This river thus has flowed thousands of years,
And may perhaps flow on for thousands more,
Under the shadows of the willow-trees,
And the black beeches hanging over it,
Making cool covert for the slumbering fish.
Nice place is this to idle in a boat
With gentle lady on a summer's morn,
While all the air is fragrant with the hay,
Plucking the simple wild-flowers on the banks,—
Forget-me-nots, and meadow-sweet and lilies—
And caring not how precious time flies past.
O to be cushioned on a silver cloud,
And float along the azure sea of heaven!

A charming place indeed is Kelvedon,
The birthplace of two famous orators,
One in the senate, the other in the pulpit.
Nor must the park of Felix Hall, near by,
Be unrecorded in my vagrant song—
One of those lovely rural paradises
Which only England in the world possesses,
With grassy downs, and clumps of oaks and elms,
A tasteful mansion, cultivated gardens,
Groves of dark pines, and pleasant wildernesses,

Where an old haughty family of rooks
Keep up a clatter on their pedigrees.
   Beneath an aged elm of noble size,
Growing beside the drive within the park,
I sit me down upon the rugged root,
And muse upon the tablet of the past,
While irresistible tears bedim my eyes;
The shadows of the grand but leafless boughs
Chequer fantastically the turf beneath;
Such are the memories of the times gone by!
The old Lord Western of my early days
Is dispossessed of all this fine estate
By Death, and all his greatness is departed.
Abbott, the gardener, too, is also gone;
So is his little rosy-cheeked old wife,
As rosy as the peaches in her basket,
And I survive to witness all the change.
Above my head two branches of the elm
Have met by some congenial attraction,
And clasped each other in a fond embrace,
Made one in sweet arboreous matrimony;
But I stretch out in barren loneliness,
No kindred being to unite with me.
   Familiar once to quaint old doggrel Tusser,
Who wrote "Five Hundred Points of Husbandry;"
And now familiar to illustrious Mechi,
The pioneer of modern agriculture—
A charming place indeed is Kelvedon:
One object above all attracts the eye,
On every side it is the central charm—

The village spire piercing the old elm-trees.
To me it is the prettiest spire in England,
Perfect in geometrical proportion,   .
Giving an air of cheerfulness and lightness
To all the rural scenery around it ;
And, when the bells at eventide are ringing,
Nothing of sylvan sort can be more charming.
  A pleasant place is this old world to live in
If we are but disposed to make the best of it,
And keep it in its place—under our feet—
Not let it get above us, and weigh us down.
Pleasant it is to pry into its history
And watch the seasons passing over it.
Every bright pebble that we tread upon
Has markings on it of the hand of God ;
A history more amazing and more ancient
Than any written by the hand of man ;
A language which no linguist can decipher ;
We only know it tells a buried history
Of the world's infant life, could we but read it,
Millions of years ago, ere man was formed.
Ours is a world of wonders.   Land and ocean
Both have their problems which we cannot solve,
The earth and sea are full of forms of beauty.
How admirable they are ! how full of life,
From the ephemeral transcendental insect
Up to man's reasoning spiritual being—
The wondrous link uniting earth and heaven !
How glorious and how vast is God's creation !
The sun is the stupendous fiery furnace

That works the engine of the universe,
Plying the shuttle of the rolling spheres,
And weaving every season in its course,
Decking the earth with flowery suits of raiment,
Clothing the trees with draperies of leaves,
Rolling the tides, driving the boisterous winds,
Doing the rough work of the changing seasons,
Yet winning from the sods beneath our feet
Beautiful flowers of every form and fragrance,
And fashioning fruits of richest hue and flavour.
A wondrous piece of mechanism is the world !
Men marvel at the Great Creator's power,—
I marvel quite as much at His supreme,
His inexhaustible inventiveness.
Each morn and eve Nature's great Decorator
Paints a new picture in the changing sky,
Not here alone, but round the world as well.
We cannot count the sands on the sea-shore,
Yet no two grains of sand are just alike.
He gives a different perfume to each flower,
A different character to every face,
To every tree and plant a different form,
And peoples earth and sea with living creatures,
Of tribes diverse beyond man's power of counting :—
How shall not man adore the Infinite God !
    Spring, Summer, Autumn, Winter, round and round
These changing seasons circle all the year.
First comes the Spring, like a young modest damsel,
Smiling, but coy, shrinking, but fresh and fair.
Spring is the time for Nature to awake
From wintry sleep, and put her verdure on,

For flowers to blossom on the green hill's side,
For merry larks to whistle up to heaven,
For bees to hum, and milk-white buds to burst,
For bleating lambs to canter down the hillocks,
And fish, flesh, fowl, and folk to merry-make.
Then comes the Summer, like a happy matron,
With all her little ones around her knees.
Summer is the time for earth to yield her fruits,
For hay-field frolics and for horns of ale,
For waggons creaking with a weight of sheaves,
For harvest-suppers round the jocund table,
For plunging headlong into limpid streams,
And courting damsels by the moon's pale light.
Then comes the Autumn, like an ancient spinster,
With frowns and smiles and storms and angry tears.
Autumn is the time for Nature to forego
Her youthful bloom, and make up for her loss,
With all the rich and tawdry borrowed hues
That fading beauty loves to deck herself,
To catch the fleeting glance of admiration;
For melancholy rains and miry roads,
For blustering winds to drive the clouds along,
For premature sharp nights and rimy frosts,
For leaves to drop off with a breath of air,
And candles lighted when the kettle sings.
Then comes the Winter, like a hale old man
Wrapped in his cloak, with frosty locks and beard,
Hedge-stake in hand, and pipe between his lips.
Winter is the time for clear, cold starlight nights,
And driving snows, and frozen roads and rivers,
For crowding round the blazing Christmas fire,

For telling tales that make the blood run cold,
For sipping elder-wine and cracking filberts,
For friendships, chilblains, fun, roast beef, mince-
    pies,
And shivering fits on jumping into bed,—
And thus the year goes round, and round, and round.
    Although I am a crusty bachelor,
I am a zealous friend of matrimony;
If I should ever be the king of England
I will lay down some very spanking laws;—
Every young man of the age of five-and-twenty
Shall have a loving wife to comfort him,
And every girl who wishes for a husband
Shall have a manly breast to lay her head on.
    'Tis sweet for loving hearts to come together!
The pleasant lottery of matrimony
Is not like other doubtful lotteries,
For here the law of chances is reversed,
The blanks are few, the prizes plentiful.
Women are not like heartless birds of passage
That share with us the summer of our joy,
But leave us in the winter of our sorrow;
They are the robins that cling round our homes.
Marriage is oft delayed by far too long;
We lose our prime in waiting to be blest;
Youth is the special time for happiness;
Neglected, only gleaning ears are left,
Instead of the full harvest of enjoyment.
We want some easier way of getting married—
Promoting marriage in a business manner. ·

How many sweet, retiring, modest girls,
With bosoms bursting for connubial joys,
Pass on through life in wasting loneliness,
Unknown, unheeded, unappreciated,
Unintroduced to honourable hearts
That might have loved them and have wedded them,
And thus are left in sadness to consume !
There are too many single men and women,—
We sacrifice to love of style in living
The very love which is worth living for.
Women regard themselves too much as toys,
To be caressed and dressed, amused and flattered,
And not as fellow-workers with their husbands
For life's chief good—domestic happiness.
The primal law of human life is labour;
Women as well as men should work to live,
And mutual effort will make labour sweet :—
There will be found enough for each to do.
How many a pale and languid sickly lady
Would catch her female servant's fine robustness
And healthy hue by helping in her labours,
And be the happier for the occupation !
   Women are abject slaves to one another;
They live in terror of each other's eyes,
And hence their efforts to out-dress their neighbours,
Their eager hankering after each new fashion,
However ugly, monstrous, and absurd.
Simple apparel is the most becoming,—
Men judge of women not by style of dress,
But by their manners and their conversation ;

It is the sweetly modulated voice,
The manners springing frankly from the heart,
As much or more than merely handsome features,
That most attract the man best worth the having,
And not the foolish ornaments of fashion.
Men, after all, although they flatter beauty,
Prefer to trust their future happiness
To women who have sense and pleasing manners,
And promise to be helpmeets to their husbands,
Not playthings to be quickly wearied of,—
Fine, but profuse, and frivolous, though fair.
  I think that parents should advise their children,
With the sound counsel of experienced age,
And aid them in the great concern of marriage;
Consult them on their tender inclinations,
And bring about the object of their wishes;
Not looking first of all to wealth or rank,
But similarity of tastes and tempers,
And healthiness, the greatest earthly treasure:
And when a young and happy couple wed,
Whether their income may be large or small,
Let them be well content to live within it.
The modesty and diffidence of youth
Too often throw a blast o'er their existence,
And destine them to dreary celibacy,
And the sad loss of life's supremest joys,
When, by a little wise encouragement,
And conference of parents in the case,
They might be wedded, and live thenceforth happy:—
The diffident are oft the most deserving.

I loved a lady in my early days,
Unknown to her and all the world around.
For twelve long years I hugged a hopeless passion,
Which was not hopeless could I have foreseen;
And when at last the clouds began to break,
And I stretched out my hands to the ripe fruit,
The selfishness of others proved our bane,
And our fair hopes were blasted fatally.
The less I say about it now the better,
But had we married, as we might have done,
She probably would now have been alive—
Instead of sinking to an early tomb,
Nursing a secret sorrow in her heart—
And been the mother of a group of children,
Gentle and good and handsome as herself!
And as for me, I might have been a man,
Instead of being, as I am, a cipher,
Snubbed by the single, laughed at by the married,
And holding no position in the world—
An outcast unto whom life is a burden.
　　It is a pity to throw away our pity.
I think I have a rather tender heart :—
I have a special pity for poor worms
That, having lost their holes amidst the darkness,
Crawl helplessly about the ground at morn;
And many hundreds I have taken tenderly,
And put their heads into the open holes,
And watched them wriggle in with heartfelt pleasure,
Praying that God would do as much for me.
And yet there are three creatures in the world

For which, I frankly own, I feel no pity—
Rats, asses, widows—and what I say I mean.
First is the rat, the very soul of mischief,
Crafty beyond the stretch of legal wit,
A real embodiment of wickedness;
And when I see one safely in a trap,
Caught by the leg, savage with rage and pain,
Gnawing the very iron that holds him fast,
I feel a lively pleasure at his capture—
Livelier and far more warrantable than his
Who hunts a timid, innocent hare to death.
Next is the stubborn ass that will not go,
Or, if he goes, will stop if he is struck,
Because his driver wants to mend his pace—
Judging inversely of the sense of things,
And acting on the rule of contrary.
The ass always takes care of Number One.
I never heard of one, in all my days,
Do as some men do—work himself to death.
His tastes are mean : he is content with thistles—
A taste not e'en a Scotchman would approve.
Corporal suffering is a vanishing quantity.
The ass has very little sense of suffering,
Or has philosophy, and disregards it,
Or if he feels the stroke he does not mind it,
Or is obtuse, and cannot understand it,
Or is debased, and knows that he deserves it,
Or is incorrigible, and so defies it.
As to a widow, I will state my case :—
When I consider how she used the man,

Before she married him, whom now she mourns,
How she rejected him with scorn and insult,
The joy she took in aggravating him,
How she despised him, laughed at him, avoided him,
Teased him and baffled him and disappointed him,
Worried him, angered him, tortured him, and mad-
     dened him—
Does she deserve one's pity at the loss of him?
And then to see her whimper and shed tears,
And make herself a fright in widow's weeds,
And plant sweet violets on the poor man's grave—
All I shall say is, I don't pity her!
   It is, no doubt, a very pretty practice
To plant sweet flowerets on a favourite grave,
It tells of gentle love and tenderness ;—
Marble at best is cold and shivery ;—
Inscriptions may describe no end of love.
No end of virtues and no end of sorrow ;
But marble strikes a coldness to the heart,
And makes one doubt whether the flattering tale,
So studied, stately, and elaborate,
Is true, sincere, reliable, and honest ;
But flowers are Nature's sweet interpreters,
Appealing to the feelings of the heart,
Symbols of truth and faith and fond affection ;
They make no fine and questionable professions,
But sweetly indicate that hearts survive,
Bound to the dead by a mysterious chain.
   I love to roam about a cemetery,
And read the names of many I have known,

And silently recount their history ;
How various are they, soon to be forgotten,
Yet full of interest and even romance !
With every man who dies a history dies,
Known to no human being but himself,
A folio volume, but in faded type,
Full of the chequered incidents of life,
Frolic and joy, sorrow and disappointment,
With a wide margin of unrealised hopes.
I know a tomb half-hidden in the grass—
'Tis not a hundred miles from Colchester—
A modest tomb, whose lonely, shelving sides
Record two names, a husband and a wife ;
They lived directly opposite my home,
Across the street.   I saw them every day.
The reckless man, when he became of age,
Inherited a small but dangerous fortune.
Having no parents to direct his steps,
He long before had wandered far astray,
And now he entered on a random life ;
And yet he did one act that might have saved him,—
He offered marriage to a gentle girl,
Beautiful, fragile, amiable, but poor ;
And she, an inexperienced child, persuaded
By foolish friends, and dazzled by his trinkets,
Threw her pure self away upon the spendthrift,
And fondly hoped that she could win him back
To virtuous ways, sobriety, and duty ;
But his delirium could not be arrested :
The fitful madness of intoxication

Hurried him on to ruin and to death,
And made him cruel to the wretched wife,
Whom he had rashly sworn to love and cherish :—
No tongue can ever tell her misery.
Ere long his vices undermined his health,
And so he coughed himself into his coffin,
Leaving behind him two sweet innocent babes
And a poor widow, only a mere girl,
With the death-arrow rankling in her heart;
But though a serpent had lain next her bosom,
Yet had he left her pure as driven snow !
She quickly died, as a dear saint should die,
With her white wasted hands folded in peace,
And looking upward towards a better world.
There they both sleep in one unnoticed grave :
And who shall say that the young wrestling saint,
Through pardoning mercy, did not save the sinner !
    This tragic story which I just have written,
Coming so freshly to my memory,
And so recalling times for ever passed,
Opened up wide the floodgates of my tears—
For I am rather womanish that way—
And now I feel so much the cheerfuller,
As brightest sunshine follows a summer shower,
And therefore I will tell another story
About the tenant of a stoneless grave,
Within a hundred miles of Kelvedon,
By name Ben Baker, an industrious man
As parish grave-digger.   His was a face
Appropriate to his serious occupation,

Grim beyond ordinary experience ;
He was an ancient, careful, prudent man,
A lonely bachelor—I know what that is—
And he at last was driven to wed or die.
Perhaps he queried who would bury him,
And this might urge him forward in the matter ;
And so he looked about him for a wife,—
Some careful, thrifty body,—one not likely
To burden him with brats and all their costs.
He found one soon. He thought that she was old :
He was mistaken,—she was only ugly.
They married, and she quickly bore him twins,
Then one by one in regular succession,
And ere the baker's dozen was complete
He threw himself in despair into the river.
    Old men should take good heed what they are about
When they allow themselves to dream of marriage ;
It is a pleasing kind of fascination,
Distorting the appearances of things,
And making sober age ridiculous,—
Like friskiness in venerable cows—
And yet to live alone and be uncared for,
Unloved, unloving, weary, purposeless,
Flouted perhaps by servants, friends, and neighbours,
Pitied, yet half enraged at being pitied—
This is enough to urge a grey-haired man
Into the nearest pond of matrimony ;
But then to marry with a worn-out heart,
Battered with all the waves of a long voyage,
Tossed with a thousand storms of sudden passion,

What hope is there of wedded happiness?
I can speak only of my own poor heart.
It has been sadly knocked about in life,
And yet it has a little kindness left ;
It has a corner, like poor Crusoe's bag,
In which there are some precious kernels left
Which yet may germinate and bring forth fruit—
A joyful harvest of domestic love.
I have been shamefully treated by the women ;—
Rejected, laughed at, scorned, insulted, slighted,
And yet with manly magnanimity
I would forgive it all for the sake of one,
If I could find her, who would love me truly ;—
Perhaps I see her now in yonder garden,
Walking sedately midst the summer flowers,—
I can but die once only—being desperate
Let me walk boldly as to the very gallows,
Or block, or altar, pretty much all one,
And rid myself of all my wretchedness.

I have loved many in my chequered life,
And some with faithful and devoted love,
Alas, too fondly for my peace of mind ;
Still loving most where love was all in vain !
But never have I felt but once the rapture,
The ecstacy of love's entrancing passion,
And that was when I was a shame-faced boy,
Even before my teens had yet begun,—
I was a school-boy, and I loved a school-girl!—
Her presence was a transport of delight,
Making the air seem tremulous with joy.

Mine was a pure and spiritual love,
A passion of the young unsullied soul,
Without the slightest taint of this low earth,
Like a clear dew-drop pendant from a rose.
A mystic change came over my existence,
Silvering the aspect of surrounding objects,—
I lived as in a blissful waking dream,
A passing dream not to be dreamed again,—
I never touched that youthful creature's hand,
It made me tremble but to speak to her,
Seldom I ventured further than a smile,
Perhaps she never noticed that I loved her,—
At least no answering passion swelled her breast :
Not long the sweet infatuation lasted,—
The proud young beauty treated me with scorn,
Which, like cold water mingling with hot steam,
Caused a collapse, and eased my swollen heart,
Changing my feverish joy to pensive sadness.

Whoever wed at least should have a home,
Humble it may be, but a sacred place,
The best of castles, where we can live snugly ;
Where we can shut ourselves securely in,
And shut the troublous world entirely out ;
A little kingdom where we can bear sway
Without dictation from proud folks outside.
How precious is a peaceful settled home !
But I have none. I am a restless wanderer,
Easily pleased but hard to satisfy,
Moving from place to place, and growing old,
Seeking a cot that I may call my own,

G

In which to settle down and end my days,—
A cheerful homestead with a fruitful garden,
Where I may watch at eve the setting sun
While my own sun is setting peacefully.
   I have a thought,—perhaps too bright a thought !
Why should I not a little meadow purchase
And build myself a dwelling to my taste,
With a snug study for my books and pictures,
And all accommodations to my mind ?
But one thing at the outset troubles me—
Where can I get the gold with which to build ?
No matter.　People love to lend their money,
Or else there would be fewer fortunes lost.
Better it is sometimes to give than lend,
For he who trusts another risks himself.
I have a notion about building houses,—
The subject has engaged my grave attention,—
Why should I not display my fair design?
The world and I are quite at loggerheads
About good taste in architectural beauty,—
A modern madness seems to have seized the builders,—
A pestilent new style affrights the sun,
All angles, ornaments, and irregularities,
Most rampant in heads quaint and clerical ;—
Horror of horrors ! what am I to do ?
Which way am I to turn lest I go mad ?
I have gone mad.　These red monstrosities,
Like the red flag waved by the *matador*
In the bull's face, described in Spanish bull-fights,
Drive me incontinently to desperation,

I can read MYSTERY, BABYLON upon them,
I feel myself already in purgatory;
On every side I see these blood-stained piles,
Top-heavy chimneys threaten to overwhelm me,
These acute angles agonise me acutely,
They pierce remorselessly into my flesh
And make me shudder for my dearest country,
The narrow windows seem to squeeze my ribs,
These pinnacles, like candlestick-extinguishers,
Serve to put out the light of other days,
Sepulchral doorways press my spirit down,
These variegated bricks make me turn sick
With recollections of gilt ginger-bread,
Go where I may nowhere can I escape them.
I am gone mad,—as mad as a mad bull,—
At every three-wont-way starts up a school-house,
Staring full at you as you ride along,
Enough to frighten any spirited horse,—
One need be well aware lest the horse shy,—
The pious rector, zealous for the Church,
And the good-natured wealthy rural squire,
Have laid their heads together seriously
To flank the growing movement towards dissent,
And built a school-house, and a mess they have made
    of it,
And stuck it where you must encounter it,
Or shut your eyelids to avoid the sight,
A horrid architectural enormity,
A sort of mongrel medieval scare-crow,
Red as the squire and heavy as the rector.

Schools, churches, parsonages, and sumptuous mansions
All are infected with this scarlet fever,
And suffer sore from osseous distortion.
Wherefore go back to Queen Elizabeth
In these good days of Queen Victoria?
  The mightiest edifices of puny man
Re-act on his comparative littleness,
And make him look more puny than he is!
The castle I am building in the air—
In other words my cot—is simple, plain,
Handsome, convenient, airy, and picturesque,
Not fashioned to attract a wondering stare,
But rather to excite a natural wish
To live and love, grow old, and die in it.
  Taste is a fashion like all other fashions,
And has as many masks as harlequin;
But truth and beauty are unchangeable.
Can any human ingenuity
Improve the beauty of a perfect flower,
Or give its perfume purer delicacy?
Artists dissatisfied with what is good
Are ever straining after novelty,
And would much rather worship the grotesque
Than not surprise the world with something new.
This leads them into endless sloughs and quagmires,
Up to their chins in gross absurdities—
Seeking with mischievous perverted strength,
The strength of ill-directed genius,
Rather to drag their wondering comrades in,
Than scramble out and free themselves from soil.

This everlasting labour for effect
Shows an unhealthy state of public taste,
Worse than black patches upon beauty's cheek.
    The whim of building for myself a dwelling
Maintained its fury four-and-twenty hours,
And then died out, leaving no sign of smoke.
In truth I am too old to think of building,
I should aim rather at a heavenly mansion;
How should I stand the plague of tiresome workmen,
Their worry, blunders, and sheer dilatoriness?
How should I bear all sorts of extra charges,
Burning like caustic through and through my purse,
And leaving it a wretched shrunken thing,
Of no more use to me or anybody
Than a dead worthless yellow cabbage leaf?
In vain should I insert my fingers in it,
And draw them back again and find them empty;
In vain should I produce it from my pocket
And look at it with seeming confidence,
And find that all its magic potency
Had melted, flitted, vanished and escaped.
Upon the other hand, to borrow money
Is pitiful to manly independence;
It has a tendency to lower one's eyelids,
And what it adds in firmness to the legs
It takes away in weakness to the back:
Let younger men, then, build if so they please,—
Fools build, but wise men buy a finished house.
    There is a goblin that bestrides the world,
A ruthless tyrant whom we all bow down to;

This ogre, this inexorable tyrant,
This trampler upon human rights is—Fashion.
Strange that mankind should love a despotism,
And while they kick against one kind of rule,
Should uncomplainingly endure another,
And while they strut with one leg gallantly,
Should with the other drag a horrid clog;
That while they beard the aristocracy,
And rail about harsh laws in Church and State,
Clenching their angry fists against oppression,
They yet should pay a tyrant to ride over them,
Saddling themselves with never ending taxes!
Ye worshippers of Fashion, what do ye worship?
Satan is the inventor of the fashions,
And they who follow the fashions follow him;—
He has a special grudge against the women
Because so nearly allied to heaven's angels;
He tried his first temptation on a woman,
And now he tortures them with love of fashions,
Makes them submit to every sort of suffering—
To inconvenience and disfigurement,
With ever-changing ceaseless restlessness,
To wreak upon them his malign revenge.
The savage paints himself with flaring ochre,
The English lady has recourse to rouge;
The savage wears his rings beneath his nostril,
The English lady hangs them from her ears;
The savage files his teeth to look like saws,
The Chinese think that little stumpy feet
Are most becoming in a finished beauty;

Our ladies think the torture best applied
To crush and render stiff the lithesome waist,
Vainly attempting to improve on nature,
And substitute a hideous ideal :—
The tyrant Fashion wills to have it so.
  This is a world of change. The seasons change,
Night follows day, and age succeeds to youth,
And fortune changes, and our friends depart,
Yet people need must add the change of fashions
To all the other changes they endure ;
They follow fast, and over-top each other,
Like idle waves breaking upon the shore.
Look at the pictures of our ancestors,
What perfect frights they chose to make themselves,
Judged by the modes that tyrannise us now,—
But fashions follow faster now than ever ;
The fashions prevalent a year ago
To-day are deemed ridiculous and stupid ;
The wickedest of women set the fashions,
The best of women quickly follow them ;
For women ever are each other's slaves,—
And thus the whirligig of time goes round.
  Slaves all ! slaves all ! slaves all ! we all are slaves !
Some to a foolish crotchet of the brain,
Some to an idle habit formed in youth,
Some to a treacherous glass of sparkling liquor,
Some to a pipe of villainous tobacco,
But most of us to other people's eyes.
  Unnumbered are the forms that slavery takes :
We choose our master when we form a habit.

I see a man looking most grave and sensible,
Day after day, and oftener than the day,
With something ugly sticking from his mouth,
A little, crooked, perforated tube,
Six inches long, black and repulsive-looking,
And having a protuberance at the end,
From which a curling quackling fume arises.
Indicative of latent fire within.
He sucks the sombre perforated tube,
And draws into his mouth the nauseous fume,
Fed by combustion of a foreign weed,
And puffs it slowly out into the air;
Perhaps he watches its return to nothing,
And finds a moral in its evanescence;
And this to this grave man is happiness!
More precious to him than his daily food!
But adding something to his natural thirst,
And leading him direct to drinking-habits!
Thus he imbibes a deleterious poison;—
If he should swallow it, it poisons him,
And if he spits it out, the waste of spittle
Spoils his digestive powers, and slowly kills him;
While wise and thoughtful men act so unwisely
No wonder boys, that would be men, do likewise,
Although it makes them puke and have the headache:—
One comfort is, the tax upon tobacco
Fills nicely full the coffers of the state,
And wise it seems that fools should pay the taxes,
If the majority of men are fools.
    There is one folly overtops all others,—

The worship of a poisonous glittering serpent
That everywhere besets our path through life;
Like Aaron's rod, when it became a serpent,
It swallows up all others round about it,—
How strange that serpent-worship should exist
In this broad day of man's enlightenment,—
This is the serpent of the sparkling cup.
I have seen beauty laid upon its altar;
I have seen youth in its attractiveness
Offered in reckless sacrifice before it;
I have seen genius with its heaven-born gifts,
Its brilliancy, its potency, its fervour,
Abandoned to it with a spendthrift's waste;
I have seen men under its fascination
Throw health and wealth and character away,
The honours, duties, sanctities of life,
Respect of friends, and also self-respect,
The joys of home, the smiles of wife and children,
And, more than all, the hope of future joy
In the bright happy world that lies beyond us!
Whoever feels this serpent's eye upon him,
Seeking to witch him with its fascination,
Let him escape from it as for his life,
Or he will be transfixed unconsciously,
And rendered helpless in the serpent's grasp,
The coiling serpent, whose encircling folds
Throttle the helpless victim to the death.
Flee from the serpent! Do not tamper with it;
Beware of its deceitfulness, and shun it,
For at the last it stingeth like an adder.

How this worn heart of mine goes pit-a-pat,
Long tossed upon the stormy waves of life!
O for the sweet repose of fond affection,
The quiet joy of corresponding love!
The doctors tell me that my heart is sound,
And so no doubt it is, though battered sore,—
What can be done? The sovereignest thing in the
     world
Is matrimony for an inward bruise.—
Lie still my heart:—Once more pluck up thy courage.—
Let's make an end of this :—I must :—I will.
I am a healthy, hearty, brisk old fellow,
A tall and well-made man, with ruddy cheeks;
'Tis true the sleepless fire within my brain
Has singed the hair off from on top my head,
Leaving a border only, white as ashes,
But yet I feel almost as young as ever.
I am a man without your vulgar vices,
I have a wise objection to tobacco,
I neither make a smoke-hole of my mouth
Nor do I make a dust-bin of my nose,
I have no taste for leaping over hedges,
And tumbling headlong into muddy ditches,
Risking my limbs, if not my life itself,
In the pursuit of a poor frightened hare,
Or worse than that, a worthless stinking fox ;
And I can trust my legs to carry me
Much better than the legs of any horse.
Nor have I any taste for shooting birds,
Which many a sportsman has left off at last

By shooting his companion or himself,
I have no taste for any sort of gambling;
I have no love for either dogs or horses,
For cats, poll-parrots, or grimacing monkeys,
By which sly nature parodies vain man;
I love to study books, and men, and women,—
Then wherefore should a woman slight my offer?
I have been humbled by adversity,
And yet I have some decent self-respect,
And I am proud to say that I have never
So far demeaned myself in my own eyes
As to solicit twice a woman's hand.
I look upon myself as quite a catch;
I have a little fortune of my own,
Enough and plenty to keep house upon
In simple wise, without the cares of business,—
Thanks to the bounteous Giver of good gifts.
Am I a fool to think about a wife?
What do I care for being called a fool?
Call me a fool if so it pleases you.

    Fools are of many sorts : some are by nature,
And some are fools from being over wise;
It is your very special clever people
That perpetrate the most egregious blunders
Which people stand amazed to contemplate.
Some clever men have so much craftiness
They over-reach themselves, and so are fools,
Grudging their shillings and their sixpences,
But prodigal of golden sovereigns.
Some men are fools in one particular thing,

And wise enough in everything beside.
I am a fool amongst my fellow men,
But in my craft they are but fools to me.
Some men are fools in hatred, some in love,—
The last a very common sort of folly.
Wise men are fools where women are concerned!
Some men are wise through all the prime of life
To the farthest verge of life's peninsula,
And knock down all their wisdom at the last
By doing some outrageous foolish thing—
Publish a book, or marry a young wife.
Some men are fools in ardent love of study,
Seeking to lay up boundless stores of knowledge,
Husbanding moments of a fragile youth
To lose by early death long years of life;
They perish in the glory of their promise.
Many may die too soon for fond affection,
But there are some men live too long for fame.
Some men are fools in toiling after wealth,
As if vain glittering gold were happiness,
Or had not, like a golden-crested eagle,
Out-spreading wings to fly away towards heaven.
Misers, like bees, lay up abundant stores,
And so are suffocated at last in smoke :—
The rich but seldom get their money's worth!
Pride often makes men fools! so does ambition!
Witness the story of the Corsican.
There is an inward rottenness in greatness,
Few would have thought of from its fair outside!
But no more monstrous folly blinds mankind

Than to think only of this fleeting life,
This gay, delusive, troublous state of being—
A meteor's flight, a moment of existence,
Unmindful of the infinite duration
Opening before us in another world,
Where there is no uncertainty of life,
And neither is there any fear of death.
O! to feel sure of being happy there
Amongst the truly wise indeed who shine
Even as the brightness of the firmament,
And as the stars of heaven, for ever and ever!
Yes, to feel sure of being happy there
Is to be happy here transcendently,
Ransomed and reconciled and heaven-adopted,
Bound in the covenant of an endless life :—
This is the only solid rock of joy.

As a tired traveller after a long journey
Arrives beneath the wall of some great city,
And speculates on all its unknown glories,
So do we stand before the lofty wall
Of blank futurity which now divides us
From the dim world of spiritual existence,
Curious and hopeful, glad of rest at last.

Here endeth Book the Second of this my Poem.
The shades of evening-time again descend ;
The sun has done his labour for the day,
And wearily retires to seek his bed
Of soft but sombre clouds piled in the west,
Like huge amorphous rocks tumbled together.

Others to right and left rear their grand forms,
As I have seen Mont Blanc at eventide,
Sweetly suffused as with a rosy blush;
While from the centre bursts a flood of flame,
Irradiating all the western sky,
Like a volcano from its depths disgorging
The pent-up volume of its fiery fervour :—
A glow of glory fading soon away.

BOOK III.

BOOK III.

A YEAR ago I plunged into this song
Head-foremost, and without premeditation;
I then was but a lonely wanderer,
Without a prospect or an occupation,
Wending from place to place to find a home.
It was at Yarmouth I began my song,   *1866*
That ancient town of many narrow alleys,
Where all I claim as mine is but a name
In the old church-yard of St. Nicholas,
Upon a half-obliterated stone.
Pleasant it was to see the sea again,
To watch the breakers beating on the shore,
Soothing the soul with wavy lullabies;
To breathe again the strengthening salt sea-air,
And watch the ships careering proudly past,
Calling up many a buried memory;
But howling gales with bitter biting frosts
Harrowed the sea, and sent the thundering waves
Dashing upon the shore with direful fury,
As if to break earth's iron ribs in pieces,
Driving the vessels from their anchorage,
And strewing all the beach with stranded wrecks.
I too was driven away from my weak moorings,
And sent adrift a homeless wanderer still.
    I came once more to dear old Colchester,
Where I had dwelt so long in times gone by,—

A wilderness abode of forty years,
Waiting and hoping for the Promised Land :—
Long tedious years borne down by wearing griefs,
Yet cheered by many a gleam of happiness.
The good old borough now felt desolate,
Where I was only but a shifting lodger.
I visited the graves of those I loved,
And wept upon them many tender tears,
Longing to let the slumbering tenants know
How lovingly I nursed their memories ;
And then I seized my pen, and wrote again
The flitting thoughts that floated through my mind ;
Seeking a refuge from my haunting griefs.
What cries were mine in groves and open fields
For help and guidance in my misery
To the All-powerful Friend of the afflicted !
Nor would I feed from any hand but His.
Ere long I struck my tent and wandered forth.
I visited the world's metropolis ;
But heartless London chilled me to the heart.
A man may be a great man in the country,
But find himself a small man up in London.
I who had felt that I was somebody,
Now found myself amidst the countless crowds,
And endless streets, the merest nobody,—
The veriest nothing humbled in the dust:
The firmament seemed brass over my head,
The earth seemed iron underneath my feet.
I wandered back as far as Kelvedon,
The pleasant scene of half my boyish days,

And there in reckless mood I hired a lodging,
And plied my ready pen from day to day ;
And Summer having now returned again
Fresh from the pearly chambers of the south,
And decked the daisy-covered fields once more,
I roamed amidst the old familiar scenes,
Myself become the stranger of the place.
Thus half a year had sped into the past
Since I began to write my careless song,
And I had written much, and liked it well ;
But now an unexpected revolution
In my existence—truly a most wonderful,
Astounding, startling, pleasing incident—
Scattered my thoughts and drove away my fancies :—
I suddenly became a married man !
  Old England is the garden of the ocean,
And Essex the most fertile of her counties,
And in that county is a pleasant village,
Known by the tuneful name of Kelvedon,
And in that village is a modest mansion ;
Behind this mansion lies a grassy lawn,
And in the distance is a little arbour,
And in this arbour on a summer's eve
I took my seat beside a gentle lady ;
We went into that bower unwittingly,
Not dreaming that our fates depended on it,
And we came out of it affianced lovers
Bound to each other by a deathless tie,
Lasting all time and to eternal life ;
How wonderful !—and yet not wonderful !

May I retrace my steps some forty years?
No law precludes a man from walking backwards—
Sometimes 'tis easier far than going forwards—
I do remember in my early life
When I resided in that pleasant village,
I used to know full well that modest mansion,
Also that bower, and, if I must confess,
The sprightly girls that gladdened all the scene.
Full oft my inclination took me there.—
I had a brother and a sister then,
And we were all a happy group together!
An ancient cheerful old-world gentlewoman
Spent in that family home her closing years,
And with her dwelt her orphan grand-daughters;
Their brother was my friend and schoolfellow:
Long since in song I told his tragic tale.
I was the junior of this family;
They treated me with all the greater freedom;
But they were fond of poetry, like me,
And genial natures soon assimilate.
One was the liveliest sylph that ever lived;
Her name was Martha—name for ever dear.
Another was more grave and talented;
Her name was Clemence; she was skilled in verse.
Then came Louisa, whose sweet ringing voice
Trilled many a good old tune enchantingly,
And she her pencil too could deftly use.
The youngest of the group was Caroline,
A heavenly saint in look and gentleness.
How deep a debt of gratitude I owe them!

They cheered the early efforts of my muse.
O happy days, and happy evening hours !
How little did we think of times a-coming—
That we should soon be scattered far and wide,
That three of them would very quickly wed,
And all of them would die an early death !
Thus did it come about : the ancient lady
Ere long fell ill, and gently breathed her last ;—
I helped to bear her coffin to the grave.
Then came the painful family dispersion.
Soon my fair sister Ann declined and died.
The charms of youth and beauty were her dower,
Genius and taste and warm enthusiasm.
Unto the outward eye and outward ear
Her deepest feelings were the most subdued ;
She died of what is called a deep consumption—
Say rather from a spark from off Love's altar,
Which fell upon her tender passionate feelings,
And, like a slow match in a hidden mine,
Burnt inwardly till it reached a vital part ;
And so, unsufferingly and peacefully,
To use her dying words, she " sank to glory."
Then my own family forsook the village,
And found a home in Roman Colchester ;
And so began my wilderness abode
Of well nigh forty dreary stagnant years,
Wherein I lived in my own little world
Of memories, fancies, hopes and aspirations,
Still doomed to ever coming disappointment.
Thrown back upon my lonely inner life

I cheered my early manhood as I might
With plaintive song, and thus the numbers ran:—
    "I was an exile once.   While yet a stripling,
A fair-faced, bright-eyed, curly-headed boy,
My father fell beneath the dreary pressure
Of odious and restrictive legislation,
And lost nigh all he had, yet lost he not
His faith, his fortitude, and truthful virtue;
Nor from the depths of soul-benumbing trouble,
Let go the cheerful heart.   His mother-country
Seemed as it were to turn her back upon him,
And bid him seek abroad for that asylum
Which she refused to yield.   The wrench was hard
That tore him and his family away
From our old friends and long-accustomed home,
And banished us across the breadth of ocean,
To buffet with a host of untried troubles,
Amidst a land of strangers and of strangeness.
My boyish heart was strong in resolution,
And I determined that I would not weep
Let come what would.   For many days and weeks
I sternly kept my sorrow in subjection,
And with unbending hardihood of spirit
Bore up against the weakness of my feelings ;
But all the while the tearful cloud was gathering,
And waiting but to burst.   At length a touch,—
The accidental touch of one small heart-string,
With its acute yet delicate vibration,—
Unpoised the hanging storm.   I thought of home,
That ever charming, ever darling spot,

The happy scene of innocent delights,
And all my fortitude of soul gave way;
'Twas there my infant tongue began to prattle ;
There too I learned to walk, and run alone,
And find the sweetest gooseberries in the garden ;
There first I learned to gaze on Nature's beauties ;
And there full often of a Summer's evening,
Before the open casement lifted up,
I stretched my arms out to the pretty moon.

   " Far o'er the dark deep sea in distant lands,
Beside the grandly-flowing Delaware,
I roamed a melancholy bare-foot boy ;
A weary weight lay ever at my bosom,
Not to be shaken off or charmed away.
My father bore his change the best ; my Lucy,
My eldest sister, playmate, friend, companion,
Sank under it ; for though so mild, so gentle,
So meek, so unrepining in her nature,
Yet in the under-current of her soul
She felt the pang of grief the most severely,
And as the heavenliest floweret of the garden
Is most obnoxious to the inward worm,
So did disease prey on her frame.   At length
The hour arrived that saw her dissolution.
We stood around her poor uncurtained bed
In all the speechless bitterness of sorrow,
And watched her soft unconscious respirations
As they grew faint and fainter, till she died.

   "My father, who had known the frowns of fortune
And with a meek and virtuous fortitude,

Had borne the loss of the unworthy trash
That men bow down to—when it came to this
When his own child—when his own darling daughter,
A part of his own being as it were—
Was torn for ever from his clasping arms,
This was a loss that touched him.   Time passed on,
But like the pebble which the brook glides over,
His grief remained behind.   He grew more silent,
But yet he shed no tears, though oft his face
Would work and quiver with suppressed emotion,
The outward language of an inward sorrow.

"A mist comes o'er my eyes, a dreary mist,
Wrapping in gloom the visions of the past.
Once more I stand amongst my native fields
The only changeling of a scene unchanged.

"And now grown old in care, though young in
        summers,
Blanched in the cheek but strengthened in endurance,
I come a wandering bard to the world's door.
Who will regard my knocks and bid me enter?
Who will stretch out to me the hand of welcome
And lead me forward to the festive hall,
Pile up another faggot on the fire,
Bid me unsling my harp and sweep its chords
In cadence to the soul-enlivening lay?
That having proved that something in me dwells
Of the pure spring of nature's inspiration,
By the out-burstings of impassioned spirit,
And warmth of words that rush out of the heart,
I may be greeted with sweet acclamations,

And having eaten at the festive table
At length may lay me down and sleep in peace."
   Thus did I sing : but the world would not listen
To notes so plaintive of the minstrel boy.
I knocked at the world's door but found no welcome.
As sing I must, I therefore sang to myself;
I fear my notes have mellowed very little
During the lapse of well-nigh forty years.
   In my new home, and new career in life,
At Colchester, so long to be my home,
My lonely home, one treasure I possessed—
A little upstairs room, that overlooked
Our pleasant fruitful and secluded garden.
Here often I composed ''immortal verse !"
This little room was called my Picture-room;
For all the walls I covered o'er with pictures,
Paintings, engravings, odds and ends of art,
A jumble pleasurable to look upon.
Amongst the rest there was a pencil-drawing
Of that same little bower at Kelvedon
To which I made especial reference.
Louisa sketched it, and she gave it me
As a memento of the happy past.
For forty years it graced my Picture-room.
I once composed a little song upon it,
And often gazed at it in pensive mood,
Little imagining that the dear old bower
Would witness the event that I have sung ;
Still less that she whom in that bower I plighted
Would be Louisa's gentle daughter Louie.

Ere long in our new home my mother died,
A peaceful parting after slow decline.
O, she was lovely as the loveliest statue
That ever Grecian chisel won from marble,
And gentle as the angels that hung o'er her
To bear her parting spirit up to heaven!
Never will she come back to me again,
But I will trust to go to her for ever.
Next died my brother, a distressful death ;
In health and strength and manhood's early prime,
A holier being did not tread the earth.
He was my sorrowing father's chiefest joy,
His favourite son, submissive as a child,
Who now was left alone with only me,
The last survivor of his family band ;
And thus it came to pass that in the ordering
Of an All-wise mysterious Providence
I, who at my poor entrance into life
Received no welcome from my burdened father,
Became the stay of his declining age :
Ever increasing duties hemmed me round,
Duties of business and domestic duties,
And also civil duties, not a few.
By trade a brewer, on a humble scale,
My father was a valetudinarian,
Who never would be left an hour alone.
I walked with him whene'er he walked abroad,
And always slept within convenient call ;
I read to him, or he would talk to me,
For he was mighty as a charming talker ;

Indeed he did the talking of the family :
And thus for thirty years I tended him,
Till he grew deaf and till his sight grew dim,
So deaf that we no longer could converse,
So dim of sight he could not see to read :
Strong in his will, but weak in mind and body,
Thus he became a poor bedridden man,
Talking and praying, or repeating Scripture,
And poetry, with a clear ringing voice,
Conversing with imaginary hearers,
Or dreaming wondrous dreams and telling them,
Until worn out with one-and-ninety years
He peacefully and joyfully departed,
A heavenly smile beaming upon his face,
Ruddy as youth and still without a wrinkle.
    While thus I wandered back to vanished times
A sacred duty bids me speak of one
To whose dear memory I owe a debt
Of inextinguishable gratitude :
A humble friend, our generous female servant,
Elizabeth, who for some thirty years,
With matchless care and assiduity,
Unfailing kindness and intelligence,
Gave a sweet sense of homeness to our dwelling.
She was my chief companion through long years,
For prudish ladies shunned a wifeless home,
And left me to my solitary pride.
Nature had given her a noble mind,
Above the usual type of common people.
Taught only in the school of early hardship,

Her little learning all was self-acquired.
I envied her her wondrous memory;
I loved to read to her books of foreign travel,
Which her acute appreciative mind
Enjoyed above all other kinds of reading,
Till she would long to visit foreign lands;
In truth as far as books would serve as ships
We went all round the beauteous world together.
Beauty she loved, and she was beautiful,
And loved to have the beautiful around her,
She was to me a sister dearly loved,
And I to her scorned not to be a brother.
Our mothers bore us both at the same time;
To me and to my father she devoted
Her energies with all a woman's ardour;
Through fire or flood she would have rushed to serve us;
Indeed she sacrificed for us her life,
For when my father grew at length quite deaf,
She strained her voice to try and make him hear;
And a most dreadful malady attacked her,
So that she could not eat, or drink, or speak:
And thus at length she perished of starvation,
After a year or more of ceaseless suffering.
The poor old man survived her a few months,
And then, worn out with age, peacefully died;
But never from my mind can be effaced
The memory of that dreadful double trouble,
The culmination of long years of grief.
    I who had sighed for freedom all my life
Was now at last enfranchised with a vengeance!

To love one spot above all other spots
In the wide world of beauty round us spread,
And feel that dearest spot made desolate—
To have its old associations ruined
As by an over-whelming flood of trouble,
And each familiar object made a weapon
To pierce us to the very heart with anguish—
To see on all things round the shadow of death—
This is an agony to crush the soul !
I could not bear the scene of my distress,
Blank memories haunted me on every side.
I gave up business, home, and my old neighbours,
And wandered forth to seek a new abode,
Alone, and in the sad decline of life,
Unable to forget the painful past.
I roamed from town to town, but found no rest.
I tried the ocean shore, I tried the city,
And then I tried the charms of rural life,
The guest of Wiffen in his pleasant cottage
O'erlooking Woburn's noble ducal park,
The only man of letters in my lifetime
Who deemed me worth his notice and regard,
And sought me out in my obscurity,—
A total stranger—patted me on the back,
Cheered me with praise and offered me his friendship ;
A heart-warm kindness never to be forgotten.
Profoundly learned in the history
Of the great Protestant movement in old Spain
Three hundred years ago, which was stamped out
By the dread Office of the Inquisition,

He brought to light the interdicted writers—
Juan de Valdés and his followers,
Printing their works again for modern use:
Not least the ALFABETO CHRISTIANO,
Which Valdés wrote for Giulia Gonzaga,
She, whose fine portrait decks our National Gallery,
Done by Sebastiano del Piombo,
A high-born dame, beautiful, learned, pious.
With the old poet and philosopher
I held delightful converse day by day,
Roaming with him through Aspley's classic woods,
Listening unconsciously to dying words;
Or by his fireside, from his own dictation,
Penning each day his learned narrative,
Snatching it as it were from the grave's mouth,
For so he yielded to my warm request.
Doubtless it was my pleasure in this task
That prompted me in my sad loneliness
To take my pen in hand again soon after,
And plunge into the torrent of this song.

Our work performed I bade my friend farewell;
I did not wish to wear my welcome out.
Again I wandered forth, but soon returned;
Sad, like myself, he wished for company,
Being a bachelor, too, and old and ailing.
Ere long my passion for the salt-sea beach
Came over me, and I once more forsook him,
And never saw his well-known face again.
Within a few short weeks, after we parted,
My friend, alas, fell ill, and gently died—

He died before I knew that he was ill—
Died, where he lived from youth to good old age,
Within the cheerful sound of Woburn bells.
Meanwhile I found my way to good old Yarmouth,
A year ago, and there commenced this song,
Leaving to chance the subject of my lay.
That which ensued I have already told,
And thus have I come round to where I started.
My tale has proved a perfect whirligig.
Some half a year, or more, had passed away
Since I began this bold discursive song,
When suddenly I ceased my task—to marry!
The fifteenth day of August was the day
On which the matrimonial knot was tied;
That great event broke off my singing mood,
And changed my fancies for realities.
I now once more resume my various song:
The heat of composition is upon me;
I am as feverish as a sitting hen;
My poem swells, for matter freely flows,
And I must write till I have had my say.
As happy married couples often do,
Away we hasted to the Isle of Wight,
That paradise of newly-wedded pairs.
We rambled on the sands of calm Sea View,
We visited the grave of Little Jane,
We sauntered up sweet shady Shanklin Chine,
We roamed about the lovely Undercliff,
We clambered up the steep St. Boniface,
And lingered long on Ventnor's sheltered sands.

'Twas fine to sit upon the soft sea beach,
And idly watch the busy waves at work ;
With Neptune's wife 'tis always washing-day.
Grand was the flashing moonlight on the deep,
And bright the sunshine on the breezy downs :
So passed with speed our joyful honeymoon.
  Happy the man that has a loving bride,
Even though sixty winters whiten him,
The All-Beneficent had given me one
To recompense me for long years of sadness ;
She seemed to drop from heaven into my arms.
Gentle I found her as the silken fawn,
And loving as the love-bird of the south ;
Her intellect was clear and orderly ;
She saw the right of things by native instinct ;
Her person was as pleasing as her mind ;
A little, delicate, weak, ailing creature,
Her nerves were tuned to nature's poetry.
She needed my strong arm to lean upon,
And I required her sweet companionship.
'Tis true my head was grey ere she was born,
But love delights in contrarieties.
Our varied natures in love's fond alembic
Projected the essential joy of marriage.
  One fact I had forgotten to record
Of far too much importance to omit :
My little wife was truly well-descended,—
A native of the famous town of Coggeshall,—
Possessing gentle blood without dispute,
A member of the most historic family

In all the realm of aristocratic England,—
The Smiths—whose property is everywhere.
  I caught my bird before I found a cage;
In truth I made "a Coggeshall job" of it.
And now we had to fix upon a home.
My heart still clung to good old Colchester;
Long years had made the town familiar to me;
I could go blindfold into any street,
And knew the accustomed faces of the people;
And though the town was linked with memories
That sent a thrill of anguish through my breast,
A year of wanderings and of loneliness
Had dulled the edge of antecedent sorrow;
And now that I was happy with my bride,
I looked upon the place with different eyes.
To Colchester we came; at first as lodgers,
But soon I bought a pleasant residence
In the Head street that forms St. Helen's Cross.
We entered it upon the shortest day,
Hoping to spend long years of happiness,
Where now I recommence my varied song.
  Again the third of March brings round my birthday!
I now am over sixty—under seventy,
Standing betwixt the confines of the two,—
A serious thing to say, or think upon;
But what a wondrous change has happened to me
Since last I ate my lonely birthday dinner!
I then was nothing but a bachelor,
And now I am a happy married man;
Then I was solitary, dull and wretched,

I

Roaming about our ample Barrack-field,
Striving to laugh my dreariness away,
And now I am contented with my lot.
Then I was nothing but a poor old nobody,
With none to care a wisp of straw for me,
And now I am a young and sprightly fellow,
A man of some importance in the world,
Not yet too old for dear domestic joys,
Fond clinging arms, and soft warm-breathing kisses.
I then possessed no settled house and home,
And now I have a comfortable dwelling,
Where I can sit at ease and stretch my legs,
Before my blazing, cheerful, social fire.
A year ago I had a landlady,
Stingy and cross, and old and mercenary,
And now I have a little tender wife,
All smiles, and amiability, and sweetness,
Who, with the magic talisman of love,
Spreads pleasantness and light and joy around her.
How blest am I !   How thankful should I be
To the Supreme Disposer of all good,
Who has at length repaid me for long years
Of secret grief with untold happiness.
　As robin redbreasts do at pairing time,
Making their pretty nests warm, neat, and cozy,
So we have sought to make our dwelling pleasant,
But not like them without a world of fuss.
Life is a chequered scene of sweets and bitters :
Full soon we found we had not done with troubles.
A pretty kettle of fish is an old house ;

I bought my house and I mnst pay for it.
There seemed at first but very little needed
To make it cheerful, neat, and comfortable,
Only a little papering and painting,
And so the men were gaily set to work.
I little knew to what port I was drifting.
A lady friend suggested an improvement;
She thought the chimney-piece by far too small
For such a large and handsome dining-room.
A proper chimney-piece was therefore fixed;
And then the stove was hardly suitable,
And so the stove was shifted to a bedroom,
And a new stove was bought to fill its place,—
And thus the bricklayers came down upon us.
The closets in the drawing-room were doomed;
They were considered out of modern taste;
It would look better to have arched recesses:
So arched recesses we resolved to have.
Thus did the carpenters come down upon us.
Then came the plumber with a serious face
To say the gutter in the parapet
Was leaky and irremediably decayed;
It might be patched, but soon would leak again,
And thus the newly-papered rooms beneath
Would be discoloured, injured, and defaced.
I am a tolerably patient man,
Being well drilled by many years of harass,
And one of my old proverbs is " Be thorough,"
And so I said by all means have it done,
For I am fearful of a leaky ship.

And next on putting ladders to the roof
The tiles were found in need of overhauling;
And now we were full swing with our improvements;
The doorway of the kitchen was so low
I always knocked my head against the lintel,—
Not a most pleasant joke by any means.
I have a way of holding up my head,
And I maintain it is commendable
To hold our heads as high as possible;
At any rate 'tis time enough to stoop
When we no longer can hold up our heads.
We therefore had the doorway raised a bit.
Our kitchen truly was a wretched place,
With casement-windows letting in the wind,
Damp, white-washed walls and floor of sweaty bricks.
All this we altered, making it dry and cheerful,
With boarded floor and gaily-papered walls,
And mantel-piece and closets neatly painted;
For I maintain that servants should be comfortable,
Who add so much to our domestic comfort.
But after all, the kitchen chimney smoked.
A smoky chimney and a scolding wife
Will sometimes drive a man to desperation.
My little wife, like a young cooing ring-dove,
Has nothing of the scold in her sweet nature,
And I resolved to take away the range,
And have a smoke-annihilating kitchener,
And do without the smoke as well as scolding;
And so this dreadful business was achieved.
    But now another very great improvement

Absorbed our daily thoughts and consultations.
The look-out from our drawing-room was dull :
How charming it would be to build beyond it
A pretty little light conservatory,
Convert the window into a glass door,
And step into a little realm of flowers !
This was my gentle wife's own bright idea ;
But how was our new greenhouse to be warmed ?
We soon bethought ourselves how nice 'twould be
To warm our greenhouse and our hall together
By skilled arrangement of hot water-pipes.
Our house was chilly in the winter-time,
And my sweet, tender wife ill bears the cold ;
And then we thought how pleasant it would be
To have a little arbour in the garden,
Where we might sit in the warm days of Summer.
I have a weakness for a little arbour.
There were no end of odd materials,
Old boards and oaken joists, to build it with,
And form a structure quite as comfortable
As Cowper's little summer-house at Olney ;
But these ulterior schemes and alterations
We thought it wiser to defer till Spring,
For finer weather and for longer days,
Having enough within doors to accomplish
To last us all the gloomy time of winter.
Most certainly it seemed the wisest plan,
Now we were settling in a house of our own,
To do whatever needed to be done,
And make it to our wishes at the outset,

According to our little whims and fancies,
And have the good at once of our improvements;
So thus at length we settled all our plans.
    I made it my own business to inspect
The daily operations of the workmen,
Not leaving this prime duty to another.
I like myself to manage my affairs:
I never yet have had a better servant.
The man who is a servant to himself
Has generally a kind and generous master
Who takes a natural interest in his welfare,
And he is better served than other people;
But he who trusts to an agent soon will find
He gets a picking out of everything,
And often only half performs his duty.
    Meanwhile another work has been progressing
Of vast concern—the furnishing our house.
What consultations, what deliberations,
What fittings, plannings, schemings, and contrivings,
What alterations and what great improvements
Have occupied our busy heads and hands!
There are few things delight a woman more
Than fitting up a house with furniture,
The more especially if for herself.
The choice of pattern papers for the rooms,
Of carpets, curtains, and of window-blinds,
Of mirrors, tables, chairs and cabinets,
Of sofas, lounges, side-boards, bookcases,
Of fenders, fire-irons, crockery and glass,
Of bedsteads, wardrobes, washing-stands and ewers—

What a most sweet perplexity it is
For loving hearts to be entangled in,
And bring forth order out of this confusion,
Making our home a little paradise.
  One thing I long had set my heart upon,
And had determined staunchly to possess
Whenever I obtained a settled home.
This shadowy object of my aspirations
Was nothing other than a monster bookcase,
With folding doors of glass, to hold my treasures :
For I had been affected from my youth
With a propensity to purchase books—
Cheap if I could ; if not, at any price—.
And I had many now to store away.
At length I found the object of my wishes ;
A noble bookcase, worth a kingly ransom.
At first Louisa entered gentle protest
Against so large a piece of furniture.
She fancied it would spoil our dining-room ;
She had not seen it, and she feared the worst ;
Imagination magnified the evil ;
But soon she yielded when she saw how strongly
My heart was set upon my noble purchase.
Polished anew and slendered to my wishes,
When fitted to its place she gazed upon it
With admiration equal to my own.
Thus do we please each other and are pleased ;
And I have filled it with my dear old books,
Companions of my solitary years.
Right glad am I to see their shining ranks.

My books are my especial worthy friends,
That never take offence if they are slighted.
The best of friends are seldom always pleased ;
A random speech, or unintentioned act,
Will sometimes wound the sensibilities
Even of kindred hearts and gentle natures.
But who can quarrel with a favourite book?
Always when I have read a work that pleased me
I never am content till I possess it.
I like to have it near me to refer to ;
It is to me a transcendental pleasure,
After the lapse of half a century,
To read a book familiar to my boyhood,
But never re-perused since those bright days.
It seems to bring one's childhood back again,
And give once more the feelings of my youth,
Reviving faded pictures of the mind
With all the freshness of old favourite scenes.
    Lonely in life, secretive in my habits,
Living unknown to my contemporaries,
I have not had my intellect refreshed
By sweet colloquial contact with great minds.
My books have been my principal companions ;
Reading has been my chief delight of life :
Thus have I communed with the mighty dead
Until my soul was knit to theirs in love ;
Not without hope that in the life to come
We might converse as kindred spirits may.
    During my sad and lonely wanderings
My books at my old home had been reserved,

Likewise the best of all my furniture,
Which now became available again,
And pleased me passing well to re-possess :
My mind revolted from a public auction
Of dear familiar household furniture.
One piece we valued much, called Cobden's bedstead,
For Cobden used it when he was our guest ;
A man whose universal sympathies
Made him belong alike to all the nations,
Who doubled England's wealth and happiness,
And taught the world how best to live in peace.
Many good men have slept upon that bed
From first to last, amongst them Thomas Cooper,
One of the lowly children of the Muse,
But gifted largely with ethereal fire ;
Who wrote the " Purgatory of Suicides,"
A poem of great power and genius,
More full of classic learning and allusion
Than any other poem in our language,
Penned in a dreary cell in Stafford gaol,
In which the gifted poet was immured,
Condemned unjustly of conspiracy ;
Thanks to the Tory tool, Sir William Follett,
A solemn jackdaw on a lofty spire
Sitting in judgment on he knew not what.
Cooper the Chartist poet was our guest
When he came lecturing all along the land,
And pleasant talk of poetry had we.
  The good old four-post bedstead now repolished,
Again arose in more than former splendour,

With curtains newly dyed in richest crimson.
I hate to lie upon a modern bedstead,
And have my body cabined, cribbed, confined :
Though not a taller man than many men,
Yet to lie down and find my feet arrested
Some halfway down the bedclothes by a barrier,
Rigid, impenetrable, impassable,
Till in a waking dream of agony
I kick and plunge against my prison wall,
This may be luxury, but it is not comfort.
No, give me rather the old four-post bedstead,
Whereon a man can stretch his weary limbs,
And sleep and dream in peace and quietude.
    Another piece of household furniture
We value much—a lady's spinning-wheel ;
A little heirloom of the family,
Handsomely wrought in good mahogany.
It stood an ornament of our old hall,
A puzzle and a mystery to many.
Our modern spinsters, who no longer spin,
Could throw no light upon the way to use it.
When Cobden came it caught his searching eye ;
He placed his foot upon the little treadle
And set the tiny wheel in harmless motion,
Comparing doubtless in his musing mind
This relic of departed slow-coach times,
With the transcendent power and enginery
Of manufacturing Lancashire and Yorkshire,
With all their world of noisy spinning-jennies.
We named our heirloom Cobden's spinning-wheel.

Some furniture I purchased at an auction,
One of the painful scenes of human life.
Most sad it is to see a happy home
By folly or misfortune broken up.
Life is a troublous sea for men to swim in ;
He who would hold his head well above water
Must keep his expenses resolutely under.
A host of people wander through the rooms
Deserted by their long-accustomed tenants,
And now in disarray and blank disorder ;
The crowd, urged on by curiosity,
Peep here, pry there, and pull the things about,
And scrutinise the lots soon to be sold,
Eagerly looking for the greatest bargains,
And letting off their cruel jokes at random,
For Englishmen are jocular by nature,
In spite of toothaches, taxes, and the weather,
And even make a merriment of trouble.
Every dull chicken has a merry-thought.
The sale-room, once the scene of sweet home life,
Is crammed throughout with a most motley crowd.
A length of table stretches down the centre ;
The auctioneer sits at the further end,
Perched on a chair and ready with his hammer,
A mighty temporary potentate,
Wielding the sceptre of despotic law.
Before his highness stands a little table
On which his sounding hammer strikes his fiat—
The quick sharp stroke that tells the assembled crowd
The lot is purchased by the highest bidder.

Each lot for sale is brought by the attendants,
And openly displayed upon the table,
Or held aloft for general inspection.
Every diverse imaginary article
Of household furniture or ornament,—
Chairs, tables, carpets, looking-glasses, pictures,
Fire-irons, crockery, curtains, beds and bedsteads,
All must pass through this terrible ordeal,
The objects of a momentary attraction,
Examined, judged of, chosen or condemned,
Till knocked down to the highest purchaser,
Amidst the jokes and laughter of the crowd.
Women are partial to attending auctions.
To them they yield a pleasurable excitement,
And wondrous bargains sometimes can be bought
To boast about to all their friends and neighbours.
The women sit on chairs each side the table,
The men must be content with standing room,
Breathing for hours the hot and dusty air,
Urged by the hope of profitable bargains.
What a sad commentary on human life
Is to be found inside an auction-room !
But all the world is one great auction-room,
In which men struggle for the various lots.
It is for them to choose which lots to strive for,
And what they are content to pay for them.
Some buy bad bargains when they hope for good,
And others good beyond their expectations.
Experience is the most expensive thing
When you are forced to buy it as you want it,

'Tis wiser far to borrow other people's.
Some trust to mother-wit to help them on,
And some to luck, and some to providence,
But Heaven helps those the best who help themselves.
  But let me turn my thoughts to affairs of state.
This Spring will be renowned for grand events.
While I have been absorbed in private cares,
Like a fat maggot feasting in a filbert,
The outer world has been in great commotion.
This is the age of peaceful revolutions;
Knowledge advances and the world grows wiser;
The daring spirits of our later times
No longer rise in civil insurrection,
With sword and blunderbus and clang of war,
Against the abuses of the Government;
We now do battle with the tongue and pen;
Talk is the staple of our ammunition;
It answers better, and it breaks no bones.
When we make head against a public wrong
We English hold at once a public meeting,
And turn a jet of our hot breath upon it;
When we promote a public benefit
We celebrate it with a public dinner:
The surest way to the heart is down the throat;
We eat and talk, and talk and print our speeches.
The Press is the Palladium of old England;
As certain as the sunrise every morning
The Press sends forth its daily fulminations;
Opinions rattle in the air like hailstones;
Steel pens are pointed deadly at each other,

And give and take is fair in argument ;
And though the contest may be long and tedious,
Yet truth at last still gets the upper hand.
Thus all our great reforms have been effected ;
And what surprising changes have I seen !
How have the old intrenchments and defences
Of arbitrary power been broken down,
And truth and liberty and right and justice
Baring their breasts against opposing wrong,
Have steadily advanced and fought and won
The only battles that are worth the winning,
The only victories to be called enduring,—
The bloodless triumphs of the human mind !
A noble right is human liberty,
Restrained and guarded by the power of law ;
Without it liberty is lawlessness,
And lawlessness soon crushes liberty,
And in its place erects despotic power.
    When I was young the Georges ruled in England,
Who dragged the name of royalty through mire :
The only law they loved was despot law,
Supported by the terror of the gallows :
The last of them he was the worst of them.
In him was seen the loathsome culmination
Of every baseness and of every vice,
The bloated type of selfish despotism.
Ill fared it with the name of royalty
In those dark days of stagnant wretchedness ;
It was become offensive to men's nostrils,
And lawless tongues reviled the name of king :

But Heaven had pity on a prayerful land,
And gave to us an innocent girl for queen,
A virtuous princess, good and pure herself,
Who shed a halo round about our country
Of truest womanhood and maiden purity,
Making herself a national exemplar.
United to a consort like herself,
Wise, virtuous, learned, noble, amiable,
Her regal influence raised the nation's tone,
And made the name of royalty beloved—
Making herself beloved at the same time
Around the humblest hearth-stones of old England,
And winning praise of peoples far remote.
Under her gentle sway despotic laws
By gradual process have been cast aside,
Yielding to peaceful popular agitation,
Without the fool's resource of sword or musket.
And as the public Press has taught the masses,
And Knowledge has descended from her watch tower,
The solid base of legislative rule
By slow degrees has deepened and expanded,
And thus at last the right of household suffrage
Has been conceded to our citizens ;
Thus drawing them still closer round the throne,
And causing them in truth to share and bear
The high responsibility and labour
Of virtuous and enlightened government.
　　Mountains of argument with endless toil,
Have been upheaved by very learned men
On the vexed question of the people's suffrage.

Some say it is a right, and some a trust;
I think it is a compound of the two.
The first without reserve would give the franchise
To every Englishman of one and twenty,
Not being a pauper or a criminal.
The other would restrict it cautiously
To only those they deem are qualified
By amount of income, rent, or education:
But then there comes the very knotty query,
Where shall we draw the line of qualification?
No well marked line of right can be discovered;
We must adopt an arbitrary line,
And household suffrage is perhaps the best.
I am in favour of a Bank-book franchise!
I honour working men who save a portion
Of each week's wages for the Savings'-Bank:
Men who exert a worthy self-denial,
And lay a good foundation for the future.
The hand that has his fifty pounds in the bank
Saved from debasing, wasteful self-indulgence
In beer, tobacco, and the skittle-ground,
Possesses in his grasp a powerful lever
By which to raise himself in his position,
And make himself a man instead of a hand.
If it is said a man of one and twenty
Is thereby qualified to give a vote,
It is his age that votes and not the man,
For he was just as fit when he was twenty;
Indeed, some knowing lads of eighteen years
Are wiser than some stupid fools of forty.

If it is said that every householder
Is thereby qualified to give a vote,
It is the house that votes and not the man ;
For if he quits the house the vote quits him.
Again, if it is said that education
Affords the best criterion of men's fitness
To exercise the said elective franchise,
Judges, like doctors, would be sure to differ
About the amount of learning which is needed
To prove a voter to be qualified ;
And so most gross injustice would be done,
For one would grant a simple pot-hook franchise,
And one demand round "Oes" and crooked " Esses ;"
Justice would fall to the ground between the two.
Again, if age, or rent, or education
Are true criterions of a right to vote,
Why should not women vote as well as men,
Who in these several ways are qualified ?
Nor will I urge a single word against it,
For female government is mostly good.
The Indian stoics of the western world
Admitted women to their solemn councils,
Because—and there is reason in their reason—
There are some women wiser than some men.
    My politics are part of my religion,
And are embodied in one single word—
One comprehensive word—justice for all.
The growing tendency of Christianity
Is to raise women to the level of men.
Why should not women sit in Parliament

K

If men think fit and proper to elect them?
Their presence would at least promote decorum,
And might conduce to wise deliberations.
A dozen women such as I could name
I think would prove a blessing to the country.
I am for equal laws for men and women,
Fair play for all and favour for the weakest.
But whether women have a vote or not,
Or whether working men enjoy the franchise,
May England ever be ruled by gentlemen.
   I like to look upon the British people
As one united happy family;
My beau-ideal-government is parental.
At first the King stands as a sort of father;
The Queen, a gentle, wise and loving mother:
To them belongs supreme authority.
Their will is absolute, their word is law:
This is the earliest type of government.
Their children, or, in other words, the people,
Are in their leading-strings, and must obey.
As time proceeds, the eldest child begins
To have its little duties to perform,
Rub down the furniture, or rock the cradle,
And exercise its judgment in affairs,
And by-and-by its parents gradually
Take it into the fireside consultations,
And grant it greater liberty of action:
This is the first idea of Parliaments,
With its fresh germs of popular influence.
The younger children, or, in other words,

The lower classes, as they come to years
Of knowledge, wisdom, and experience,
Are one by one admitted into council,
Acquire a greater share of liberty,
And take their part in household government,
Until the whole, admitted to the franchise,
Form as it were a family republic.
This is the law of gradual advancement
In education, liberty, and power;
But if the parents keep all power to themselves
The children in the end—that is, the people—
Will rise rebelliously against their rulers,
And sometimes it has fared must fatally to them.
On the other hand, if there were no authority,
And all the children in a family
Were just allowed to have their wilful ways,
And rise in arms and claim to make the laws,
And all the noisy boys kicked up a racket,
Clamouring to have plum-pudding every day,
And eat as much as ever they could stuff,
And barring out the cook until she yielded—
Orderly rule could never be maintained,
Domestic government at once would cease,
And anarchy and ruin must ensue.
   Most beautiful is sweet domestic life
Where mutual love and mutual forbearance
Drive all discordant sentiments away,
And heavenly elements of harmony
Confer a grace to cultivated nature,
And gentleness and kindliness and peace,

Like flowering climbers o'er a sunny window,
Throw round a home a halo of enchantment.
  How venerable evils stick to us !
What desperate work it is to stamp them out!
We have to overpower them one by one.
Reform appears an everlasting work.
One of the rampant scandals of our time
Is the rude way we manage our elections.
What can be more debasing and degrading
For gentlemen to soil their fingers with
Than a sharp contest for a rotten borough?
Whatever beer and bribery can accomplish,
Or foul intimidation can effect,
Or even fisticuffs can do, is done.
For days and weeks before the election comes
These evil influences are set to work ;
Both parties generally do their worst ;
They dodge the humbler class of the electors,
And seek to influence them by every means ;
Entrap them into dirty public-houses,
And make them prisoners till they give their votes,—
Pay their expenses to some distant town,
Or frighten them with threats of loss of trade,
Want of employment or of patronage :
Debtors are driven headlong by their creditors,
And men are worried to engage their votes,
Till they are mad that they have votes to give.
  At length arrives the day of nomination,
A wasted day of jangling, noise, and riot :
A motley crowd of men surround the hustings,

Where stand the candidates amidst their friends,
Bowing, grimacing, bandying badinage,
And making speeches, or attempting to,
Amidst the plaudits of their partisans
And the fierce hootings of their adversaries.
Sometimes a shower of rotten eggs is thrown,
And sometimes something even harder still,
A brick-bat, or perhaps a faggot-stick,
Or something softer, a dead cat, or rat:
Disorder is the order of the day.
At length the uproarious show of hands is taken,
The Mayor proclaims the candidates elected,
The losing candidates demand a poll,
And then the tumult closes till the morning;
But all night long the tug of war goes on.
Watchers of either party prowl the streets,
For foulest influences are brought to bear
To win the election of the coming day.
    At eight o'clock a.m. the poll begins.
"Rush to the poll" is heard on every side.
One vote recorded during the first hour
Is worth two votes recorded afterwards,
For those who get ahead can keep ahead.
Some ride, some walk, and some are fairly carried;
Coaches and cabs race wildly through the streets;
The lame, the blind, the halt must have no rest;
The dying man is hustled from his bed;
The drunkard is supported to the poll;
Many a poor man votes against his conscience,
And many a workman votes to please his master;

While many a tradesman will not vote at all
Rather than thus offend his customers;
Fighting and wrangling, uproar and confusion,
Intimidation, drunkenness, and bribery,
These horrors signalise a borough election.
What eagerness possesses every body
To ascertain the progress of the poll;
What cheers are raised as every vote is given
By one or other of the opposing parties!
And as the closing hour of four draws on,
What frantic efforts either party makes
To turn the quivering scale of the election!
   St. Peter's clock strikes four.   The struggle ceases.
All has been done that mortal man could do;
The Wires and Aylets have achieved their best,
And nothing now can alter the result.
Men breathe again, confer upon the contest,
The victors triumph, and the vanquished sulk;
Vengeance is vowed against the renegades,
And harsh reproaches lavished on the false;
Family feuds afresh are fed with fuel,
And jealousies and rivalries revive.
   Meanwhile the Mayor comes forth upon the hustings,
The golden chain of corporation glory,
Glittering afar, suspended from his neck,
And having counted up the numbers polled
Reads the result, and tells the multitude,
Who crowd beneath him thick as swarming bees,
On whom the election of the day has fallen.
Then each successful candidate steps forth

With hat in hand, amidst uproarious cheers,
With cat-calls, groans and hootings intermixed,
Smiling and bowing to return his thanks ;
Making the usual speech on such occasions
About the proudest day of all his life,
And duty to his new constituents.
The beaten candidates make parting speeches ;
Thanks to the Mayor are then proposed and carried ;
The crowds retire to talk and drink and feed,
While bands of music march with colours flying
Throughout the town followed by ragamuffins.
   A few days afterwards the poll is published
When all the world can see how each man voted,
And act against him as they find occasion.
   Such is the picture of a borough election
In this so proud and worshipful old England ;
But old abuses stick as close as pitch.
Those who have power cling to the means of power,
And these foul scenes are still maintained by statesmen
Who climb to power by practices so shameful ;
And thus are boroughs eaten up by faction,
The public good exchanged for party ends,
The peace of private families rent asunder,
And local efforts for a borough's welfare
Weakened and neutralised by the spirit of faction.
   All these abuses might be remedied,
And men might live in harmony and peace,
By a well-ordered plan of secret voting,
Conducted in a simple honest way,
By dropping folded tickets in a box,

Having the names on them for whom you vote ;
No one needs know for whom you give your suffrage,
Unless you choose to tell it to your neighbours.
    Election contests call to mind old times,
When Daniel Whittle Harvey was our champion.
I have heard orators of great renown :
O'Connell, Follett, Palmerston and Russell,
Brougham, esteemed the mightiest of his day,
And later lights, Cobden, and Bright, and Spurgeon ;
But none of them could stand by Whittle Harvey.
Tall and proportioned finely, with a face
Beaming with lofty intellectual power,
He was a very king in personal appearance,
Casting all common men into the shade ;
In mien and port he seemed a demigod ;
His was the highest polish of his art ;
His dignity surpassed all other men's.
Clear and melodious was his ringing voice,
His action and his utterance full of beauty,
Most ready was his ever playful wit ;
His memory was something wonderful ;
He could call every voter by his name.
How admirable he was in argument,
How keen in satire, terrible in invective !
He was a master in the school of oratory,
He knew the art and science of it too,
The practice and the theory, matter and manner ;
His language was refined and beautiful.
The matter and the manner of his oratory
Were not the dull results of memory,

But the spontaneous efforts of his mind.
It was a glorious treat to listen to him,
A memory to be forgotten never.
He lived before his age, when despot power
Frowned down the daring radical reformer;
They gave him a bad name to ruin him,
Their slander crushed him all his better days,
And when at last his character was cleared,
Slow-coached acquittal came too tardily
To do him justice and retrieve the past;
And thus a patriot chief, who might have vaulted
Into the highest seat of human power
Beneath the throne itself of England's monarch,
Had he but worldly suppleness enough—
For he had talents for the loftiest place—
Lived to old age in the cold shade of fortune.
    When last I looked on Harvey he was standing
Upon the unstable shifting sands of Brighton,
Looking intently on the expanse of ocean,
Whose restless, glittering, treacherous, lovely billows
Delusively came dancing to the shore;
Who now shall tell the thoughts that filled his soul?
    A noble gift it is to have the power
To sway, as with a hurricane, the minds
Of multitudes of thinking, breathing men;
A noble thing it is, and worth ambition,
To stand upon the floor of Parliament,
The centre of all eager eyes and ears,
And by the cogency of burning words
Shed light and truth on sacred principles;

To rend the tangled webs of sophistry,
And proudly shape the destiny of nations.
A very precious gift is oratory;
It is the handmaid as it were of power,
The scaffolding by which men climb to greatness,
A glorious gift when dedicated to truth,
To right and justice and the good of men ;
If otherwise, a dangerous quality,
Corrupting him who basely uses it,
And leading those who hear it far astray.
It has one great reward paid down instanter :
Applause, which all men love, rolls in upon it
In a tumultuous overwhelming flood,
Not like the lonely poet's recompense,
Which comes in echoes from his secret heart,
Or if it comes at all from the outer world
Most often comes too late for him to hear—
In fitful whispers o'er his mouldering urn.
Poetry, like virtue, is its own reward ;
Oratory gives wealth and fame and power.
It is a rapture to an orator
To guide an audience like a charioteer,
Lashing his prancing steeds which way he pleases;
To feel that all who hear him have one heart,
Whose chords he sweeps by magic influence.
When an accordant feeling holds an audience
How powerful is the sense of sympathy !
A single pulse beats faint and timidly,
A thousand pulses joined throb violently;
A smile inspires a smile, a yawn a yawn ;

A word that would not touch us when alone
Will bring out tears when uttered to a crowd ;
A repartee that would not wake a smile
Uttered in private life 'twixt man and man
Will raise a roar of laughter in a speech.
But all these gifts of mind are vested powers,
To be exerted for the good of others,
Not for one's own vain selfish gratification,
Carefully cultivated and discreetly used.
Where there is power there is responsibility.
What a most melancholy thing it is
To see the richest gifts debased and squandered,
Like to some ghastly ruin after a fire,
Charred, tattered, broken, blackened and consumed.
'Tis well to know our capabilities,
And not attempt the unattainable ;
Some men who merely have the gift of words
Imagine they can shine as orators ;
Dull lamps that have no burning light within.
Others, who have the knack of stringing rhymes,
Suppose themselves to be immortal poets,
But have no vital sympathies of soul
That bind them to the living breathing world.
Absurd it seems to be, to try to be
What nature never meant that we should be ;
A monkey, we all know, is twice a monkey
When it is dressed and imitates a man.
Doubtless the sphere most proper for the many
Is safe domestic life with all its duties
Of business, social cares, and homely pleasures.

In this small sphere a man can be a man,
Live wisely, virtuously, usefully, and happily,
Gain the respect and praise of other men,
And, better still, enjoy a peaceful conscience.
  Deep in the human bosom is the passion
To go beyond all others in achievement,
Doing or daring what is difficult.
Nothing impels men onwards like resistance ;
The school-boy loves to climb the loftiest tree,
To run the swiftest in the eager race,
To jump the highest, throw a stone the furthest,
Or shoot a marble with the greatest skill ;
And so it is with boys when they are men ;
The sense of danger is the charm of daring ;
They rush into the thickest of the battle,
They tempt the perils of the Arctic regions,
Bearing fatigue, and cold, and greasy food,
Or traverse sultry lands where English feet
With irksome steps have never trod before,
Seeking the grand old sources of the Nile ;
Or climb the slippery icy pinnacles
Of the inhospitable and barren Alps,
Doing again the Duke of York's performance,
Who with his valiant army at his heels
Marched up a hill and then marched down again.
Fool-hardiness is not true noble daring ;
Daring is noble when its aim is noble.
  Endurance is a priceless quality ;
Hope may evaporate like boiling water,
And faith may melt like iron in a furnace,

But true endurance is imperishable ;
It is the fire-brick of humanity
Which fits us for the trial of our manhood
When overwhelming dangers close us round,
And all escape appears impossible ;
It is pre-eminently the characteristic
Of the true-hearted strong-willed Englishman ;
It gives him spirit under difficulties
That might appal the unsupported heart.
Such was the pluck of my sweet Louie's brother,
The surgeon of a whale-ship, the " Diana,"
When she was drifting helpless in the ice,
And the old weather-beaten captain died,
And the starved mariners dropped one by one,
And the crushed ship was sinking gradually.
Our Charlie tended and cheered up the sick,
Worked at the pumps to animate the rest,
Submitted to the same most meagre rations,
Piled up the frozen dead men on the deck,
A dozen ghastly relics of hard suffering,
And when the ship was freed at last from the ice
Brought her, scarce floating, back to dear old England,
Laden alone with dead and dying men,
While all the bells of Hull rang out for joy
To see the long-lost ship return to port !
   This noble energy of Englishmen
Enables us to take the lead of nations ;
Our race rides over all opposing races ;
Our tongue is silencing all subject tongues.
We settle colonies in distant lands

Midst hardships, sufferings, difficulties, and dangers ;
Wear out the hatred of opposing fortune,
And triumph ultimately in well-earned success.
   We English, therefore, love athletic sports,
Which brace our souls and sinews for great deeds.
Nothing can pluck the pluck out of brave bosoms.
The game of cricket is an English game,
The fine invention of a hardy race,
Requiring skill and tact and promptitude,
Strong arms, swift legs, and an unerring eye.
A stirring sight it is to watch the game.
We islanders must dabble in the water ;
There's nothing can exceed an English boat-race,
When our proud Universities contend.
Oxford and Cambridge meet upon the Thames,
They cast Thucydides unto the dogs,
Euclid is laid upon the dusty shelf,
And either party sets to work to drill :
All England stands on tiptoe to look on.
Long weeks and months must see the preparation,
The practice and the training of the rivals.
The contest is the universal talk ;
Grave men discuss the question on the Exchange,
Friends in the street shake hands and ask each other,
After remarking duly on the weather,
About the prospects of the coming Boat-race,
Knitting their brows with eager earnestness ;
Cabmen, costermongers, omnibus conductors,
Dining-room waiters, and commissionnaires,
Bankers, bank-clerks, tradesmen and shop-assistants,

Gentlemen living in the sleepy suburbs,
All of them bubble over with the subject;
Lads in the kennel who know naught of letters,
And construe nothing but policemen's forms,
Bet on their favourite Universities.
The ladies, still more ardent than the men,
Talk o'er their tea-cups of the coming contest,
Discuss the training of their favourite crews,
The beauty, strength, and skill of the competitors,
And wear the colours of the side they back.
    At length the day and hour have come about
Which must decide the honours of the race.
London, which is so difficult to move,
And where King Mob may riot at one end
For a whole day, and turn things upside down
Before the other end knows aught about it—
All London is this day moved by one impulse.
Members of the Imperial Parliament,
After the night and morning's long debate,
Snatch a short nap and haste to see the contest;
Ladies who only left the ball-room late,
Are early up and dressed and off to the race;
The four-in-hand, the costermonger's barrow,
The smart barouche, the humble shandydan,
Cabs, omnibuses, every sort of equipage,
Gentlemen in the saddle, snobs on the saddle,
Blue-busted ladies mounted upon horseback,
Full rivers of pedestrians from all quarters,
Flow down their several channels towards the Thames
To furnish the spectators of the Boat-race;

The very windows open wide their mouths
To see the grand exciting spectacle;
Crowds upon crowds block every point of view,
While daring youngsters perch upon the house-tops,
Or sit astride upon the edge of walls,
Or hang like autumn swallows to the bridges;
Each person shows the colours of his side,
For Oxford dark blue or for Cambridge light blue,
Giving an azure brightness to the scene;
The very babies in their nurses' arms
Wear in their chubby hats the party favours;
The dark blue terrier in a lady's lap
Barks at the light blue spaniel at a window;
Hundreds of thousands of all ranks and ages,
Cling round the neck of Father Thames and choke him,
In eager expectation of the race.
The crowd of people feel the electric thrill
Of one inspiring common sentiment.
    The young athletes are seated in their boats:
The dark blue Oxford and the light blue Cambridge.
Putney, the starting point, is in a fever;
The word at length is given, "Off, gentlemen,"
And momently away they bound with speed,
Springing like eager greyhounds from the leash;
A burst of cheering roars from either side.
With bows abreast they fly along the water,
Each seeking eagerly to outgo his rival:
Now one boat spurts ahead and then the other,
At every lifting simultaneous stroke
The rapid boats half spring from out the water.

Behind them throng a lumbering rout of steamers,
Laden with gazers to the water's edge,
Who aid the exciting scene, and add their cheers,
Pay rather dear to view the famous Boat-race,
But only see it in imagination,
Yet can at least talk learnedly about it.
Fulham and Chiswick give them all their eyes;
Four miles of gay spectators urge them on,
Royalty shares the exhilarating scene;
The hopes and fears of many an anxious month
Have now arrived at their heart-beating crisis;
All eyes are straining to obtain a glimpse,
All heart-strings tightened with exultant hope,
All bosoms throbbing for their favourite crews.
'Tis not a competition of brute horses,
But of athletic youthful Englishmen,
Testing their well-trained manhood in the race.
A little lapse of time, say twenty minutes,
And the great contest of the year is over;
The rivals reach the destined point at Mortlake,
The long strong springing pull decides the day,
And the blue riband of the Thames is won!
The victors take their honours quietly,
The vanquished brace their nerves to try again.
Never say "die;" that is the coward's word.
With Englishmen to be content is baseness;
The beaten but look up to beat in future.
    Life is a race: it is an old comparison,
But not less true for being very old.
The prize we seek to win is not a riband,

The emblem of a brief and fading honour,
Nor the vain plaudits of an idle crowd,
But an immortal and a priceless crown.
For this we well may daily train ourselves,
Lay aside every weight that hinders us,
Make every little sacrifice required,
Live wisely, virtuously, and self-denyingly,
Running with patience our appointed course,
And never yield till the great prize is won,
Aided by Him on whom all help is laid,
Who will not see us too hard put upon,
But will support us by His heavenly grace,
And give to us the palm of victory,
And that most excellent of all rewards,
The sweet participation in those pleasures
Which are reserved for us at His right hand.

Here endeth Book the Third of this my Poem.
The gates of day are closing in the west,
The crimson curtains of the east are spreading,
Silence is softly falling over earth,
The setting sun is wrapt in gorgeous clouds,
Like a menagerie of uncouth wild beasts,
Lions and elephants and hippopotami,
Stretching their giant forms along the horizon,
And melting their resemblances away,
Slowly and harmlessly, but gloriously,
Like the phantasma of an idle dream.

BOOK IV.

BOOK IV.

OLD Colchester enjoys a history;
No mean and beggarly inheritance;
A history to look back upon with pride,
If age can give a sanctity to places
Whose date is lost in pre-historic times.
The capital of a line of ancient Britons,
And afterwards a Roman colony,
Here Cleopatra—no, it was Boadicea,
Queen of the Britons, in her patriot wrath
And womanly revenge, conquered the Romans,
To be herself ere long conquered in turn,
And eighty thousand of her warriors slain,
While she sought refuge from despair in poison.
And old King Coel lived here, that merry old soul,
Whose jovial spirit dwells amongst us still;
Witness our annual native oyster-feasts,
To which I never had an invitation,
And therefore only speak from common report.
Old King Coel's kitchen still remains near by,
A puzzle to befool the antiquary.
Ancient remains abound on every side ;
The earth is rich in precious buried treasures,
If we knew only where to dig for them.
The Romans seem to have had no breeches-pockets,
Judging by how they dropped their money about!

Here Helena was born, that pious princess
Who found the True Cross at Jerusalem.
Here too her son Great Constantine was born,
The earliest Christian Roman Emperor,
Who tied the fatal knot 'twixt Church and State.
Here flourished for succeeding centuries
The conquerors of the world, the powerful Romans,
Built themselves stately palaces and temples,
Which time long since has swept away as rubbish—
And reared stout walls around the lofty town,
And built a castle of enormous strength,
Which still remain to tell of ancient days.
    The Saxons, then the Danes, and then the Normans,
Each in their turn bore sway in Colchester.
Those were the feudal times of vassalage,
Of greedy monks and half-starved artisans.
The Reformation came, and altered all things.
The streets of Colchester were then baptised
With martyrs' blood, which never flows in vain.
Great principles must always have their martyrs,
And truth must be baptised in innocent blood.
Then came the war of King and Parliament,
And Colchester endured a desperate siege,
Sore pressed by Fairfax and by Ireton,
Till the beleaguered town ate cats and dogs,
And so were starved at last into submission;
And then the Royalist chiefs, Lucas and Lisle,
Were led forthwith into the Castle Bailey,
And there inhumanly, in cold blood, shot.
    I have but little faith in history;

All history is a yarn of contradictions.
I read some grave historian's learned pages,
And meekly form my own opinions from him,
Believe his facts and feel quite satisfied.
After a while I read another history,
And find a very different narrative;
The facts that I had built my faith upon
Are now shown to be falsehoods or perversions.
I stand amazed to find the noblest men
Set down as base and selfish knaves or fools;
And know not in my conscience what to believe.
When I read history I feel 'tis fiction;
When I read fiction, if 'tis true to nature,
I read with pleasure, for I know 'tis true.
Was Richard the Third a hump-backed reprobate,
Or was he a quiet gentlemanly person?
Was Bacon one of Nature's noblemen,
Or was he a mean mercenary wretch?
Was Cromwell a great saint, or a great sinner?
Was Mary Queen of Scots a virtuous woman,
Or was she an inhuman murderer?
Different historians tell us different tales,
According to the passions which inspire them,
The party or the sect which they belong to,
Or else the colour of their spectacles.
No human character has proved too sacred
For these ingenious men to anatomise:
Witness the purest and the noblest minded
Of English statesman and philosophers,
The founder of the State of Pennsylvania,

A man at once of piety and genius,
Accomplished, eloquent; a Christian gentleman:
And yet Macaulay, a mean crawling viper,
Snapped at him with his fangs, and bit himself,—
The just reward of his malignity.
To such a pitch of daring have men come
That even Christ Himself, the Son of God,
Who bore, for us, atoning agony,
That we might be His fellow-heirs of glory,
Is laid upon the cold dissecting-table
For heartless jackanapes to cut and hack,
And try to prove him nothing but a man—
Yet only prove themselves not men, but bloodhounds.
    I have no unity with gifted men,
However learned or however clever,
Who set aside the truths of revelation
As often as they clash with their opinions,
Bringing the doctrines of the Holy Bible
Unto the fallible bar of their vain minds,
And setting up a standard of the truth
That even Lucifer himself must laugh at.
As blowflies busily hum about a carcase,
Seeking for crevices to lay their eggs in,
So do these learned transcendental sceptics—
Biblical blowflies—with persistent zeal,
Not to discover truth, but seeming error,
Believing naught save their own unbelief,
Buzz round the Bible to find out its faults,
And so insinuate into every part,
Their little, loathsome, mischievous, infidel eggs,

Which, when they hatch, become devouring maggots.
These daring sceptics kick away our stools,
And give us nothing else to stand upon;
They rob us of our faith, our hope, our comfort,
And offer us dry husks that swine should eat.
Puffed up with notions and with spiritual pride,
They vainly think that they are rich and full
Increased with goods—yea, and have need of nothing,
And know not all the time that they are wretched
And miserable and poor and blind and naked,
Having no hope, and without God in the world.

Honour and majesty are before the Lord,
Strength and beauty are in His sanctuary.
The Bible tells us much, but tells not all.
It tells us quite enough for our instruction,
In heavenly truths to fit us for hereafter;
It is a book so full of heavenly wisdom
That all the sermons, even of all times,
On all its glorious texts, cannot exhaust it.
It sometimes checks our human curiosity,
Yet gives us glimpses of deep hidden things,
Which prompt the human mind to daring search;
And man's untamable and restless spirit
Is prone to spend its strength on mystery.
There is a tempting charm in the mysterious
Which fascinates the warm imagination.
Whether we wish or not the mind will wander,
And thoughts unsought will crowd upon the brain;
Opinions upon mysteries unrevealed,
Unasked, usurp possession of the mind,

And I have my imaginings of deep things,
Though how I came by them I cannot tell.
I often meditate on man's relation,
Not merely to the future but the past;
His being is surrounded by enigmas.
Whence does he come and whither does he go?
Existence is not bounded by this life;
Man is immortal.   Can his being therefore
Have either a beginning or an ending?
Is he not clearly of angelic type?
Perhaps mankind were once the fallen angels;
Ours is a strange mysterious mingled nature;
We have some traces of divinity
Woven with our propensities to evil.
Some men seem little lower than the angels;
And some appear not far removed from demons.
Perhaps the gracious Ruler of the world,
Designing in His mercy and His goodness
To reconcile unto Himself again
The least offending of the fallen angels,
By opening wide the door of true repentance,
Planned the transcendent scheme of man's redemption
To bring about these rebels' restoration.
The Almighty never could assume the nature
Of fallen angels and rebellious spirits,
But might He not uplift them to the platform
Of human nature, clothe them in the flesh,
Even as He could stoop from heaven's height,
In love to man, and clothe Himself in flesh,
And condescend to meet them thus half-way,

Shedding atoning blood in sacrifice,
For the transgressions of a fallen race?
If finite man is called on to forgive
Seventy-times-seven the offences of his fellows,
Who shall set bounds to infinite forgiveness?
This key would seem to fit a thousand wards,
And yet perhaps it is an evil fancy.

  How vain are all such idle speculations;
That which is unrevealed concerns us not;
To fabricate such bold and baseless theories
Is all the same as putting out to sea
In a frail unsubstantial paper boat,
Which cannot bear the brunt of stormy weather;
Or blowing empty and yet gaudy bubbles
Out of the suds of our imagination,
Which burst ere long and leave no trace behind.
How greatly better is it to employ
The powers of mind with which we are endowed
In learning the great truths within our grasp,
And teaching them to those that are around us.

  The broad High street of good old Colchester
May match with any street in any town,
Ending in old East hill—where once I dwelt,
And which I have climbed some twenty thousand
      times—
A somewhat formidable hill to mount,
Where old St. James's church-tower mocks old Time,
And where in warlike long-forgotten ages
Many a sanguinary and stubborn fight
Was vainly fought, and triumph vainly won.

The streets and lanes of good old Colchester
Have been well trodden by some men of mark.
Daniel Defoe the true-born Englishman,
Who suffered for truth, and wrote the tale of Crusoe,
Which has bewitched our school-boys ever since,
Once tenanted our Corporation farm.
In Colchester the painter Lance was born,
Whose luscious pictures of most tempting fruit
Exceed the works of any other artist ;
His mantle rests upon my friend Ladell,
From early youth a dweller in our town,
Who now stands foremost as a painter of fruit,
Whose imitative touches rival nature.
Here dwelt in his young days Professor Airy,
Distinguished now as the Astronomer Royal,—
A credit to the air of Colchester,—
Whose climbing intellect explores the realms
Of lonely, trackless, interstellar space,
Treading with firm and mathematic steps
The topless ladder of the universe,
With steady hand and penetrating eye,
Taking calm note of heaven's exhaustless wonders,
Where common intellects would fail to follow.
   If I were not an easy-going poet,
But loved to rack my brains with calculations,
And strain my eyes with nightly star-gazing,
I should like well to be an astronomer,
And probe the hidden wonders of creation.
This pigmy world is not half big enough
For man's inquiring spirit to disport in.

It seems a very pleasant occupation
To go a-roaming through the universe,
Riding perhaps upon a comet's tail.
I should not care to tarry at the moon,
The cold and starving dream-land of the poet,
With naught to eat or drink or warm one's self;
·But I should take a bolder, loftier flight;
Knock at the sun, and see his apparatus
For heating and illuminating space;
Look at the sweaty beads on his warm brow,
And the dark grimy spots upon his visage,
Seeking to find if over exercise
And ceaseless toil had given him the vapours;
And asking where he gets his stock of coals.
Then I might sweep across the realms of space,
Dodging a flight of meteors in my way,
Looking for hidden undiscovered planets,
The ancient elder brethren of the earth,
Rolling their lonely courses round the sun,
Amidst the dimness of remote existence;
And calculate their distances and periods.
Then I might journey onwards to the stars,
The suns to other systems of fair worlds,
And ascertain what metals they are made of;
And reckon up their heat-affording powers—
Fixed stars, that like to ships far out at sea
Seem fixed, and yet are ever moving onwards
With our own sun to some mysterious bourne.
But chiefly would I like to make acquaintance
With those small nebulous spots which crowd the sky

Far in the dark profundities of distance,
Unseen except through lenses of vast power;
Spots of star-dust, expanding, as the range
Of artificial vision spreads them out,
Into fantastic and capricious forms,
Rhomboid, or volute, or trapezium,
Or streaming far like our own Milky Way;
Clusters of stars forming new universes
Like this of which our sun is but a part;
Bewildering finite man on earth's small stand-point
With glimpses of the infinite power and goodness
Of the Eternal All-creative God.
   When I was young the holy William Marsh
Was the loved vicar of St. Peter's Church;
A man of goodly presence more than common,
And a good man beyond the common sort;
His loving face was equal to a sermon;
He was a preacher mighty in the Scriptures;
He had them in his head and in his heart,
He had them also at his fingers' ends;
He preached unwritten sermons fluently,
And when he made a reference to a text
Turned promptly to the chapter and the verse
In his great Bible, ere he quoted it,
With a most marvellous celerity:
A man of many admirable gifts
And lucid, sweet, persuasive eloquence.
He did not preach for pelf, but for the love
He bore to Christ, and to the souls of men,
Preaching with words and teaching with his works.

He was a man of large beneficence,
Beyond his means of liberality,
A man of catholicity of spirit :
He sought to spread the Bible through all lands,
And overthrow the power of Antichrist ;
His heart beat warmly for the good of all,
Not only for the free man but the slave ;
A cheerful man who made religion lovable,
He dwelt within a fragrant atmosphere
Of heavenly sweetness and benignity :
Were all the clergy of the Church like him
Surely there never would have been dissent !
    In Colchester, three hundred years ago,
A great and true philosopher was born,
Who trod the path of sound experiment
Even before the illustrious Lord Bacon ;
Gilbert, a sturdy questioner of Nature,
Who took in hand that fiery principle—
That tricksy spirit—Electricity,
Which permeates the air, and earth, and ocean,
Unrecognised by man for countless ages,
Save when it flashed in thunder from the clouds,
But which has now become through modern science,
A kind, benignant fairy, doing our bidding ;
With its light wand, annihilating space,
Stretching its tendril feelers round the globe,
And binding all men's hearts in sympathy.
    Our grand old Castle overtops the town
With walls that promise to stand firm till doomsday,
Built with cement-stones dredged off Harwich harbour.

Who shall reveal its undiscovered records?
One tale of modern days I chiefly heed.
Here in the rough times of the Commonwealth,
When Cromwell ruled the country as Protector,
And Independents had their glorious swing,
Parnell, the boy-apostle of the Quakers,
Endured their persecutions to the death.
The little oven in the Castle wall,
In which he was confined, may still be seen,
Cold, cheerless, stony, crampt, where cruel hatred
Wore out his mind and body with hard usage,
And doomed him to a holy martyr's fate
For the pure light of truth and holiness.
   Beneath the Castle on the northern side,
Beyond the Roman ruinous town-wall,
Where the small river winds along the meadows,
An old lop-sided humble flour-mill stands ;
Behind it is a clump of ancient willows,
So large and venerable that any artist
Would notice and enjoy their fine effect ;
Beyond them is a small but cheerful meadow,—
Middle Mill Meadow is its well-known name,—
Brilliant and gay with buttercups and daisies
When the warm breath of Summer, comes each year;
The playing-place for countless generations
Of the small population of the town—
Delighted childhood kicking up its heels.
I love to watch the happy little creatures
Rolling about amidst the grass and flowers,
And gathering all their little hands can hold.

There are more golden cups in this small meadow
Than in the palaces of all earth's kings,
And they afford more exquisite delight.
Here the fat baby-grandfathers and grandmothers
Of these fat babies also gathered flowers.
Small generations thus succeed each other,
Each happy in the golden age of youth,
Unconscious of the past and of the future,
And innocently absorbed in the bright present.
Here in the mill-dam boys and grown-up men,
Gifted with large development of hope,
And blessed as well with admirable patience,
Angle for fish that never will be caught;
Yet generation after generation
Here may be found still watching for a bite.
The fish, if fish there be, are cautious fish,
Fish that have smelt the bait and felt the hook,
Wise fish that are too crafty to be caught.
      We have some pleasant field-walks round the town.
I value them, and fought for some of them.
The prettiest walk of all, that led to Lexden,
Most picturesque of Essex villages,
Was lamentably diverted and despoiled
By one who loves himself more than his neighbours,
The man who owns the land—that is to say,
The man who owns it till another owns it;
A man who has the heart to shoot the cuckoos!
May not a man do what he likes with his own?
A man may do with his own just what he likes,
But not to the injury of other people.

M

In this advancing age, when public bodies,
And private gentlemen of generous minds,
With an enlightened sense of what is right,
Give parks and playgrounds to the common people
To minister to popular enjoyment,—
This dull unsocial being, with a soul
Cooped up within the palings of his park,
For his own private gratification ruined
The ancient path of twenty thousand people,
In order to enclose his grounds more snugly,
Not for his lifetime only, but all time,
And not against his own contemporaries
Alone, but all succeeding generations.
    What daring deeds are done by country squires,
Great men whose word is good as Parly law,
Who ride high-horse over us common people !
One of these squires has sown his fields with soot,
Lest folks should trample on his precious grass,
Too good for any but black butterflies ;
And tarred his fences to keep off poor people
From rambling through their old accustomed paths
To breathe the country air free from town smoke,—
And thereby lost his seat in Parliament.
Another squire throws glass into the river
To cut the naked feet of venturous bathers,
And keep them from intruding on his land,
Forgetful that old rights are sacred things,
And that he gained his temporary tenure
Subject to these inalienable rights.
Another squire, an upstart of the law,

Of small importance as a landowner,
Has put a stop to boating on our river
By driving piles across the ancient stream,
Lest those who row should trespass on his grass,
And hires a bully, twice his own size and strength,
Armed with a pitchfork to resist aggressors.
Fine doings for a squire who would forget
The humble cottage out of which he sprang,
Who has no son his money to inherit,
But would deprive for all succeeding time
His native townsmen of their boating pleasures.

    The great Unpaid make us pay dear for justice,
Laying down rural law right absolutely.
Before them every rustic humbly cringes,
And touches ruefully his tattered hat ;
Their politics are sound Conservatism.
And what is sound Conservatism ? you ask.
Conservatism is a very simple creed ;
Its faith is in our glorious Constitution,
Which means the Church, the State, the Army and Navy
Hares, rabbits, pheasants, partridges, and foxes.
Great is the country Justice of the Peace ;
A king without the cares of royalty,
Who, living on the fatness of the land,
And ruddy with the wines of Portugal,
Fares sumptuously every day he lives,
And when he dies—no one speaks ill of him,
For, happily for him, he is forgotten.

    The town looks very nobly from the north
When the descending sun gleams richly on

Strange that the Queen has never been to see it!
There proudly stands the ancient Roman castle,
Half hidden by a grove of stately trees;
There is St. James's ivy-decked old tower,
And there St. Peter's lifts his lofty brow,
While old St. Mary's rears her battered form,
Telling to all her story of the siege,
Her fine stone tower being topped by vulgar brickwork,
From whence the one-eyed gunner smote the foe,
Until himself in turn was smitten down.
Far o'er the town ascends St. David's spire,
The modesty of Nonconformity
New built where stood the old round Meeting-house,
Aping the exaltation of the Church.
Beautiful to the eye it doubtless is,
· And ornamental to the good old town,
But the reflection forcibly arises,
How many a lofty and ambitious structure
Has no foundation but a mortgage bond!
And ah, how many an organ peals to Heaven
With music tuned to promissory notes!
   In Angel Lane once dwelt a pair of angels
Who could not rest without imparting good.
They left before I knew that dismal lane;
Their memories now have nearly passed away
From all the busy dwellers of the town,
But one or two can just remember them.
· They wrote the simple " Hymns for Infant Minds,"
And pleasing "Nursery Rhymes for Boys and Girls,"
Which gained such universal popularity,

And have contributed so much to bend
The little twigs of English intellect
In the most excellent and true direction,
And thus have left their impress on the age.
Jane and her sister Ann—these names are dear
To many a one who never saw their faces.
I often think of them in my field rambles
In the green meadows over Sheep-pen foot-bridge,
Or in the pleasant grove at Lexden Springs,
And fancy they have lingered there before me.
Old paths are haunted by old memories.
Long since I found a vivid trace of Jane
At the sweet rural hamlet of Bere-Church,
Within the shady sacred edifice.
It is "the Squire's pew" of which she sang,
And the grand tomb on which the old knight lies
In marble hard and cold, and underneath
His numerous offspring kneeling, with clasped hands,
As if to expiate his past transgressions,
By mutely saying endless prayers in stone.
    Jane had a garret where she sat and worked,
And where she saw the western sun go down
Over the glowing fields afar outspread
Beyond the intervening chimney-pots.
I look up at her window as I pass,
And fancy her still gently musing there,
Working at once with busy head and hands,
Haply not dreaming of the countless millions
Her simple lays were destined to instruct.
I once ascended to her favourite attic

Up the dark narrow staircase leading to it,
Not without serious risk of broken bones,
And if I caught no inspiration there
It was my own, and not Jane Taylor's fault.
A funnier study I have never seen :
It had at least the merit of seclusion,
Which is of great importance to a poet,
Who sees, like owls, the better for the twilight ;
Fitter it seemed to smother inspiration,
Rather than call it forth into existence ;
A room whose ceiling sloped from either side,
Yet in the highest part was still so low
My bare head touched it as I stood erect ;
A garret with a window which commanded
A fine view of the sky, and a small glimpse
Of distant fields far in the fading west ;
And yet her genius consecrated it ;
For what is place or space to genius !
But ah ! the light of genius had fled
And left behind a miserable blank !
   It is not the most laboured poetry
Which is the most executive of good,
Nor yet the grandest or the most poetical
That lays the strongest hold on people's minds.
The gorgeous clouds of heaven roll over us
And win but little of our admiration ;
Men want the intellectual pabulum
Which comes the nearest to their daily life ;
The cares, the fears, the joys, the hopes of men—
These are the subjects which engross them most ;

And hence the reason why so many poets
Fly over people's heads and are unheeded.
What do the populace care for ancient knights
And ladies of impossible perfections,
Of times that have completely passed away,
And fashions that are now ridiculous?
What do they care for fine philosophy,
Which is too fine for common comprehension;
Twaddle of anything or everything,
Except the heart of man and the heart of nature?
Poetry must come down from off her stilts,
Not pride herself on what is difficult,
Playing the philosophic acrobat;
Move gracefully upon her natural feet,
Not dance in air on intellectual wires,
If she would wish to please intelligent people.
  Jane Taylor left the town of Colchester;
And so I have observed in my long life
That various gifted men have done the same.
A country town can hardly hold a genius;
Such people mostly break away to London,
Where they can find fair scope and elbow-room.
I well remember one in humble life
Who wrote a pretty essay upon Taste;
His name was Carter. How he loved to talk!
He was a poor asthmatic jobbing tailor,
Who had but vague ideas of worldly business,
And had a weary struggle with ill-health,
Badness of trade, sick wife, and lots of children;
He dwelt near by St. Botolph's Priory,

That rugged relic of the olden times,
One of the curious sights of Colchester,
A sort of architectural skeleton
Of some great fossil old-world edifice,
Whose huge gaunt bones have partially escaped
The dreadful wear and tear of war and time.
Well, Carter also took his flight to London,
That vast receptacle of struggling men,
And there he wrote an interesting book :
The simple " Memoirs of a Working Man,"
In which he tells the story of his life,
And has some words to say of Colchester.
Long lost to sight, but not to memory,
I know not what at last became of him :
A little while he held his head aloft,
Then sank obscured beneath the smoke of London !
    A borough is no pleasant place to live in,
Where party politics run mountains high,
And everybody knows his neighbour's business.
I have been snubbed and hustled in my time
Because I laboured hard to win Free Trade,
And always stood for radical reform ;
But I was never one to cringe or yield,
Though mostly in the ranks of the minority,
And those who would have trod me in the dust
Gave up the game when they found out 'twas useless,
And only shunned me when they could not crush.
    Colchester has its share of party spirit ;
It has within it sixteen parishes,
And every parish has its special church,

And every church its own political parson,
And often-times the parson has his curate
To keep the church machine in going order,
Some four-and-twenty blackbirds altogether.
O why should sacred things and holy truth
Be tarnished by the touch of politics,
Dragging consistency knee-deep through mire?
Has not religion strength enough of limb
To walk alone without securely grasping
The strong but baneful arm of temporal power?
And must the secular State convert religion
Into a subtle engine of support?
   We have our share as well of cunning lawyers,
Without a single grain of principle
Beyond the common run of legal men,
Who howsoever times and terms may go,
And howsoever other men are ruined,
Mostly contrive by wriggling well, like cats,
To fall upon their feet and take no harm.
We have great bankers, too, who love obeisance,
Who bolster up the needy tradespeople,
And screw them to their party purposes.
Great men who cannot see beneath their chins,
Or notice meaner people right or left,
And tread upon the earth that soon will cover them
As though they had forgot the dust they sprang from.
   Besides all this we have a garrison;
A regular manufactory of soldiers,
Where raw recruits, poor, simple, ignorant fools,
Are drilled into the ordinary ranks.

Hard work it is, as many of them can tell,
And when they thus are polished into soldiers
They then are shipped abroad to rust or die;
But here, or wheresoever they may be,
They spread a moral pestilence around them.
'Tis pretty to behold their uniforms,
Their handsome figures and superior bearing,
Their polished weapons and their docile horses,
Their measured movements and their stately march,
And listen to their military music ;
But what an utter waste of men and money
They offer to a thoughtful contemplation;
And what a waste of homely happiness
And native virtue marks this soldiering.
If all our soldiers were at home at work,
Earning their daily bread by honest labour,
And married, as God meant that men should be,
How many an outcast and unfortunate girl
Might be a happy and respected wife,
The loving mother of a family,
And these poor slaves of war be grateful freemen !
    Women and sheep are very timid creatures ;
A single dog will fright a flock of sheep,
Yet if a pack of hounds go racing by
With whoop and holla and the noise of horses,
A flock of sheep will follow them like mad,
Urged headlong forward by some occult influence:
So women who would shriek to meet a mouse,
And have such cause to hate the name of war,
Which makes them widows and destroys their homes,

And sacrifices England's finest sons—
Women, by some perverse propensity,
Delight in war, and run mad after soldiers!
  When Christian nations settle their disputes
They seem no wiser than the Greeks or Romans!
They set about it by the clumsy method
Of killing one another out of hand:
The merits of the quarrel go for nothing;
Might, as in heathen countries, still makes right.
Grave statesmen can discern no better way,
And send forth hosts to kill, and to be killed;
Bishops encourage it as—"the correct thing,"
And bless the banners of the slaughtering armies.
Both sides appeal to God, their loving Father,
Implore His blessing on their barbarous efforts,
And thank Him for their victories o'er each other!
  All war is waste, and yet grave men defend it,
Because they foolishly believe it necessary;
But why should neighbouring states keep standing
          armies,
Threatening to injure and destroy each other,
Whilst neighbouring towns do very well without them,
And live in perfect harmony and thrive?
Men who wear daggers are too apt to use them.
A standing army is a standing menace
Courting the danger it is paid to quell.
Here are these rival towns, Ipswich and Colchester,
In opposite counties, with the river Stour
Forming a hostile boundary between them,
What greater cause of quarrel could they wish for?

Why should not Colchester, the smaller town,
Maintain an army of five thousand men
To guard it from invasion by its rival?
And wherefore should not Ipswich, being the stronger,
Maintain an army of seven thousand men,
Commensurate with its wealth and its importance,
To overawe the town of Colchester?
Depend upon it if these towns had armies
To gnash their spiteful teeth against each other,
A single twelvemonth would not pass away
Before their leaders, eager for advancement,
Glory and pelf, would find, or make occasion,
To pick a foolish quarrel with each other,
And war, with all its horrors, would ensue—
Burnings, bloodshed, death, waste, and all wickedness!

   Men are their own inveterate enemies:
They go to war and lose their limbs or lives,
Make targets of themselves for fools to shoot at,
Ruin themselves in other peoples' quarrels,
Lose their possessions in wild speculations,
Break down their constitutions with their vices,
Burn their insides by drinking fiery poisons,
Wear out their brains with over-straining study,
Their strength with toil, their spirits with anxiety,
Squander their wealth in foolish dissipation,
And cheat themselves by cheating other people!
Good gifts are heaped upon them in profusion,
Which they accept merely as matters of course:
Things of most use to man are most abundant—
Food, fuel, fire, water, iron, sunshine and air;

So are the things that form men's chief enjoyments;
Religion, love, health, offspring, and the five senses:
Yet men throw all these precious gifts away,
And go down to their graves but little the wiser.
  I often roam about our Barrack field,
Where, being shy, I need meet nobody,
Delighting in the broad expanse of grass,
And freshening my mind with the sea breezes:
For though the sea is some ten miles away,
Yet the high ground is free to all the winds,
And sometimes sea-gulls pay the ground a visit,
For sea-gulls sometimes like to look inland;
And I recall the time when cultured fields
O'erspread the spot instead of barrenness,
And waving corn repaid the farmer's toil
Where all is waste, trodden by soldiers' feet.
  The post of power and influence in a borough,
And the chief prize of profit and of honour,
Is the town-clerkship of the Corporation.
The man who wins this prize must be a lawyer,
And therefore with as many wits as fingers.
He has the handy salary of his office,
And all the honour and prestige that it gives,
And all the business following in its train;
His policy is therefore obvious,
To keep what he has got against all comers.
He therefore seeks to make the borough Council
Mere puppets, by whose means he holds his own;
For this he puts up men of the baser sort
As candidates for borough councillors,
And by election arts attains his end.

They gain their seats and they become his tools;
He gives his voice for choosing aldermen,
He recommends his private friend for mayor,
And when a parliament election comes
He throws the weight of all his influence
Into the scale of his exclusive party,
And works with all his tools to win the day.
A gentleman of independent feeling
Would hardly care to be a councillor,
And if he were a Yellow politician,
Although he were John Howard or Joseph Sturge,
The Blues with tooth and nail would try to oust him :
Such are the secrets of municipal craft.
It is not thus in every English borough,
For England is not ruled by Colchester,
A very happy circumstance for England.
　　As to the honours of a borough council,
Such honours have for me no fascination ;
I'm not the fish to rise to such a bait ;
I never sought to wear the chain of office,
Although it is a glittering golden chain,
Nor do I care to march along High-street,
Behind the mace, clothed in a scarlet cloak,
To the gay sound of military music,
With gaudy banners flaunting in the sun,
To church, to listen to a man-made priest.
It is enough for me to be a poet,
And help to shape the opinions of mankind,
Snug in the home which Providence has given me,
And happy with the ringdove at my side.

What is the use of a municipal body,
Its mayor, its aldermen and office-bearers,
Its mace and chain of gold, and scarlet robes ;
Its council meetings, dinners, and processions,
Unless it vindicates the public rights,
Aims ever to advance the public good,
Rules by just laws, and guards the public morals ?
   The bane of party spirit in a borough
Poisons and weakens public enterprise ;
And energies, which, if they were combined,
Would work a boundless benefit to all,
Drivel to nothing and are wholly wasted.
Our Corporation is political,
Not popular—applied to party aims—
And not devoted to the public good,—
Like grim St. Runwald's Church, an ugly eye-sore
That stands in our High-street,—it blocks the way.
I speak about it in the spirit of love.
The noble relics of the Roman times,
Of which our town may rightfully be proud,
Are left to go unheeded to decay.
Children are free to scramble on the walls
And daily dislocate the stones that Romans
With toil built up two thousand years ago ;
The Roman guard-room by the city gate,
Where Roman soldiers played at pitch and toss,
Is made a dwelling-place for English pigs.
I say these things in honesty of speech
To shame the men who thus neglect their duty,
And bring a burning scandal on the town.

We have a castle of enormous strength
Built by the Romans, or I know not whom,
A wondrous relic of antiquity,
And round about it is the Castle Bailey,
Disfigured by wretched buildings on one side,
And left a barren waste upon the other.
The whole of it is private property,
But yet the public have an ancient right
To use the Bailey for their recreation.
('Twas there we townfolks all went mad together,
And roasted frantically a bullock whole,
When Albert Edward, Britain's youthful heir,
Wedded the sweet and captivating Dane.)
Some while ago the town authorities
Sought to convert it to a cattle-market—
A very intelligible appropriation
Were it to sell themselves for Essex calves—
A desecration which I fought against,
And with the help of others overthrew.
Now if there were a spark of public spirit
In those who have authority to act,
What a delightful place of recreation
Might of this Bailey be eliminated.
A lovely garden with delightful walks
And shady seats and beds of various flowers,
A lawn where Lisle and Lucas in old times
Shed their heroic blood for Royalty,
An ample green for children to disport in,
With the old Castle standing in the centre,
Like reverend age smiling at youthful joys.
    Did Lisle and Lucas shed their blood in vain?

These gallant gentlemen have left their names
On history's bloody page, and is that all?
The boys who make a racket on the green
Care not the least, and hardly give a thought
About these chiefs who died to save their king.
When some inquisitive traveller treads the spot
He listens with some interest to the story,
Of which perhaps he never heard before;
Nine people out of ten who pass the place
Are thinking only of their own affairs,
And not the ghastly martyrdom of heroes.
Is this the proud reward of noble deeds?
Ungratefully does war repay its friends—
A breath of praise for life-blood thrown away!
 This is the story of these hapless chiefs:
In the sad civil war, that ravaged England,
Between the Parliament and Charles the First,
The starving garrison of Royalists
That held the ancient town of Colchester,
Having consumed eight hundred of their horses,
At last were forced to yield themselves as prisoners
To the besieging army of the Parliament,
Upon the famous twenty-eighth of August,
In the year Sixteen hundred forty-eight,
A day in Colchester to be remembered.
 A council of war was held at the Moot Hall
By the victorious general, stern Lord Fairfax,
And his subordinate chiefs and officers,
Who to their presence summoned Sir George Lucas
And Sir Charles Lisle, the conquered Royalist chiefs,

N

And upon hasty consultation told them
That after so long and obstinate a defence
It was most needful for the example of others,
And that the peace and comfort of the country
Might not hereafter be disturbed by traitors,
Some military justice should be executed,
And therefore that the council had determined
They two should presently be shot to death.

   Then were these chieftains taken to the castle
And placed together in a gloomy dungeon,
And left to think upon their sad estate.

   Meanwhile the other captured officers,
Who had partaken in the town's defence,
Fearing not for themselves but for their friends,
Spake low to one another of their state,
Breathing the broken prayers of dying men.
Ere long there came a message from Sir Charles,
Begging a chaplain might be sent immediately.
This message struck a death-chill through all hearts,
Showing the sentence that hung o'er their friends ;
They therefore sent by a comrade in great haste
An earnest message to the council of war,
Imploring that these gallant gentlemen
Might nowise suffer more than they themselves,
Because, that all being equally concerned
In the defence of the town and Royal cause,
It was but just that all should suffer alike ;
And for themselves they thereby begged permission,
Whatever might be their worthy comrades' fate,
To share it with them, as was right and just.

The council of war regarded not this message :
And that there might be found no sort of slackness
Or time for interference with their will,
Ireton, the illustrious Cromwell's son-in-law,
Forthwith proceeded to the castle dungeon,
And told the prisoners to prepare for death,
For that the sentence which was passed upon them
Was straightway to be put in execution.
Sir Charles inquired by what law they must die,
Whether by ordinance of the Parliament,
By the decision of the council of war,
Or by the order of the general :
Whereupon Ireton replied to him
It was by order of the council of war,
Taken by vote according to an order
Of Parliament, by which those found in arms
Against the Parliament were adjudged as traitors :
To which Sir Charles immediately replied,
Like to a man proceeding to a banquet
Rather than unto death, showing no fear,
And scorning death, just as he held in scorn
Those instruments of death who sought his life,
" Ah, you deceive yourselves, but me you cannot ;
But we are conquered and must bear your sen-
    tence ;
We only ask that we may live till morning,
That we may settle some few worldly matters,
And above all prepare ourselves to die."
But Ireton answered sternly unto him
That his request could no way be complied with ;

To which Sir Charles replied, "Sir, do not think
I ask this boon because I wish to live,
Or that I fear the death you doom me to;
I scorn to ask my life at hands like yours;
But I would fain arrange some business matters,
And I desire to make my peace with God,
And not be thrown out of this jarring world
With all my sins about me unforgiven;
But since that you refuse this charity
I must submit me to the mercy of God,
Who doth hear prayer.   His holy will be done.
Now do your worst; I shall be ready to die."
   Likewise Sir George desired a little respite
That he might write unto his father and mother
To tell them what was happened unto him,
And comfort them in their so sore distress.
This being refused he yielded silently.
   And so a chaplain being sent to them,
These most unfortunate but gallant gentlemen
Devoted the short time remaining to them
To prayer and to religious exercises,
And the great work of the soul's preparation
For an admission to a better life,
A work that never should be left till last;
Both of them breathing forth from their full hearts
Such sweet and heavenly ejaculations
They seemed translated to another world.
Religion reconciles discordant things,
Diminishing the importance of the present
By magnifying the glory of the future.

It was about the evening hour of seven,
The very day on which the town surrendered,
That the two chieftains were led forth to die
On the green sward behind the gloomy castle,
Where Ireton and his brother officers
Received them with three files of musketeers,
Whose duty was to do this bloody deed.
Sir Charles was fixed upon to suffer first;
His friend meanwhile being shortly led aside
That he might not behold his comrade fall.

Sir Charles at length being placed in due position
To meet the volley of the musketeers,
He told them it was no new thing to him
To look death in the face on the field of battle,
And said, "You now shall see that I dare die."
He then fell down upon his knees and prayed
For a few minutes, and, soon rising up,
He, with a cheerful face, opened his doublet
So as to bare his bosom to the foe,
Then placed his hands boldly upon his sides,
And calling to his executioners,
He bravely said, "See! I am ready for you;
Now rebels do your worst!" and at these words
They fired at once. Four bullets pierced his body.
He fell, and in a little while expired.

Sir George was then brought forth to the fatal
spot
Where lay the bleeding body of his friend,
And, kneeling down beside the corpse, he kissed it,
And said, " Dear friend, thine was a noble heart,

A reputation of unspotted honour,
An understanding worthy of thy rank.
We have fought side by side in this great conflict,
And now are doomed to perish here together,
By the atrocious act of guilty rebels,
But for a cause for which we gladly die."
    Then standing up, and taking from his pocket
Five pieces of gold, being all he had about him,
He generously bestowed one piece of gold
Upon the soldiers who were murdering him,
And the remainder handed to a servant,
Whom he desired to give them to his friends
In London, as his last sad legacy.
Then, turning round to the spectators, said,
" How many of your lives who here are present
Have I, in hot blood, saved, when we have fought
In open warfare, and must now myself
Here, in cold blood, be barbarously murdered !
But what atrocious act dare they not do,
Who willingly would sentence to the block
Their king ! whom they already have imprisoned ;
For whose deliverance from his enemies,
And for the peace of this unhappy nation,
I dedicate my latest prayers to Heaven."
    Then looking at his executioners
Full in the face, and thinking them too distant
To do their bloody deed effectually,
He asked them to approach him somewhat nearer ;
To which one answered, " Sir, I'll warrant you
We'll hit you," whereupon he smiled and said,

"I have been nearer to you when you have missed
    me."
He then kneeled down in prayer for a few minutes,
And, after uttering many invocations
In the most precious name of the Prince of Peace,
Rose up again, and resolutely exclaimed,
"I now am ready, traitors! do your worst."
    These final words had hardly passed his lips
Before they fired. One of the fatal bullets
Passed through his noble heart, and he fell dead.
    The bodies of these valiant gentlemen,
United in their lives and in their deaths,
Were buried in one vault unitedly,
In old St. Giles's church in Colchester,
Where to this present day may still be seen
Their marble tomb, showing a proud inscription,
And carved too deeply ever to be effaced.
    Truly I should not like to be a soldier,
And have my limbs torn off, or be shot dead.
It may be pretty to be dressed in scarlet,
And look as showy as a paroquet,
To strut about like an old turkey-cock,
And march in rank behind a band of music,
While all the servant girls from doors and windows
Are staring open-mouthed with admiration;
But I possess no taste for fields of battle,
And have peculiar notions about courage.
There are at least a hundred sorts of courage;
The sort that bares its breast to sword or rifle
Is not the sort of courage I possess;

I have a horror of corporeal pain;
I do not like the feeling of cold iron,
Though only playing with a rotten tooth,
It sends a painful shiver through my frame.
   England has been a foolish fighting country,
Quick at offence but tardy at forgiveness,
A little country with a mighty spirit,
Seizing the sword rather than yield a word,
And what has been the upshot of it all:
The loss of her best blood in civil wars,
And foolish quarrels with surrounding countries;
And now she stands a hardened, shameless bankrupt,
Pressed with a debt that never can be paid
Until she grows potatoes made of gold;
And if an army of her creditors
Sent in their Christmas bills on New Year's day
The bubble of her credit must be burst:
So much for all your military glory,
Bathed in a sea of proud but wasted blood.
We now at length begin to see true daylight,
And from past history learn the mighty lesson,
Which may be put into the smallest nutshell,
"Leave us alone, and we'll leave you alone."
Long will the name, "Crimea," turn us sick,
And, "Abyssinia," spoil our appetites.
   War's greatest heroes are they really heroes?
Look at Napoleon in his latter days,
A captive on a rock in the Atlantic,
Quarrelling about his soups and omelettes;
While Wellington in his declining years,

The soldier who dethroned Napoleon,
The iron Duke who won at Waterloo,
Had like to have had his life of glory ended
By being choked, within an ace of death,
By a poor little innocent chicken bone !
   War is the worst of self-inflicted evils;
Its wasteful and illimitable cost
Baffles and staggers human calculation.
The sum we have to pay merely for interest
On our expenditure on foreign wars,
All which were fought in vain and are forgotten,
And what we have to pay for current costs,
For standing armies and for ships of war,
Comes to a hundred pounds for every minute
Of every day of four and twenty hours.
Talk about lawyers' bills, they are bad enough,
But 'tis our army bills that ruin us.
The preparations for prospective wars,
Which those who live by them alarm us with,
Eat up the rich resources of the state.
The system will continue to exist
So long as soldiers are allowed to rule us ;
This scourge of military armaments
Is the great blight upon the nation's growth.
The army and the navy of the country
Form genteel cribs for idle gentlemen
Fond of their ease, and pleased with rank and station,
And not averse to an immoral life.
   I have beheld abroad two thorough-bred bull-dogs
Hang on the nose of an infuriate bull,

Their sharp teeth buried in the creature's flesh,
From which they hung with all their horrible weight.
In vain the bull plunged hard to throw them off;
Carry them he must, but humbled, helpless, doomed.
Such to old England are her Army and Navy,
Which dangle with their fangs in the nation's nose.
    England will never have good government
Till her constituencies refrain from sending
Soldiers and lawyers into Parliament.
This is the nail; hammer it well on the head.
Hanging of rogues is going out of fashion,
And I confess that I am glad of it;
But what are we to do with these sad knaves?
Some course 'tis certain we must take with them;
Teach them, I say, to live by honest labour.
'The lawyers thrive by multiplying laws,
Of which we have a thousand times too many,
And thus they often contradict each other.
These laws are just so many crafty snares
Which lawyers set to catch and trip us up;
'T were well to make a bonfire out of them.
As to the soldiers, they are twice as bad;
They suck up half the taxes of the country;
Their lavishness most truly knows no bounds;
They squander millions of the public money
With just as much compunction and no more
As I should cop a sixpence in the sea.
The Army and the Navy are our lions,
Show beasts that England keeps for fools to stare at,
Most ravenous beasts devouring up the country!

These creatures over-ride all governments,
And get the upper hand in every state !
'Tis from among these lawyers and these butchers—
Butchers, that word came foremost to my pen—
I mean these gaudy and cocked-hatted soldiers,
That peers of Parliament are mostly made;
It is not men who make discoveries
In art or science, and confer a blessing
Upon their country and the world at large;
It is not writers whose exalted thoughts
Fashion and guide the intellects of men;
It is not the sublime philanthropists
Whose bounty is a blessing to all times,
And whose example elevates the nations;
But it is lawyers crawling on all fours,
And using politics for scaling-ladders,
Who clamber into powerful peerages—
It is these bloodstained military men
Who mulct us for these costly armaments,
And having got them, urge us on to use them,
And thus involve us in the horrors of war,
By which they profit and the people suffer;
Filling the papers with their victories,
And caring nothing for the blood they shed,
But glorying in the grandeur of their crimes,
And earning stars and garters for themselves,
Honours, emoluments, and, worse than all,
The power, as noble peers of Parliament,
To keep this vicious system in full play,
And thus perpetuate the ills they cause.

The monstrous wrong of standing armaments
Surpasses all the follies of mankind;
And first there is the cost of keeping them,
And then there is the cost of their equipments,
And last, the waste of all their time and labour,
Which otherwise might have enriched the land;
Besides all these there is the enormous suffering
Borne by the soldiers in encampment life,
And worse than this the vices that attend it.
Cannot this mammoth folly of the nations
Be superseded by a grain of sense?
Why should the various states composing Europe
Stand in more terror of each others' aims
Than neighbouring towns should stand in mutual fear,
And keep up armies for their mutual safety?
The whole device of standing armaments
Is all a sham, an empty base pretence,
Contrived to furnish pay and privilege,
Honours, rewards, and power to needy men:
Too proud, though poor, to gain an honest living
By industry and virtuous enterprise.

If nations stand in fear of one another
A guarantee of peace may soon be found.
Let them give hostages to one another,
Two or three men of noble family,
To be relieved by others every few years,
Their lives the sureties for enduring peace;
And let them be rewarded for their services,
By garters, peerages, or ample bounties;
Just the odd thousands of our annual outlay

Would form a large and ample recompense,
Saving the millions that are wasted now
On guns, redcoats, cocked-hats, powder and shot.
    And lest disputes arise 'twixt different nations,
Let them in time of peace when men are calm
Establish a High Court of Arbitration,
Composed of noblemen from all these States,
A court of sacred justice and proud honour,
Whose verdicts shall be binding upon all,
Under the penalties by all agreed to—
The solemn sacrifice, by axe or gallows,
Of the devoted, guiltless hostages.
This is the plan of wise and virtuous jurists,
And when mankind are wise 'twill be adopted.
Would any Christian nation in all Europe,
Under a State Alliance such as this,
So far forget the sanctity of Treaties,
Its fame, its dignity, its sacred honour,
As to break faith with any other nation—
Basely allow its noble hostages
To suffer in cold blood, a horrible death,
And plunge into the miseries of war
To gain some favourite object? Never ! never !
    A noble principle is patriotism !
Right noble in a virtuous statesman's breast
Who faces all the angry frowns of power.
The truthful poet singing in his garret
May well be called a lofty patriot ;
He elevates the nation's sentiment
With earnest song that blends with our heart's blood.

But patriotism, like another Proteus,
Takes many curious and fantastic shapes.
Who cannot but admire its startling form
When it leads peaceable painstaking men
To undergo the risks and toils and hardships
Of soldiers of a Corps of Volunteers,
Ready to shed their blood for England's safety ?
Kind-hearted men who never shed a drop
Of human blood, except when they were boys,
Cutting a stick with a blunt pocket-knife ;
Plain men who never touched a gun before,
Not even to knock down an impudent sparrow
That would not try to fly away from them ;
Whose fingers tremble but to touch the trigger;
Men of exemplary self-abnegation,
Who scruple not to make themselves look fools
For the protection of their dearest country,
Belted and padded like a pig in harness,
Stiffened and choked with a self-torturing collar,
And dressed so droll they do not know themselves ;
So that a meek-eyed man looks vulturish,
And the bland, smiling, smirking counter-kicker,
Bewhiskered up, fancies himself a lion.
The more ferocious they appear the better.
And then to undergo the daily drill,
And give themselves a borrowed martial air,
Heads up, backs straight, legs stiff, and arms in form !
Sometimes to take a march into the country
In all the mimic pageantry of war,
With fife and drum and such tom-foolery

Tramping along the slushy public road
All in the pelting rain or blinding snow,
Wet through and shivering to the very marrow,
Enduring hardship, as becomes good soldiers,
And the grim smiles of the snug lookers-on—
Men who, as mere civilians, would have shrunk
From venturing forth without a silk umbrella,
A stout great coat, and woollen comforter,
Lovingly knitted by an anxious mother ;
Yet braving all these hardships and these risks,
Not of the bullets of an enemy,
But of sore throats, catarrh, neuralgia,
Chilblains, swelled face, and chronic rheumatism,
To shield us from imaginary foes :
If this is not most noble patriotism,
Why then it is the silliest vanity.
　There is a town ten miles from Colchester,
The town of Coggeshall, lying in a hollow,
Famous throughout the land for " Coggeshall jobs,"
A town by some folks called the city of wisdom,
Of which a number of strange tales are told,
Blunders absurd and misadventures various,
Of which I here shall mention only one.
When Bonaparte tried to frighten England,
By threatening to invade our island shores,
The men of Coggeshall, full of public spirit,
Resolved to form a Corps of Volunteers
For the defence of their beloved country ;
But none of them would serve as private soldiers ;
All of them wanted to be officers !

Yet they agreed upon the point of tactics.
The town of Coggeshall forms a triangle
With Colchester and Maldon on the coast ;
So they resolved that if the pig-tailed French
Should make a landing on the coast at Maldon
Then they themselves would march to Colchester ;
In order to protect that ancient port.
If, on the other hand, the French should come
Up the broad Colne, and land near Colchester,
Then they would march immediately to Maldon !
So sang the luckless bard of Coggeshall town,
In burlesque verse, " The Coggeshall Volunteers."
He was a clever thriving schoolmaster,
But gave such umbrage to the men of Coggeshall
By the hard-hitting satire of his poem,
He lost his school, and so, poor man, was ruined ;
In short he made a " Coggeshall job " of it.
 This is the twenty-second day of April,
A day of mark upon my calendar,
And I remember in my early youth
A scene half-way across the Atlantic Ocean,
Never from memory to be effaced.
A gale swept fiercely o'er the tumbling waves
That rolled before it in their ponderous strength :
Their frothy tops caught up into the wind,
Flew hissing forward like a pelting rain.
The ship with just a sail to steady her
Pitched o'er the billows like a living creature,
Or plunged into the intervening valleys.
I watched the scene with boyish ravishment.

The weird mysterious daughters of the wind,
Seated securely on each tall mast-head,
Waved their thin robes and whistled mournfully.
On a sudden the gale tore from the opposite point!
The waves not knowing the way they were to go,
Ran helter-skelter, dashing against each other
In mad disorder and enraged confusion,
Like the grand army routed at Waterloo;
The ship shrank back trembling in all her joints,
And reeled and staggered like a drunken man;
The eager billows rushed upon the deck,
Burying the half-stunned vessel in the deep.
Would she go down, or would she right herself?
A moment, like an age, and all seemed lost.
I, ere the worst, though loth to quit the scene,
Was ordered down below, out of harm's way,
To join the silent group within the cabin,
Where we were all shut down, and made secure
From inundation of the flood above us.
Grasping a firm support I stood and viewed
The faces of the seated company,
Awe-struck and breathless, waiting for the end;
And there were spirits there who could look up
In humble trust, not unprepared for death.
No fear felt I.   The excitement strengthened me;
The grandeur swallowed up the sense of danger;
I felt the struggling ship bend under me
As though she were about to snap in twain,
And tremble like a helpless guilty creature,
Until at length the sturdy mariners,

Blessed in their efforts by a Power Divine,
Brought round her gallant bowsprit to the wind,
And lashed the helm to keep her to the mark,
And then, the danger past, we breathed once more.
  How exquisite is the return of Spring !
When the awakening earth puts on its mantle
Of tender green, studded with star-like flowers !
What dewy freshness glows in every tint !
The earth appears to be restored again
To its original new-born purity
Ere man rebelled and brought a curse upon it ;
The uplands heave their shoulders of green wheat ;
The trees unfold apace their budding leaves ;
The hedges show in all their lovely freshness ;
The ferns and velvet mosses on the hedge-banks,
Mingled with primroses, enchant the eye ;
The commonest weeds are beautiful to look on,
Clad in the delicacy of opening life ;
The apple-trees are all a-pink with bloom,
The cherry-trees seem wreathed with feathery snow !
The birds are busy with their nest-building,
And cheer their pleasant toil with songs of joy ;
Sparrows chirp passionately amongst the bushes ;
The sun sheds balmy warmth on all alike,
Infusing into all new life, and hope,
And love, the moving instinct of all nature ;
While nature seems to send its reflex back
Upon the throbbing heart of erring man—
The reflex of its chastened purity,
Inspiring him with holy thoughts and feelings ;

Enamouring him with love for the Creator,
Of so much beauty and sublimity,
The source of so much bounty and lovingkindness ;
And prompting him to worship at His footstool.
Yes, nature to the meek and chastened soul
In all its manifestations is devout.
The sun, the symbol of the Deity,
Worshipped indeed as God by heathen nations
In their obtuse, uncultured ignorance,
Displays His infinite life-imparting power,
His glory and His rich munificence.
The stars that deck the sky, and the broad ocean
With its perpetual roll of sounding waves,
And the unnumbered sands on the sea-shore,
These all are types of God's infinitude,
And lead the adoring spirit up to Him.
The mysteries of the winds and of the tides,
The marvellous growth of flowers, and plants, and
  trees,
Display the inscrutability of God.
The fragrance of the summer-blossoming fields
Is a sweet-smelling-sacrifice to Him ;
The songs of birds are anthems to His praise ;
The freshness of the landscape clothed in sunshine
Is but the glow of nature's gratitude ;
The mists that float on high from the hill sides
Ascend as incense to the throne of God ;
The reverential hills with their bare heads,
White with the snows of age, they worship Him ;
The waving trees bow their high heads in worship ;

The tiny brook, falling from rock to rock,
Half hidden in a wilderness of leaves,
Sounds like the lisping praise of babes and sucklings;
All nature issued from the hand of God,
And pays eternal tribute in return!
    The beautiful, the true, and the eternal,
Linked in the golden chain of love divine,
These are the elements of heaven on high,
As here below are fire, air, earth and water.
The beautiful, the beautiful, the beautiful,
The beautiful, the true, and the eternal,
And love, the ocean in which heaven is bathed!
The exiled soul pants for you evermore!
There are magnetic pulses of the soul
Vibrating momently 'twixt earth and heaven,
Sympathies wedded to the Infinite.
The beautiful, the beautiful, the beautiful,
The beautiful, the true, and the eternal,
And love, pure love, the sum of heavenly joy!
Whatever is your reflex here below,
Charms like the notes of music from afar,
The glory of the sun's declining rays,
The exactitude of nature's primal laws,
The equal boundlessness of time and space,
The goodness scattered everywhere about us,
These all are types of Heavenly antitypes
Beyond all measure of comparison.
The beautiful, the beautiful, the beautiful,
The beautiful, the true, and the eternal,
And Heavenly love, the bond of purity!

Ere the creation dawned—before the sun
Illumined all the trackless realms of space—
Ere yet the stars bedecked the dome of night,
Or ever the moon walked forth in bridal sheen—
Ere man in Eden dwelt in innocence,
Ye were coeval with the Deity !
The attributes of His divinity !
Shall we not therefore cling to you in life,
And seek to be embalmed in you in death ?
The beautiful, the beautiful, the beautiful,
The beautiful, the true, and the eternal,
And love, the odour of Heaven's sanctity !

Here endeth Book the Fourth of this my Poem.
Sweet is the close of the young summer's day,
Sweet as the heavenly smile of dying saints ;
The air is calm, the very clouds repose ;
The beamy sun sinks peacefully to rest.
O, what a pity that a sun so bright
Should fade so soon ! but vain are our regrets.
The prism of the horizontal air
Subtends the red rays of the setting orb
Upon a panorama of rich clouds,
Whose gorgeousness is the despair of art.
The western sky is like an emerald sea
With golden islands floating on its bosom,
Islands of purest transcendental joy,
Peopled with happy angels in bright robes ;
But while I gaze entranced the pageant fades.

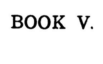

BOOK V.

BOOK V.

May day ! May day ! This is the first of May ;
A day that thrills all hearts with welcome promise
Of coming summer, and of softer airs ;
Of cowslips, daisies, buttercups and whitethorn ;
Of cuckoos, with their mellow double notes ;
And happy nightingales with hearts so full
They warble all the day and all the night.
Though clouds may intercept the sun's warm beams
We know the wasteful ocean of his glory
Is flowing o'er the boundless realms of space.
An early summer brings a fruitful season.
May, of all months, is dedicate to love ;
But May-day games are going out of date ;
The Queen of May is only seen in song.
The Pagan sports that have come down to us
From the dark ages of gross superstition
Are dying like the darkness of their birth ;
The lofty Maypoles garlanded with flowers,
Round which the youths and maidens used to dance,
Are superseded by tall factory chimneys ;
And toil, with profit, is more thought upon
Than idle sport with scanty sustenance.
We now look forward to the first of May
With feelings which are altogether modern.

This is the day the Royal Academy
Throws wide its portals to the shilling public,
And manliness and beauty crowd the rooms.
Most hard it is to say which are most charming,
The pictures or the fair realities.
Beauty in every form is seen around—
Landscape and seascape, portraiture and architecture,
Historic group, or literary presentment,
Scenes in the world, and scenes beyond the world,
Domestic scenes, and street and rural scenes,
And fruits, and flowers, and birds and animals,
Painted in styles as various as their subjects :
Some, wasting excellence of execution
On subjects with no mind or story in them ;
And some, evincing with uncultured vigour
A genius which excuses everything.
How has the morning been anticipated !
How many a pale and anxious youthful artist
Has thought, and wrought, and eaten scanty bread
To place a picture on those honoured walls !
Perhaps to find it ruthlessly excluded,
And all his proudest visions ended in ruin—
The last bright ray of hope dashed to the earth,
Like the red gleam of the descending sun
Thrown on the tomb of a Plantagenet !
And not his hopes alone.   Perhaps a mother
And gentle sister may have buoyed him up
With ardent love and sanguine admiration,
Looking on his success as though their own,
And now hang over him to comfort him,

Dropping warm glistening tears of sympathy,
While they extol his merits o'er again,
And thus console him for his disappointment,
And cheer him with the hope of future triumph.
Perhaps the artist is a delicate girl,
But with ambition almost masculine ;
With skilful fingers and a cultured mind,
Urged by the stern necessity to live,
But sensitive as woman's soul beseems.
She finds this day her picture is rejected :
That picture which has cost such anxious toil
And tender skill ; on which she has built up
Such a fine airy castle of fond hopes !
She bursts into a flood of bitter tears,
And having none to give her sympathy,
Yields up for just a moment to despair.
  But there are artists who have potent names,
Who, somewhat like young, rich, and handsome lovers,
Who have but to propose and be accepted,
Are sure to have their works received and hung,
Though they may be the thirty-ninth dilution—
Watery and thin—of former excellence.
What disappointments, jealousies, and hatreds,
What fears of failure, hopes of good success,
And raptures of attained appreciation,
Are interwoven with the Opening Day !
The trembling artist mingles with the crowd
To watch the effects his landscape may produce,
And hear the observations made upon it.
Many pass by and never notice it.

The art of connoisseurship is to see
Merits or faults which others cannot see.
One burly gentleman in sombre broadcloth
Levels his eye-glass at it seriously
For half-a-minute, trying to comprehend it.
The artist hopes he is about to praise it
To the stout lady leaning on his arm ;
But her tired eyes are wandering far away ;
Her thoughts are with her servants left at home
Down at the rectory in Hertfordshire.
The rector pauses, and then passes on,
Giving no symptom of decided judgment.
Another gentleman, whose long, sharp nose,
Surmounted by a pair of spectacles,
Gives the idea of critical acumen,
Shrugs up his shoulders and extends his hands,
And tells his friend the colouring is too warm.
Ere long another comes with easy air
And droll expression of self-satisfaction,
Well dressed, well fed, with note-book in his hand ;
The fashion of his face is critical ;
Perhaps he scribbles for the leading journal.
The artist sees, and trembles for his fate.
With lips compressed, and eyes peering obliquely,
The critic views the picture for five seconds,
And mutters to himself decisively,
"The sky and water are most cruelly cold !"
Jots down his *ipse dixit* in his note-book,
And passes onward to another picture.
A group of ladies next draw round the landscape,

But neither praise nor blame the sky or water,
Nor yet the ruddy brilliance of the scene,
Nor seem to observe the skilful light and shade,
Nor yet the fine perspective of the distance,
But are delighted with a pair of doves
Billing and cooing in the foreground trees !
The disappointed artist hurries homeward,
Trusting that some Review will do him justice.

   I wonder what becomes of all the pictures ;
Year after year there is an inundation.
The good ones doubtless are in great demand ;
Where all the bad ones go to is a question ;
Perhaps the limbo where dead donkeys go.
But every exhibition—every picture—
If it could speak, could tell a history
But little dreamt of by the passing throng.

   How many long and learned dissertations,
Essays, and lectures have been writ on Art !
And yet these volumes never made a painter.
All our great painters have been great without them.
May I not sport my little dogmatism ?
The secret of success is genius ;
True genius studies in the best of schools,
The school of nature and of actual life ;
And what is genius but an inborn power,
Creating by selecting and combining ;
A power that practice carries to perfection ?
True art is nothing but selected nature,
Not its mere superficial aspect only,
But its inherent inward spirit of beauty.

All art is bad that has no living soul.
Mind is the highest attribute of nature ;
In man alone it is pre-eminent ;
And yet there lurks around us everywhere
Its seeming counterpart in things inanimate,
Types of the different phases of the mind :
The sun, an emblem of unbounded power,
The ocean, of illimitable goodness ;
Motion and magnitude in combination,
Impress us most with true sublimity ;
Darkness is saturnine, and light is cheerful ;
The opening buds are emblems of our hopes ;
The weeping willow is funereal ;
The yew is sombre with the hue of death ;
The spreading oak betokens steadfastness ;
The primrose and the lily of the valley
Are innocence and purity itself ;
A field ablaze with buttercups and daisies
Is a fine type of youthful happiness ;
The evening hour, when all the moon-lit sea
Is frosted over with a silvery sheen,
Sweetly accords with tenderness and love ;
While sunshine dancing on the summer ocean
Reflects a fine embodiment of gladness.
These infinite resemblances of nature
To all the feelings of the human mind—
These outward symbols of an inward spirit
Become the painter's powerful accessories
In working out his contemplated meanings :
A store of inexhaustible materials.

All art is therefore but a manifestation
Of actual or implied humanity,
Developed in a clear and natural form;
It treats of mind, or mind enlivens it.
A painting must be always full of meaning,
And, if it undertakes to tell a story,
The story must be both intelligible
And worth the telling by the painter's art.
The excellence of fiction is its truth ;
So also is the beauty of a painting.
A painting is the offspring of much labour,
Of deep reflection and protracted practice ;
It is the height of art to hide all this ;
The aim of art is to conceal itself
Under the flowing garb of simple nature,
And give the impression of unstudied ease.
All art and labour must be unperceived ;
Nature performs her mightiest miracles
Without apparent toil or painful effort ;
The sense of effort soon grows wearisome.
A waterfall is always beautiful,
Whether it trickles softly down the glen,
Or dashes playfully from rock to rock ;
The eye is never tired of gazing on it :
It does not labour, so it does not weary.
How different is it with the man-made fountain
Squirting a column of water to the sky !
Its novelty surprises for a moment,
But soon the sense of effort palls upon us,
And so we turn dissatisfied away.

Nature is simple, and so art must be,
Especially when art would picture forth
The faces and the forms of human beings.
True art can catch unconscious attitudes ;
The mere pretender deals in studied airs,
Fit only for grand actors on the stage,
To please young gentlemen and pretty ladies
Come home from boarding-school in holiday time.
In one thing Art and Nature oddly differ :
An echo is most beautiful in nature
And yet it is an odious thing in art.
We value an original composition,
But turn away indifferent from a copy.
   Every true genius is a lawgiver ;
At least he is a law unto himself,
Winning from life its latent poetry.
For every individual character,
Sees all things through a prism of his own,
And hence the strange varieties in taste
Which are effected by a thousand causes,
Chiefly by natural bent, by education,
And more than any other cause by fashion.
Good taste in dress in Regent Street is one thing ;
Good taste in dress in Pekin is another.
France regulates our taste in many matters.
The French being poor and short of cutlery,
Acquired the art of pimbling all their food
With forks and spoons instead of manly knives ;
So, spooney-like, we eat with forks and spoons.
   What freaks of taste have I beheld in my time !

Until the era of the Exhibition,
In the year Eighteen hundred fifty-one,
Which did indeed intoxicate all England
With its fair treasures in a Crystal Casket,
And brought outlandish people from far climes,
With flowing beards, and marvellous uncouth dresses,
Who stared, themselves, and also made us stare !
Till then it was considered only decent
To shave our chins, and make ourselves look clean.
All that is altered by these foreigners.
We now have retrograded back to barbarism,
Abolishing the business of the barbers,
And men appear in public with long beards,
Black beards, and white beards, beards of grizzly hue,
Or straggling hairs, the apology for beards,
Or beards that might belong to billy-goats ;
Some, like the beard of ancient Hudibras,
Described by Butler, red as any tile ;
Some, sombre like a cluster of dark bees,
Burying the mouth of a pale yellow bee-skip :
Such is the potency of public taste.
How fond men seem of playing with their beards ;
I hate to see them paw the nasty things ;
And yet 'tis all a matter of mere taste ;
But then what contradictions we behold !
Men let their beards grow long and rough and ram-
    pant,
Yet shave their garden lawns as smooth as carpets !
Our flower-beds all seem plastered with a trowel.
O ! rather let men cultivate themselves,

P

And polish off the roughness of their nature,
And let their gardens grow to wildernesses.
I do love wildness in its proper place;
I love the rich luxuriance of foliage,
The wildness of deep groves and shrubberies,
The bold exuberance of weeds and wild flowers;
For savage nature has a matchless grace.
Yes! let us shave and christianise ourselves,
And leave our heathenism to the face of nature;
And thus reverse the fashion of the day.

How small a place has reason in our tastes!
And yet we never want for good excuses
For either what we like, or what we do.
An Englishman is a peculiar creature,
And you may drag him through the Atlantic Ocean
Before you rid him of his prejudices
And favourite notions upon things in general.
And yet how often we deceive ourselves,
Or rather suffer ourselves to be deceived,
By false appearances of outward things!
We fancy that the world is rolling westward,
When it is rolling eastward all the while.
One common error always vexes me—
It is the way in which men comb their hair,
A grand discovery which I made in youth;
They comb it from the left, and not the right.
If you take twenty men promiscuously,
You mostly find that nineteen out of twenty
Stupidly comb their hair from left to right.
From right to left is the plain law of beauty;

And how does this gross blunder come about?
'Tis simply by an act of self-deception.
Men stand before a glass to comb their hair,
And in the glass, by an old law in optics,
The spectrum of one's face is just reversed ;
The right appears the left, the left the right ;
And so they comb their hair contrariwise,
Perverted by an optical illusion,
Combing their hair from left to right demurely,
When they imagine they are combing it
From right to left, and never see their error.
And yet it is an error that wise men
Have fallen into, as well as common people.
Sir David Brewster and Lord Brougham and Vaux—
I knew them both, and I can speak of them ;
They both are dead, and I may speak of them—
Both these philosophers had studied optics,
And written learned books upon the subject,
Yet both were cheated by their looking-glasses,
And combed their hoary locks from left to right,
And died, and never knew they were deceived !
    I like not modern taste in many things.
One error of the age is over ornament ;
This was the legacy bequeathed to England
By the great Crystal Casket Exhibition !
We are almost suffocated with over ornament ;
Everything now is made absurd with it.
I do abhor this artificial taste—
This everlasting straining for effect,
This toil for what is called originality,

However ugly and brimful of faults.
It may be daily seen in architecture.
The birds are satisfied to build their nests
After the fashion of their several kinds,
Just as they built them in the days of old,
And what can be more beautiful and perfect ?
The bees, that build their cells so skilfully,
Are quite contented with the good old style,
And never think of trying to surpass it.
To prove a thing by means of illustration
Is not I know like proving it by logic;
The argument by illustration only
May easily be made to prove truth error;
And yet there is a living germ of truth
In the position I have here advanced.
When we have reached a style of architecture,
Handsome, convenient, durable, and healthful,
Adapted to the nature of our climate,
Not formed by instinct but by sober reason,
It is far better to adhere to it
Than strive ambitiously to go beyond it,
And sacrifice convenience to ornament,
Or healthfulness to durability,
Or all of these to some fantastic notion.
I am no Goth, and love not modern Gothic :
Gothic was very well in Gothic times ;
But who can bear the brand-new imitation ?
Who now would walk about in Gothic coats ?
This medieval taste is covert Popery !
This passion for the quaint and the grotesque—

This taste for tawdry over decoration—
These grand appealings to the outward senses,
Instead of to the oracle within us—
This love of legends of unreal life,
Of paste-board heroes, and of duck-trussed dames,
The crude in art, the false in poetry—
Is all sheer retrogression back to Rome !
   Of taste in dress I find no fault with men.
We have improved upon our ancestors ;
Gold lace and ribbons long have been discarded,
Or used by menial lacqueys of the rich,
And garments of a quaint and graceless form,
And costly and elaborate workmanship,
Somewhat resembling ancient suits of armour,
We only see in paintings of the past ;
We dress with plainness and simplicity,
In clothes adapted with consummate skill
For free and easy exercise of limb.
Machinery now supplies us with materials
Far better than our old forefathers dreamed of.
   Of women's dresses I forbear to speak,
Although a satirist with a sharp steel pen
Might find in them materials for much sport ;
I only think they change the fashion of them
With a remarkably bewildering speed,
And make them far too much a constant matter
Of occupation to the mind and fingers—
To mention nothing of the mercer's bills.
The toes of Fashion kick the heels of Custom.
What a relief 'twould be to any lady

Who had the strength of mind which it demands,
To dress in one, becoming, simple fashion,
Wisely adapted to her age and rank,
Without being driven into modes of dress
Ugly, preposterous, irksome, and disfiguring.
Simplicity of dress is most engaging ;
A meek and quiet spirit more adorning
Than rich apparel or the gaudiest colours.
    I like not much the public taste in music :
Rattle and clatter is the favourite fashion ;
That which is difficult in execution,
Not what is musical, is most esteemed ;
I would as lief hear poker, tongs, and shovel
As half the music we are favoured with.
My nerves ! my nerves ! can this be meant for music ?
Is this the natural concord of sweet sounds ?
Call you this noise the flow of harmony ?
Away with it, and let us file some saws !
I hate the roaring, grunting, growling organ
That stuns you with its awful mass of noises :
Music without the attribute of cadence,
And poetry without the charm of metre,
Are of the same unwelcome category.
Music must be allied to melody,
And be the breathing of a sentiment,
To touch my feelings and delight my ear.
Mine be the simple stirring melodies
Of ancient times that came by inspiration,
Of which the heart and ear can never weary ;
Old tunes that thrill us into ecstacy.

I like one voice without accompaniment,
Singing distinguishable and heartfelt words,
That sense and music may go hand in hand ;
Or else I like a single instrument,
The plaintive clarionet above all others—
Perhaps the effect of old associations ;
Its touching music suits my simple taste.
In music, as in many other things,
Especially in poetry and painting,
That which affects us with the dull impression
Of effort and laborious execution
May make us stare, but wearies very soon.
How sad it is to see a fair performer
Seated in state before a grand piano,
Doing the wonderful with voice and fingers,
But failing to detain tired-out attention,
Or stop the infectious yawn that circles round !
  We have in this our northern English clime
Many delightful twilight evening hours,
Too dark to work, too light to bring in candles,
When family music is a sweet resource ;
Not soulless music from dumb instruments,
Tedious to learn and wearisome to hear,
The mere result of misdirected skill,
But the sweet human voice attuned to song,
Not drowned by twanging strings or jingling keys.
Sweet is the music of a family group
Singing the holy hymn, or tasteful ditty,
Varying in age, as well as power of voice,
From lovely childhood to parental age,

Blending their voices in sweet harmony,
Yet so distinctly that the melting words
Are clearly and articulately sounded,
So that the music and the sense combine
To wrap the soul in pleasing ecstacies;
Such music is a charming social bond,
Uniting a whole family in love,
And sweet dependent harmony of life;
So that should death or distance intervene,
And separate one member of the group,
And thus the happy fireside bond be broken,
One voice being wanted in the family choir,
The absent member will be always missed;
The silent voice recall the absent face.

But taste in literature is more my hobby.
This is the era of light literature;
To me the lighter the bookmakers make it
It is the more intolerably heavy.
What a tremendous pile of words they give us
To consecrate their small and stale ideas,
Like the Egyptians building pyramids
To enclose the carcase of a sacred beetle!
It seems to me a strange anomaly
That in this age, when time is everything,
And speed the general order of the day,
When railway trains convey us rapidly
From one end of the country to the other,
And the electric telegraph, like magic,
Transmits its mystic pulses through the land
As fast as beat the pulses of our veins,

That literature should be so slow and heavy,
Using a page of common letter-press
Just to describe the singing of a kettle,
And a whole volume to tell less than nothing.
O verbiage !   O endless verbiage !
O wearisome repletion of fine words !
O everlasting beating round the bush,
And putting off the upshot till the end !
I do not wonder at the bookmakers
Making a ham extend in sandwiches
Over an acre of thin bread and butter,
They being remunerated by the acre ;
But what I wonder greatly at is this :
That readers can be found with time enough,
And taste depraved enough, to stomach it :
Big words transplanted from their usual sense,
And usual place, to dignify mean thoughts,
Doing base duty as substitutes for wit ;
And pompous fustian making its solemn mouths ;
But what is infinitely worse than this,
Our authors grin themselves to make us laugh,
Retailing the vile slang from streets and alleys,
Degrading thus our noble English language,
And substituting gross buffoonery
For natural and unaffected humour.
Sense is a solid article of freight,
So out they heave it, and away they sail.
How differently our charming Goldsmith wrote,
The prince of humourists, and Johnson's friend,
The friend of all, most lovable of wits,

Whose liquid pages flow so artlessly ;
A sweet and clear perennial rivulet.
I enjoy wit when it falls naturally,
Gracefully bubbling over from the lips,
Like limpid water dropping from a spring ;
Not squirted upwards from a grinning mouth,
With painful effort and elaborate art.
   I hate your popular but vulgar authors,
However bright their gifts of genius,
Who turn the sewers of slang into our language,
And thus pollute its sweet and crystal stream.
Our language is a great inheritance ;
Its strength, its beauty and simplicity,
Fit it for every range of human thought,
Enriched with handy words from foreign countries.
The vulgar comic is the popular taste :
I hate baffoons who travesty plain nature,
And with their wearisome exaggerations,
With low tom-foolery, and with broad grimace,
Burlesque the true simplicity of language,
And give us twaddle, and perverted humour,
For truthful, easy, natural narrative.
Thus is our language lowered and debased,
And the young men of England are corrupted
With an impure unhealthy style of thought,
False wit, low pompousness, and vulgar slang,
The sweepings and the garbage of the kennels.
   I hate the morbid taste of modern authors,
Who gloat on Vice just like a surgical operator
Over a pestilent and loathsome corpse,

Who contemplates the stark revolting spectacle
As a most beautiful subject for dissection
And critical ingenious commentary,
Turning it round in half a dozen positions,
And playing with it with his keen-edged knife,
Laying bear all its ghastly mysteries,
And peering into all its foulnesses,
With a calm magnifying microscope,
Regardless of the stench beneath his nostrils.
   Some people only like far-fetched ideas,
Deeming of them as others do of doctors,
The further they are brought the better they be.
Some write in riddles to attract attention,
Brimful of learning and obscure allusions,
Affecting such a quaint and crabbed style
That those who read their writings and admire them—
For there are always people who are ready
To admire whatever is obscure and strange—
May be excused for swallowing them in faith,
Without exactly understanding them;
A scrap of Latin goes for much with many:
I know a little, *merus scholasticus,*
Merus asinus, volumes in one sentence.
   The spread of literature is fragmentary;
Its tendency is not to grow to books,
But dwindle into periodicals.
These flat-fish of the sea of authorship
Come forth in shoals, like mackerel or white herrings,
Sickening us with their wonderful abundance:
And yet the public readily devour them,

Thriving but little on such watery food.
How infinitely better would it be,
Instead of feeding on diluted nonsense,
To study and adopt into one's nature
The solid substance of a few good books.
Much time is wasted upon daily papers,
Some eighty-and-forty columns for a penny;
Whether there may be news, or whether not,
The ready authors always fill them full.
These practised writers for the public press
Can write on any subject that they please,
According to the wish of their employers;
Can make a text of any fleeting topic,
And therefrom squeeze their column and a half;
Can preach a sermon or dissect a play,
And prove that white is black, or black is white;
Can skilfully distort the plainest statement,
And make it mean whatever suits them best
To ridicule and damage their opponents,
And make a Solon gabble like a goose;
With banter overpower the force of reason,
And laugh at sense with the most serious face;
Or they can make a goose talk like a Solon,
And praise his empty twaddle to the skies,
And really seem to believe what they are saying;
Or, if they wish, they can be sensible,
Lucid in statement, admirable in argument,
Dealing in truths that cannot be gainsaid:
They can trot east or west, or north or south.
　　How eagerly we seize upon the papers,

And open them to read the last intelligence,
And when we have expended, say, an hour
In running over all the various columns,
We lay the paper down dissatisfied,
And sighing, murmur " There is nothing in it."
Even the special tidings of to-day,
The most acute and telling " editories "
(I fain would coin a word before I die,
A word much wanted by the daily press),
Are stale and probably forgot to-morrow.
What do we care for tidings nine days old ?
And yet it is a right and proper thing
To have an insight into public matters,
And know a little how the world goes round,
And help it onwards in the right direction.

    Time was that authors only wrote for fame,
Anxious to charm or to instruct mankind,
Urged onward by the force of intellect,
Which could not rest supine in indolence,
But must be heard, or perish of the strain.
Authors write now for bread, and not applause ;
Thousands write well whose names are never known,
Content with creature comforts for reward.
How many a brilliant article delights us
Whose authorship we feel disposed to envy !
Yet we are saddened with the mournful thought
That all his brilliance will be soon forgotten ;
That he who wrote it will remain unknown,
And that it was produced merely for pay.
But probably 'tis better as it is,

For in the ardour of impassioned youth,
The noble and unselfish days of boyhood,
How eagerly we pant for fame and glory;
And if they could be won too easily,
How would our heated heads be overset
By notoriety's intoxication,
And all our well-trained manliness of character
Be often sapped and ruined beyond hope!
  In my young days I wrote much poetry,
And dreamt of fame and all its fascinations;
I longed for friendship with superior minds,
And love from kindred hearts to cheer me onwards;
Not to be stared at as a vulgar wonder,
Just like a double-headed Essex calf,
But to indulge an honourable ambition.
The publishers looked coldly on my labours:
They would not risk a farthing upon poetry,—
The veriest drug in all the labour market.
A proof that modern poetry is bad,
Because our standard poets still are prized,
Or else a proof that modern taste is bad,
Ruled only by the senseless freaks of fashion.
I struggled long and hard against my fate,
But had no money of my own to spend
To undergird my poems through the press.
I could not burst my egg-shell and take wing.
How many a gay and roaring chanticleer
That might have waked a village with its crowing,
Is boiled in the egg to make some booby's breakfast!
So I retired defeated from the field,

Waiting and hoping for some brighter day,
And laid my precious manuscripts aside,
In a dark corner of my secretary,
For thirty or some five-and-thirty years,
Till they are spotted with the damp of time,
Most probably—I dare not look at them—
Crude early fruit unfit for modern taste,
And worthless, bearing no great author's name.
But now, when I am old and past my prime,
And I have seen the havoc made by years—
And it is only we who live to be old
Can estimate the wondrous transformation
From youthful bloom to venerable wrinkles—
Now, when my setting sun gleams in the west,
And I have lost the friends whose gratulations
Would have been sweeter than the breath of fame—
When those are dead and gone whose proud contempt
Rankled within my breast long years ago,
Who never now can feel repentant shame—
Now, when I see how vain is men's applause,
I now at last am master of myself,
And I can print upon my own account,
And shame the stupid purblind publishers
Who crushed me in my youth and poverty.
We have got rid of ancient grievances;
But modern grievances spring up instead.
Books multiply beyond our power of reading.
Banks break, and so must bookshelves presently;
But hungry authors will keep scribbling on,
And, like the persecuting fleas of Egypt,

When one is done for, two more take its place.
No marvel we are overwhelmed with books;
It is a vain attempt to read them all.
What can be done with all these dreary volumes?
Shall we begin to pave our footpaths with them,
Or use them up to build our houses with?
No! books are hard to read and very heavy,
But are not of the gritty stuff to build with;
And yet perhaps they might be valuable
To pile up as a barrier round our coast
By way of earth-work or dull fortification!
No enemy would be likely to get through them.
    One would suppose that authors would be puzzled
To know what subjects to dilate upon,
And yet this very seldom seems the case.
They know their market, and they write for profit.
Poetry stands no chance with cookery books.
Philosophy is forced to bow to Bluebeard.
The art consists in making something new—
New in appearance—out of something old.
They give new lanterns to us for our old ones.
    I often wish that one of our compilers,
Seeking a novel subject for his labours,
Would execute a favourite scheme of mine,
And bring together in one pleasant volume
The current incidents of any month
That happened, say, a hundred years ago,
Day after day, according to their dates:
A lively conversation at the Club
'Twixt Johnson, Goldsmith, Reynolds, Burke, and Boswell;

A witty letter writ by Horace Walpole ;
A smart adventure told by Fanny Burney ;
A speech delivered in the House by Burke ;
A letter from the gentle bard of Olney ;
And hundreds of contemporary doings.
How vivid could the spectacle be made !
A month's events brought clearly to one focus !
  I have a somewhat awkward, dangerous habit
Of concentrating what I have to say
Into a few severe hard-hitting words,
Or figure of poetical expression,
But which sometimes, I fear, may give offence ;
Caused partly by my way of bringing up.
Perhaps I have expressed myself too strongly
In matters of acquired artistic taste.
When I was but a boy I was a man
In thoughts, in habits, feelings, and pursuits.
I cared but little for the sports of children ;
From early life lonely in all my ways.
To fish, to swim, to skate, and pore o'er books—
These were the pleasures of my boyish days.
When I became a man I seemed a boy,
With all the ruddy bloom of early life,
And all my youthful feelings fresh within me ;
I cared not for the aims of other men :
Business, and the pursuit of gaining wealth.
The married snubbed me as a bachelor,
My youngers shunned me as no mate for them ;
Treated at home as if I were a boy
By my old father, as he grew in years,

And shunned by boys because I was a man ;
I was a fish out of water from my youth,
And have been knocked about in my past life,
And had my faults dissected by my friends.
Why should not I condemn the faults of others ?
I will be heard ! yes ! I must have my say.
Unless I come to blows with somebody
No one will take the trouble to abuse me.
If no one deems me worthy of attack,
It were as profitable to be nobody ;
I would not be a common flatterer,
And neither would I be a general censor ;
But speak the truth as I believe in it,
And pay no heed to either fear or favour.
Some men esteem it reprehensible
To speak about the faults of other people,
And salve them over just as if they had none,
But are unmerciful upon their own.
I think the truth commands to speak the truth ;
Frankly condemn what ought to be condemned,
And praise whatever is deserving praise.
In what way else, in this mixed state of being,
Are men to be instructed and advised
To choose the good and to reject the evil ?
I seek to propagate eternal truths :
I have a purpose, therefore do I sing.
   London has come into a pretty fortune,
A fine estate derived from Father Thames,
Lying along beside her noble river ,
Just in the midst of the metropolis,

Forming a graceful amphitheatre,
Raised and supported by a grand embankment.
What will she do with it ?   Will she fool it away ?
It would not be her first time to act thus.
Will she bestow it, and herself besides,
Like a rich, lovesick, spoilt, intractable lady,
Upon an idle and presumptuous footman ;
Or will she, like the wealthy heir of Hastings
With his possessions, lay it down in turf?
Everyone asks what she will do with it.
Let her not make herself a laughing-stock
For future ages to throw scorn upon,
Or well-earned censure, which would be more sad.
Her new possession is a stately platform,
With the broad river flowing at its feet,
Forming the grandest crescent in the land
On which to build a range of palaces.
Here then let her erect her Palace of Justice,
Her Courts of Law, and other public edifices,
And make herself the beauty of the world,
As she is now the richest of all cities.
But let her still be wary how she builds ;
We want no grinning Gothic architecture ;
No heavy monkish dark monstrosities ;
No dismal caves for new Adullamites ;
And let us have no more gilt gingerbread.
We have our chaste and handsome Somerset House
Already standing in the crescent line,
Airy and light and cheerful to the eye.
Let her then build in harmony with that pile,

And show the nations that her taste is pure.
That which is done, do well, for it will stand
For evil, or for good, irrevocably,
A specimen of the taste of these our times,
The praise or censure of succeeding ages.

   I should not like to be an architect.
A man of genius and of cultured mind,
Long patient study, and expert invention,
Designs an admirable public building—
Convenient, light, proportionable, and stately—
Foreseeing, with the eye of practical taste,
Effects and merits inappreciable
To those who only look with common eyes,
Yet have abundant notions of their own,
And having absolute control of funds,
Possess the power to thwart him every way,
And use their power to alter all his plans.
What can be meaner slavery of soul
Than to be driven to submit to this?
If I were a horse, I'd be a brewer's horse ;
If I were a pig, I'd be a miller's pig ;
If I were a slave, I'd be a woman's slave,
But not the slave of half a dozen fools.

   I should not like to be a metaphysician.
He spins a theory like a spider's web,
Elaborate, unsubstantial, beautiful,
Just fitted to entangle a weak fly,
But yet not strong enough to hold a mouse.
A metaphysician builds his airy castle
Of fair proportions and enormous bulk,

With spacious uninhabitable rooms
Adorned with endless ornamental tracery,
But with no hearths (like hearts) to keep them warm.
Stairs up, stairs down, low doors to knock one's head,
And narrow passages that wind on for ever;
A marvellous piece of human workmanship;
And all the world admires the wondrous structure.
Some men look wise and talk and write about it
As if they understood it perfectly,
And comprehended all its intricate parts,
Which probably the builder never did.
Up jumps at length another metaphysician,
And with the well-aimed stroke of a stout folio,
Knocks the whole fabric into countless shivers,
And builds another castle in its place,
Just like the last one, only different.
This gains our admiration in its turn.
Ere long we are blessed with another metaphysician,
Who serves the last just as he served the other,
Annihilates him without benefit of clergy,
And sets to work to build a different fabric,
And so successors run *ad infinitum*.

Nor would I be a statesman and hold power,
And have uneasy days and sleepless nights,
Living a feverish, fast, and heartless life.
Exposed to gross misjudgment and abuse,
And jealousies, annoyances, and hatreds;
Disgusted with the flatteries of the selfish,
And worried by the whim-whams of the vain;
Bored with the turmoil of conflicting parties,

And harassed with perplexities and labours ;
Having not even time for joy or sorrow.
Death snatches from him, it may be, a wife,
Perhaps a daughter, or a favourite son ;
But public matters, great concerns of state,
With exigency press on his attention,
And so he seizes on a bit of crape,
And wraps it hastily around his hat,
And sets his rigid face to public cares,
Thrusting away the sorrow from his breast.
    The three professions that bestride the land,
Law, Physic, and Divinity, are guilds,
Privileged, at their own price, to make their market
Of our defenceless, secular ignorance !
    I never had a wish to be a doctor.
Having a tender conscience against murder
I feel a scruple against killing men—
Taking their lives, I mean, " professionally,"
According to the law of dull routine,
That happens for the time to be in vogue,
Purging, or sweating, or phlebotomy.
Nor could I finger money for " attendance"
On a death-bed, that had been robbed already ;
Or squeeze the pocket of a weeping widow,
Or fleece the orphan's poor inheritance.
'Twould do despite to my compunctious feelings.
Nor should I like to visit beds of suffering,
Horrid diseases and pestiferous fevers,
To set arms out of joint, or saw off legs ;
Or, after a long day's distressful toil,

When snug and warm in bed dreaming of nothing,
To hear the door-bell ringing violently,
And be compelled in a cold winter's night,
To mount my horse, and face the frosty air,
And travel weary miles to a frightened patient,
With nothing perhaps the matter but a colic,
From over-stuffing at the dinner-table.
O, I would rather buy a three-penny broom,
And sweep a crossing than submit to it !
　　But least of all would I be bred a lawyer,
Because I have a humble hope of heaven.
Let law alone, that sword which cuts both ways !
A lawyer, if a fool, is good for nothing ;
And if a clever fellow he is worse ;
The loftier his grade in the profession,
The more illimitable is his extortion;
The best of them are just the worst of them ;
He may not knock you down and steal your money,
But he will surely worm it out of you.
He holds the key by which the law is opened ;
If you want law you fain must go to him,
And he will soon unlock it with a vengeance,
And run you up a regular lawyer's bill.
For instance, if you simply buy a house,
He will take note of every interview,
And charge you for receiving your instructions,
Charge you likewise for drawing up the same,
Eight folio pages with a world of margin ;
Charge you likewise for copying the same ;
Charge you likewise for reading you the same,

And sending of it to the other party ;
Charge you likewise for reading long reply
From London lawyer with a draft agreement;
Charge you likewise perusing of said draft,
Charge you likewise for copying the same,
Attending you, informing you thereof ;
Charge you likewise transmitting draft agreement,
Along with letter, to the London lawyer.
Having received fair copy back for signature
Charge you for reading and examining same ;
Charge you likewise attending you therewith,
Getting your signature and attesting same ;
Charge you likewise attending London lawyer,
Exchanging forms of mutual agreement,
Instructing him to send abstract of title.
Having received the abstract of said title,
Charge you likewise perusing of the same ;
Charge you likewise for making an appointment
With London lawyer to examine abstract,
And reading his reply, naming a day ;
Charge you likewise for journey up to London ;
Charge you likewise attending London lawyer,
Examining the abstract of the title,
Engaged four hours (making their little plant) ;
Charge you likewise for share of the expenses,
(Oysters and porter very probably) ;
Charge you likewise for making out fair copy
Of the said abstract after due correction,
And careful examination with the deeds ;
Charge you likewise for drawing observations

Upon the aforesaid abstract of the title ;
Charge you likewise fair copy of the same ;
Charge you likewise transmitting of the same,
Along with letter, to the London lawyer.
Having received said observations back
From London lawyer, charge you for perusing
Answers thereto, informing you thereof :
(No doubt these answers from the London lawyer
Made out these observations were all humbug) ;
Charge you for the instructions for conveyance ;
Charge you likewise for drawing the conveyance,
Just four and thirty folio pages full ;
Charge you likewise attending upon counsel,
To settle same in legal conference.
Charge you again attending upon counsel,
Receiving of the same from him as settled ;
Charge you the counsel's fees, also his clerks ;
(All of them greedy crocodiles alike) ;
Next charge you for fair copy and perusal ;
Charge you likewise transmitting the conveyance
To London lawyer to peruse the same,
With precious letter to him on the subject.
Having received conveyance back again,
Charge you perusing sundry alterations ;
Charge you likewise engrossing said conveyance ;
Charge you likewise for stamps and also parchments ;
Charge you likewise examining the skin ;
(No doubt to see if there were holes in it
Big enough for a lawyer to creep through :
A pin's point hole is amply large enough) ;

Charge you for sending same to London lawyer
To get him to attend upon the owner
To execute the deed, and pass the estate;
Charge you likewise writing to London lawyer
To make appointment to complete the business;
Also perusing letter in reply,
Attending and informing you thereof;
Charge you again for going up to London,
Attending London lawyer to complete,
Taking the deed, and giving receipt for same;
Charge you likewise for share of the expenses,
(The champagne dinner that they had together).
The title not complete without an extract
From Probate of a certain ancient will,
Charge you a journey to obtain the same;
Charge you likewise for copy of said extract;
Charge you likewise for drawing out a schedule
Of the old deeds to place with title writings;
Charge you likewise for paying London lawyer
For the agreement as agreed upon,
(No doubt this means they had agreed together
To bleed both parties to their hearts' content);
And charge you also for attending you,
Delivering up the precious deeds to you,
Taking receipt, and finally completing
This roundabout and complicated business,
And also handing you this little bill.
    I make no charge whatever for this fair copy.
This bill is nothing but a common sample
Of lawyers' bills in any part of England:

But this particular bill belongs to Colchester ;
It was presented to my good old father,
And duly settled, when he bought his house,
Some twenty years ago, by a keen lawyer,
Well known in Colchester, named Samuel Tillett,
A man whose portrait I will here preserve.
Like several of our Lawyers, in his childhood
He was a hunger-bitten charity-boy,
And swept a lawyer's office for small wages.
These men become important personages,
And when they offer to shake hands with you
They do you honour with a pair of fingers ;
This boy was soon promoted to a stool,
And so at length became himself a lawyer.
He was a little active bustling man,
Extremely neat and dapper in apparel,
Ignorant of books except his books of law,
But with a fund of hearty cheerfulness,
And with a ready boldness of behaviour
That made him popular with Tory squires,
Although his brother kept a barber's shop.
Self-confidence, however, bore him onward.
He never lost advancement through timidity ;
There was a charming frankness in his manner ;
He had a clever knack of doing business ;
He entered heart and soul into the subject,
As zealously as if it were his own.
It was a pleasure to do business with him,
And I employed him in my own affairs.
O how a little puff of bland prosperity

Swells out a man too bulky for his harness !
Ere long as he advanced in his profession
He built himself some handsome offices
In the Church-lane, which made his brethren jealous,
And moved into a mansion which he bought
At lovely Lexden, near by Colchester,
And kept his horse and gig and livery servant !
His weakness was the weakness of Napoleon,
An overpowering passion of ambition.
All are left-handed in some way or other.
He gained the status of Town Councillor,
And, by and bye, the dignity of Alderman,
And strutted grandly in a scarlet cloak
Behind the mayor and mace to old St. Peter's.
He freely talked of being Mayor himself.
If he caught sight of gentleman or noble
Across the street, he rushed to speak to him,
Seizing him cordially with outstretched hands,
And talking to him on familiar terms ;
He loved to be connected with the great.
Sometimes he managed to appear by name
In the " Court Circular," or some such paper,
As having had an audience on business
With the Prime Minister, or at least Home Secretary ;
And this was copied into all the papers,
To the astonishment of common people,
And made the most of to his country clients ;
But his ambition made him enemies,
And led him blindly onward to his ruin.
Men often clamber to a mountain's top

With labour and with danger and with bruises,
And, having reached it, find that it is barren;
So it is with the heights of worldly glory !
His love of splendour needed ample wealth,
And he had little scruple how to get it ;
Stories leaked out of various lawyer tricks,
Especially of making death-bed wills,
And coming in for lumping legacies.
There lived in Colchester a certain lady,
A lonely, single, unprotected woman,
Who owed us something in the way of business.
After a lengthened period of delay,
My father called upon her for his money,
When she gave utterance to a piteous tale.
She said she was an independent lady,
And would most gladly pay him what she owed ;
But said that her affairs were in the hands
Of Samuel Tillett, who would give her nothing :
She could not get a single shilling from him.
At length some creditor, I know not who,
Clapped the poor lady into Chelmsford jail.
Whene'er I see that gloomy-looking place,
I think of that poor unoffending lady,
And what she suffered in that dismal prison,
Unjustly suffered through a heartless lawyer ;
But when the world around us yields no pity,
Pity comes down to us direct from heaven,
If we look up for it with earnest hearts ;
And so it happened unto her, poor lady ;
Her Heavenly Father took her to Himself,

Away from this world's inhumanity.
In her lone cell in that dark jail she died.
    A few short years elapsed, and then there came
A curious transposition of affairs,
And Samuel Tillett, through his crafty doings,
(For even sharks themselves sometimes get bitten),
Was relegated from his country mansion
Into the calm abode of Chelmsford jail.
I know not whether they imprisoned him
In the same cell in which that injured lady
Wasted away, and died in her distress ;
I know not whether in the dead of night
Her wandering spirit ever came to him,
And laid her shivery hand upon his heart,
And with her mocking eyes looked in his face;
But when, after some years, he gained his freedom,
And left that doleful jail, his head was grey.
He went to London, that unfailing refuge
Of clever men with damaged reputations,
And there contrived to live upon his wits.
But the old Adam still was strong in him,
And he became a celebrated man,
A one day's subject for the daily papers,
Though not perhaps in the " Court Circular ;"
He had the audacity to attend a Levée !
By dint of tact and boundless impudence
He gained admittance to the Drawing-room,
As spruce and trim as any noble there ;
But as bad luck would have it, or misfortune,
The grim old judge who tried him down at Chelmsford

Set his hard eyes upon him in the crowd,
And thought he had some knowledge of his face;
For judges are good judges of men's faces.
He looked again, and recollected him,
And was amazed to see the crafty culprit,
On whom he had passed sentence in the dock
At the assizes several years before,
Mixing complacently with lords and ladies
As though he felt himself completely at home!
The end of the affair was rather tragic;
For he, who thus gained entrance unattended,
Walked out attended by a man in blue!
   Supremely sweet and beautiful is June:
At night the moon lights up a silvery hall;
By day the sun gilds all things with his glory;
The freshening breezes give new health to life;
The waves roll lovingly upon the shore;
And the salt sea sparkles with new-born joy.
On land the trees are all full sail with foliage,
And flags and union-jacks of various blossoms;
The fields are in their gayest holiday dress.
Sweet smells the pleasant hay a-down the meadows,
And richer still the bean-fields by the grange.
The blackbird whistles his most dulcet notes
The lark, the cheerfullest of living creatures,
Fluttering its little wings, soars up to heaven,
Singing as with an over-gushing heart,
Dear, dear, dear, dear, dear, dear, dear,—de-ar—de-ar
   —de-ar!—
Filling the air with joyous ravishment.

Red cherries promise soon delicious baits ;
The tender ears of corn burst from their sheaths ;
Industrious bees hum merrily at their work,
And idle butterflies flit gaily by;
The meads are full of buttercups and daisies.
By day the skylark carols in mid heaven,
By night the nightingale attunes the grove.
O would that I could sing like thee, sweet bird !
That I might please all tastes ; then to the pensive
I should be pensive, cheerful to the cheerful.

   Though men may argue by the rule of reason,
They act too often by the rule of contrary.
Our legislators set us the example.
Two things engross the attention of our statesmen—
The making of our laws and hunting foxes ;
The last, the most important of the two,
Is winter work when days are short and dark.
Making our laws is work for any time,
Or so our statesmen would appear to think ;
Thus they perversely, when the days are short,
Leave the snug city and its myriad comforts,
And dive into the dull and leafless country,
Subject themselves to wintry winds and rains,
Ankle-deep mud and sometimes knee-deep snow,
Wet coats, damp feet, and sharp rheumatic pains ;
And spend the warm and blessed summer-time
Cooped up in London, hammering at their laws,
Roasted with sunshine in the sultry streets,
Losing the country in its pride of beauty,
Its hayfield fragrance and its wealth of flowers,

And the cool breezes of the grand sea-side,
To sit, half-stifled with the dust and heat,
In the dark chamber of the House of Commons,
Tired of long speeches and the strife of party :
So much for senatorial common sense.

The rival parties in the political circus
Stun the arena with their noisy contests ;
The Tory minister of State—Disraeli—
Resists the champion of the Liberal party,
The stern and the indomitable Gladstone.
The first is like the serpent of old Nile,
Powerful of muscle, but without a backbone,
Twisting and twining in all sorts of ways,
Subtle and smooth, and full of artifice,
And using every kind of trickery
To gain the advantage in the angry fray,
Hissing, and darting venom from his tongue,
And hurling fiery glances on his foe.
His rival, calm and full of noble courage,
Assails him boldly, like an English mastiff,
Amidst the ringing cheers of his own friends,
Seizes him, shakes him, tosses him in air,
And flings him helplessly upon the floor ;
And, confident in his superior strength,
Plays with him like a kitten with a mouse !

To be in office must be something pleasant,
For those who climb to power cling fondly to it.
When a Prime Minister becomes obnoxious,
How hard it is to thrust him from his seat :
Three courses it is clear are open to him ;

R

For, firstly, he may kick the table over
Which stands before him, and may thus smash others;
Or, secondly, he may kick his chair of state
Right over backwards, and so smash himself;
Or, thirdly, he may sternly keep his seat
Till his opponents rise with indignation
And kick him from his stool, and thereby smash him.
    When I look round upon the names of men
Who flourished in old England in my time,
And try to find the wickedest of the lot,
The man who did the most amount of evil,
Who broke most hearts by long protracted grief,
And wronged the widow and the fatherless,
I should not pitch upon a murderer,
Or any vulgar rogue that had been hanged,
And neither should I pitch upon a soldier,
Although I hate the hands of bloody men;
But I should pitch at once upon a lawyer,
Eldon, the Lord High Chancellor of England,
Familiarly depicted in a novel
By a distinguished author, as " Old Bags,"
The virtual head of the Established Church,
Who managed its preferments at his pleasure.
He was a man who, in a legal way,
Without offending against courtly modes,
Contrived to agonise the British people
More thoroughly than any other man,—
A modern Draco, whose delight was blood,
Who punished the misdeeds of other men
With the most unrelenting cruelty.

Long tedious years he sat upon the woolsack,
The head and shoulders of the English law,
A cold, unfeeling, mercenary man.
His heart was harder than the nether mill-stone ;
His mind as narrow as a needle's eye :
A mind that weakly wavered in the balance,
While tortured suitors waited his decision,
And justice was inhumanly denied;
A canting hypocrite of high professions,
For ever coddling men about his conscience;
It might indeed be called his stock-in-trade :
A creature who could weep salt tears at pleasure,
As easily as any crocodile,
But cared just nothing for the tears of others :
A man who had no faith in anything
But sanguinary laws to serve the State.
The gallows was his favourite hobby-horse,
Preferring that an innocent man should suffer
Rather than one suspected should escape.
He was the ready tool of despotism,
For tyranny to him was meat and drink,
And laid more grievous burdens on the people
Than any modern Minister of State.
He vindicated every evil law,
And zealously resisted all reform ;
A minister who stuck to power and pelf
Tenaciously, as long as he could stick,
Till the old placeman seemed at length to fancy
The world could not go round without his help.
　　When a man dies and can do no more mischief

His very enemies speak well of him ;
But who has ever said a word for Eldon?
I recollect but one good thing of him :
He ran off with a girl when he was young
And married her—a very canny stroke ;
But whether out of love, or for her fortune,
Most probably he never could decide,
No record being found in his decisions.

    Our processes of law are antiquated ;
They savour of the dungeon and the thumbscrew.
A grand career is open to the statesman
Who works a reformation in our code
Of civil and of criminal jurisprudence,
Adjusting punishment with righteous hands,
According to the turpitude of crime,
And not allowing great culprits to escape
While small offenders suffer rigorously ;
Nor yet permitting a sanguinary wretch,
Invested with the dignity of governor
Of some ill-managed distant colony,
· To murder hundreds of defenceless people
Without the least authority of law ;
While a poor labouring man who snares a hare
Is sentenced to relentless punishment.
The forms of trial need to be revised
That justice above law may be supreme,
And rich and poor be equally protected.
The rule of law is now the rule of contrary ;
Crimes must possess respectable dimensions
To escape their due and well-earned retribution.

How much one man may make or mar the world !
Here is a man after my heart of hearts,
John Bright, the tribune of the British people !
A name which in all gatherings of the masses
Strikes through men's hearts like an electric spark,
And brings down ringing cheers from roof to floor.
Every begrimed and toiling artisan
Smiles proudly when he hears the name, " John
      Bright ;"
The cobbler, sitting in his narrow stall,
Tugs his wax-ends with increased energy
When John Bright takes the floor of Parliament.
I knew him ere the world had heard of him ;
His handsome face then wore a haughty scowl,
Which many a triumph since has chased away ;
The wrongs of England weighed upon his heart,
And he had not yet scope to battle with them ;
But now he stands forth first in Parliament,
The bold assertor of the people's rights,
The conqueror in many a glorious cause,
Dragging monopoly and bigotry,
And old misrule, like unclean birds of prey,
From their high nests and antiquated perches,
And trampling them beneath his scornful feet ;
Frightening the cormorants of Church and State,
Shaping anew the form of government,
Making his enemies to do his bidding,
Sending the trimmers to Adullam's cave,
And giving breadth and strength to popular rule :
A man of many gifts.   Rich every way ;

Rich with an ever-teeming intellect,
Cultured and balanced by long exercise,
Endowed with burning eloquence of speech,
Yet with a soul attuned to poetry.
A bold true man with something of the lion
Depicted in his broad and massive head;
A man to stand before the cannon's mouth
Of opposition and unjust abuse;—
Not to be purchased, not to be cajoled,
Not to be daunted by the fear of man—
A heart devoted to his country's good!
  Here endeth Book the Fifth of this my Poem.
Calmly the evening sun sets in the west;
So calmly that the glorious pageant seems
Not like a quickly-passing spectacle,
But a fair scene that never would fade away.
How splendid is the purple-tinted sky!
While all the floor of the outspread horizon,
Dotted afar with little golden clouds,
Seems strewn with burning coals from off God's altar,
Such as once touched the inspired prophet's lips!
So radiant is the rich magnificence
It seems the very vestibule of heaven!

BOOK VI.

BOOK VI.

I have been writing under difficulties
These last few months, to me of novel kind.
The ringing trowel of the bricklayer
Has made enlivening music to my ear;
The hammer of the noisy carpenter
Has startled every spider in the house;
The painter, with his overpowering brush,
Has put a smarter face upon affairs,
But choked us with the palling scent of paint.
Then came the grainer and the varnisher,
And gagged us with another kind of perfume;
And after them arrived the paper-hanger,
And soothed us with the scent of paste and glue;
But now the tedious work at length is done;
The workmen have departed with their tools;
The rooms are neatly carpeted and furnished;
The floor-cloth in the hall is neatly laid;
The statue of Aurora fills the niche;
And the conservatory, my Loüie's hobby,
Is finished, too, and also nicely furnished
With flowers and creepers to adorn its walls.
Our pleasant dream at length is realised,
And it surpasses all our expectations.
Our drawing-room that once was dark and dull
Is now enlivened by a cheerful paper,

And finished in accordance with our taste;
The ugly cupboard, now an arched recess,
Contains a cabinet of precious china,
Relics and heir-looms of the family,
Which never have been so displayed before,
Nicely arranged by Louie's gentle hands.
We sit within our pleasant drawing-room,
And look into our sweet conservatory;
The glass-door opens, and we enter it,
And find it quite a little paradise.
Each day we watch the opening of the flowers,
And mark the growth of every little tendril
Clasping the iron lattice fast and lovingly.
How nice it is to sprinkle all the leaves
With Louie's small refreshing water-pot,
Or gently nip away the dying flowers:
These little matters are great things to us.

   There is a foil to every happiness.
Midsummer day is overpast and gone,
And now the little bills come dropping in.
In blank astonishment we view the totals.
O vanity of workmen's estimates!
O danger of departing from our plans!
Alas! these alterations and improvements
Have upset all our little calculations;
Behold our bills doubled, and even trebled!
What must be done? The hook is in my gills.
I may be angry, and may make a splash;
I cannot get away from these demands.
Painters and glaziers, bricklayers and carpenters,

Gravely maintain that every charge is right.
With solemn faces they declare to me
The regular price is charged for everything;
No doubt they may be regular to them,
But they are quite irregular to me.
Can I by County-Court appeal oppose them,
And shame these tradesmen into fairer charges?
I can appeal; but would that mend the matter?
I fear in that case I should fare still worse,
And have as well a lawyer's bill to pay;
The remedy is worse than the disease.
There are the bills! No doubt they must be paid;
I'll pay the bills! and so have done with them.

   We have 'tis true our little paradise,
In common prose a comfortable home;
But good and evil ever will be mingled
In this imperfect mundane state of being.
Joy lasts not long, it is not made to last;
Sweet, but soon gone, like a plum-cake at school.
Two nuisances disturb our equanimity:
Rats and blackbeetles, creatures pestilent,
Apt to infest old houses everywhere.
The rats assail us from the common sewer,
And gallop gaily underneath our floors,
Making a racket, like a coach and six;
Gnaw through the wainscot right into the pantry,
Having an instinct where good living is,
And being of malicious dispositions,
Not only rob us underneath our noses,
But do us all the mischief that they can.

I set my traps, and bait them skilfully;
The baits are taken, but the traps not sprung;
The cunning rats are far too clever for me.
They see a rat-trap in the dark as clearly
As I can see this writing-desk by daylight.
Could I but only catch one by the leg
I'd tar his coat for him; but I despair.
As to blackbeetles; they are loathsome creatures
That sally forth by hundreds in the dark,
And run about the kitchen floor in swarms,
Invading pantries and exploring cupboards,
Feasting upon whatever they can find,
Like locusts in the Oriental countries.
We catch them in a trap in countless numbers,
Destroying them remorselessly by drowning,
But do not seem to waste the teeming swarms.
They come! they come! and evermore they come!
   England, which is the whole world's paradise,
Is just as much invaded as our house
With cunning rats and odious blackbeetles.
The lawyers which infest both town and country,
And gallop over us by night and day—
Gnaw holes in our estates remorselessly—
Make warm nests for their young out of our parchments,
And are by far too cunning to be caught—
These are our rats; while our political parsons,
That swarm so thickly over all the land,
For ever seeking for fat benefices
And never satisfied, these are the true blackbeetles.
   This may be called the age of ingenuity;

Science and art accomplish everything !
The mighty modern Revolutionist,
The steam-engine, has changed the face of things.
This Samson, which we Philistines have captured,
Is now our willing and obedient slave,
Ready at all times to perform our bidding.
Hard work to us is only play to him ;
And we do well to use his giant strength,
To grind for us, and turn our heavy wheels,
Help us to overcome our difficulties,
And fight our battles against time and tide :
Only we must be careful of his tricks.
    The motto of our engineers is this :
" You give us money, we will give machinery
To execute whatever work you need."
And, truly, mighty marvels have been wrought ;
For as it is our fools who own the money—
And there are many fools to one wise man—
The world must needs be greatly benefited.
Our railways are the wonder of the age ;
It was our fools who chiefly paid for them,
And everybody rides at their expense.
We therefore have great cause to thank the fools ;
We may have reason yet to thank them more,
And have a tunnel underneath the Channel,
And railway trains, laden with sightseers,
Careering to and fro 'twixt France and England,
Making the different families of Europe
Better acquainted with each other's ways,
And thus promote the general harmony.

As the scared natives of some Indian shore
Gaze on the passing ship far out at sea,
And wonder what strange animal it is,
So did our country bumpkins open their mouths,
And stare to see the strange and wondrous sight,
When first a railway train went thundering through
The calm seclusion of a rural hamlet.

Our poor behind-hand pitiable ancestors
Were unresisting slaves to wind and tide;
We now set wind and tide both at defiance,
And, calling in the aid of fire and water,
We get up steam and merrily plough the waves
Wherever we incline to ride the deep;
We cross the mighty ocean in all weathers,
Outstrip the idle and inconstant wind;
The hissing engine beats the hissing waves,
Snuffles and pants and sends forth clouds of smoke.
The noble steam-ship, like a great sea-serpent,
Speeds through the sea with irresistible strength.

We use our men of genius scurvily.
We feel too proud to own our obligations.
Gratitude is a very humbling virtue,
Raising the giver—lowering the receiver.
Men do not really love their benefactors.
Our great inventors and discoverers,
Born with the mighty talisman of genius,
Who wore their brains out, and their purses too,
To benefit mankind all round the world—
Who gave to modern every day existence
New life, compared with life in olden times,

Ere Steam, and Gas, and Iron, transformed creation ;
We shovel their dust away remorselessly !
But our great law-makers, who grind our bones
Between the upper and the nether millstone ;
And our great chieftains who mow down our sol-
　　diers,
By tens of thousands on the field of battle,
And drain the nation's coffers of its millions,—
These are the men that we delight to honour
With statues, monuments, and lofty columns,
Because they do not claim our gratitude,
But only flatter our pride and love of folly !
　　The ninth day of July : a joyful day !
This is the day on which we caught the rat.
Early this day the servants of the house
Came tapping loudly at my chamber door
To tell me a great rat was caught in the kitchen,
And begging me to come immediately
For fear the savage creature should escape !
Right gladly I responded to the summons,
And, bundling out of bed with eagerness,
I meditated on the impending battle ;
All my worst feelings of revenge possessed me
For injuries and annoyance long endured,
And justice, disappointed hitherto.
Resolved to make him pay for his misdeeds,
I settled in my mind, in the first place,
To serve him with a writ of *habeas corpus :*
That is, a gripe with a stout pair of tongs ;
And then a *capias executione :*

That is, in other words, a blow with the poker.
My ideas of a rat and of a lawyer
Are mixed inextricably in my sensorium.
To close with a sharp lawyer, or a rat,
Requires great prudence and consummate skill.
To strike him while he wriggles in the trap
Is injudicious and most dangerous,
Lest in attempting to despatch the rat
You strike the trap and let the rat escape.
My method is a safer course than this;
I first contrive to grasp him with the tongs—
No easy matter, for the vicious brute
Twists round and bites the iron with his teeth
Savagely, violently, though all in vain;
But, having griped him safely with the tongs,
A little tap upon the head with the poker
Will stun him, and he then may be despatched.

   Soon I descended in shirt-sleeves and slippers.
Entering the kitchen all was in confusion;
The rat-trap, over night, baited with meat,
Had, with due care, been set down in the kitchen.
The rat's hole entered from a corner closet.
During the night, the rat being caught by the leg,
Had made most frantic efforts to escape,
Tearing the mortar down, gnawing the wood,
And putting all the place into a litter.
Soon as the servants made their first appearance
The frightened rat retreated to his hole,
Dragging the trap behind him to the entrance,
Hiding himself, but powerless to escape.

Thus was he hidden when I reached the scene.
Opening the closet door there crouched the rat,
And screeched with fear—for rats are arrant cowards.
I quickly armed myself with poker and tongs,
And cautiously proceeded with my tactics,
The servants looking on with trembling interest.
Grasping the rat-trap firmly with the tongs—
Not with my hand, lest he should turn and bite—
I tried in vain to coax him with the poker
Backwards again into the open kitchen,
Where I could easily have mastered him ;
But he refused to move from his position.
I did not dare to pull him by the trap,
For fear his lacerated leg should part,
And he escape, as I have known rats do,
For rats will gnaw their legs off frequently
When they are caught, and thus contrive to escape.
Not being able to dislodge the enemy,
I gave his body a slight push with the poker,
While, with the tongs grasped firmly in my left hand,
I tugged the trap, perhaps convulsively ;
But so it was I felt the trap give way,
And instantly methought the rat was free !
I only had him pinned to the ground by the poker ;
A momentary fear flashed through my mind,
That I should lose him, and be thus defeated.
The juncture was intensely critical,
But, summoning up my utmost resolution,
I gave him a tremendous thrust with the poker
Which seemed considerably to stupify him,

S

And, bringing round the tongs to bear upon him,
I soon despatched him satisfactorily.
A very shocking story, is it not?
But what is this compared to Waterloo,
Which men can read of with complacency,
Where human victims, thousands upon thousands,
Poured out their life blood in one maddened slaughter !
   Dragging my rat by the tongs into the light,
He proved to be a rat some three parts grown,
A young and therefore rather silly rat.
An old rat is too crafty to be caught.
   Under my cherry-tree I buried him,
Where he will do more good returned to dust
Than ever he had done while he was living,
Fit only to manure his parent earth !
   One noiseless triumph of advancing science
Is worth a hundred victories of the sword.
These last too oft retard the march of mind.
We now compel the sun to draw our portraits,
And make the lightning run with messages.
How wonderful it is that the bright lightning,
Which used to be a puzzle to the learned,
And a dread terror to the ignorant,
Should now be made our quick and active servant,
To go of errands at our beck and call,
And fly along a hundred miles of wire,
Whispering our secrets at the further end !
The kite-string with which Franklin drew from heaven
The zigzag, terrible, cloud-rending lightning,
Inveigling it from its sky-sanctuary,

And taming it for everybody's use,
Has now become the electric telegraph,
With which we speed intelligence afar,
Much faster than the flight of time itself.
The electric wires, extended through the land,
Are like the nerves throughout the human body,
Conveying instantaneous report
From one extremity unto another,
Spreading like cock-crows on a summer morning,
So that a rumour from Bread-street in London
Flies in a moment to the Land o' Cakes !
　But this was not enough for man's ambition;
Nothing would do but we must compass ocean,
As well as earth, with an electric chain,
And thus unite the old world with the new;
And so the great achievement was accomplished
Of laying the renowned Atlantic cable
From shore to shore beneath the surging sea,
Whose world of briny waters could not quench
The electric sparks that darted to and fro
Across the lone dark depths of the Atlantic.
A very clever scheme it was indeed
To tickle Neptune underneath the ribs,
And thus come over the old gentleman,
Who never had been coaxed that way before,
And was too old to gambol with the mermaids !
How men devoured the story of this feat:
And when the triumph of their toil was won,
And messages of peace, goodwill to man,
Were flashed from the old world unto the new,

And every one rejoiced at the event,
What disappointment clouded every brow
When the great oracle ceased to utter speech !
And then, after the lapse of years, we read the story
With a warm outburst of enthusiasm,
How the great steamship sailed on its grand errand—
For Englishmen will never brook defeat—
And with her grapnels raked the ocean's bed,
Where it was two miles deep, so men assert,
Though never such a thing before was dreamed of,
And hooked the cable in its darksome lair,
And drew it with consummate skill and labour
On board the steamship, and repaired its fault,
And then returned it to its watery home
To speed again the interchange of thought
Between far distant sea-divided worlds !
    Nature ! thou art a wasteful prodigal.
How many ages have thy boundless plains
Grown noxious weeds instead of waving corn !
How many thousand unrecorded years
The lonely ocean rolled its waves in vain,
Ere Commerce sent her fleets to foreign lands
To bring abundant treasures from afar ?
What floods of glorious sunshine have been lost
Ere Science, with her magic camera,
Taught it to fix the images of things
In exquisite and life-like portraiture,
By which our shadows marvellously become
Creations more enduring than ourselves !
We are the shadows, they are the immortals.

How precious are the bright resemblances
Of absent friends, or friends that are no more ;
Friends that are snatched for ever from our arms !
Among the inventions of these happy times
No one affords more rational enjoyment
Than this delightful one of sunlight portraits.
O that the powers of all-inventive science
Over the capabilities of naturè
Had been discovered many ages past !
How excellent,—how passing capital
It now would be to have the true presentments
Of Chaucer, Spenser, Shakespere, Milton, Bunyan,
And hundreds more of the immortal dead,
Just as they lived and looked in homely life !
If I had only but my mother's portrait,
How great a treasure it would be to me !
O she was beautiful beyond comparison :
Noble in features but yet feminine,
Supremely delicate in her complexion,
With soft dark eyes as gentle as herself ;
The lines across her undulating forehead,
Like the twin arches of an undrawn bow,
Though lines of age, yet added to her beauty.
How many are there who can say with me.
Alas, for the irrecoverable past !
    Why our forefathers dwelt in old-world darkness
So long, remains a problem unrevealed ;
Eternity alone will solve all riddles ;
No doubt it was the will of Providence.
I have a little theory of my own :

There still are nations steeped in heathenism,
Deprived of many blessings we enjoy—
Are not the disabilities and sufferings
Of these, and also of our predecessors,
The pains and penalties and punishments
Of antecedent sin and disobedience
Of some remote and pre-existent state,
According to some wise divine gradation;
While we in this broad day of Christian light,
With all the rich appliances of science,
Are blessed as nation never was before?
We come into this life without our choosing;
Come we not therefore from some previous being?
For who would willingly accept of life
With all its fearful risks, here and hereafter,
Unless to expiate some past existence?
Life seems a link in being's endless chain,
Which we behold exemplified in nature.
We see the base and creeping caterpillar
Transmuted to a helpless chrysalis,
Like the imprisoned soul in human life,
And then at last changed to a beauteous creature,
Winged like an angel flying in mid heaven!
We know not what we are, nor what we shall be,
Nor what we have been in some previous state.
Is it not likely that we are connected
As closely with the past as with the future
In some retributive mysterious way,
Known to the Great Creator of us all,
Who knows our history, and assigns our stripes

According to our various shades of guilt?
Who fashioned us according to His purposes,
And gives to each a different form and face,
Voice, manner, mind, spirit and understanding!
He knows our different degrees of guilt
As perfectly as He knows our different persons,
With all our various individualisms,
And in His infinite fatherly compassion
Has planned a glorious system of redemption,
By one supreme atoning sacrifice,
To reconcile unto Himself again
(After that we have suffered for awhile
The tribulations of this mortal state,
If we accept the proffered terms of grace,)
All kindreds, peoples, nations of the earth
In one eternal covenant of love,
Joy without end and heavenly rest and peace!
This life is but the tuning of the strings
Before we join the chorus of the skies!
   It is a privilege to live in times
When science has made life four times as pleasant,
And living twice as easy as it was
In the slow, heavy, stupid days of old,
When prudent people settled their affairs
And made their wills before they went to London,
An awful journey of some fifty miles,
Beset with robbers, ruts, and various dangers;
And when the postman from the country village
Went duly to the post town once a week
To bring the letters, not so many as now;

And always in returning with his budget
Had orders to go homewards by the Hall,
Where, by the stately lady's strict command,
He had to join the large and pious household,
And listen to the lengthy morning prayers,
Ere he proceeded further with his letters,
While all the village had to wait in patience ;—
And very heavy was the charge for postage,
So that the poor could seldom use the post.
I knew a widow who was old and destitute,
Who had a son who lived in Edinburgh,
That handsome city of old memories,
Three or four hundred miles perhaps from hence ;
On being asked if she had heard from him,
She shook her head, and mournfully said, "No."
A letter had arrived from him, she said,
But as she could not pay the charge for postage
The sonless widow could not take it in—
A cruel torture to a mother's heart.
Now, we have only just to write a letter,
And place upon it a pink penny stamp,
Being a portrait of our Gracious Queen,
And pop the letter in the pillar post,
And the next day, by an ingenious system,
Elaborately contrived, and worked with skill,
It will in safety reach its destination
In any corner of our happy England,
And be delivered to the hands we wish.

  This is the age of science, not of song.
How would our old great grandmothers exclaim

"Hey! hoity! toity!" if they could but see
The wonders now performed by mechanism :
Machines to wash the linen of the family,
Machines to wring the same when it is washed,
Machines to smooth it too when it is dry,
Machines to milk the cows with expedition,
Machines to cut the meat for sausages,
Machines to peel the apples for a pudding,
Machines to do the sewing of the household,
And, best of all, machines to nurse the babies!
But these are nothing to the mighty engines
Invented to relieve the toil of man,
And supersede old sources of propulsion,
Machinery has at length fairly invaded
The last redoubt of stubborn old-worldism,
The once poetic realm of Agriculture.
The farmers formerly supinely trusted
For their advancement and prosperity
To specious laws to keep out foreign corn—
Delusive laws that could not bear the strain
Of treacherous weather and deficient harvests.
(Cobden and Bright at length dispelled that nonsense
By dint of argument and eloquence ;)
They now with better reason trust to science,
And seek the aid of skilful enginery.
  Each county has its Agricultural Show,
One of the striking features of the age,
Where implements for every farming purpose
Are brilliantly displayed to wondering eyes ;
Machines to reap and mow by stout horse-power,

And do the work of half a score of men,
Without the toil and back-ache of past ages,
Thus expediting harvest operations,
And making hay in fact while the sun shines.
Here engines worked by steam astound old men,
The stolid, bent day-labourers on the soil,
In antique coats and modern wide-awakes,
Who stand and fumble in their breeches' pockets
To find the sense not found within their brains ;
Who never dreamt of any implement
Beyond the two-horse plough and ancient sickle.
In short we see a peaceful revolution
Wrought out by science and necessity,
And an amusing sight it is to witness.
I will not dwell upon the fine fat cattle,
Straight-backed, short-legged, and broad across the
       chest ;
The horses, sheep, pigs, poultry, dogs, and donkeys ;
Nor yet describe the bustle and the hubbub,
The heat, the dust, the music, and the banners ;
I only care about the men and women,
And I shall leave the latter to themselves,
Although perhaps they go there to be noticed,
And certainly deserve to be admired.
The English farmer is my present study ;
The farmer lives upon his outspread acres,
Looked up to by his ignorant farm servants,
With no one to dispute his sovereign sway,
Or contradict him in his strong opinions ;
No need has he like a rich shopkeeper,

To bow and smile and prattle mincingly
To every two-penny-half-penny customer.
His wealth is all spread out before his eyes;
Also before the eyes of all the world;
How therefore can he keep from being proud?
And certainly he is a little proud,
And having his own undisputed sway,
He might be called a very happy man,
If it were not for one cantankerous matter
That dogs him day and night, thwarts all his plans,
Pays no attention to his will and wishes,
Nor will be ruled by him do what he may—
This is the weather—the ever-changing weather—
That rules him by the rule of contrary;
Sure to come cold just when he wants it hot,
Sure to come rainy when he wants it dry.
He cannot have his way and rule the weather;
This makes of him a discontented man,
For ever grumbling like a fat spoiled child.
Poor man; he cannot, or he will not, see,
Or if he sees, is yet too petulant
To own the comforting and obvious fact
That when the weather does not suit one soil
It is exactly what another wants;
That when it is too sultry for the barley
The warmth precisely suits the breadth of wheat;
That when it is too dry for swedes or mangolds
It is delightful weather for the haysel;
And when it is too rainy for the corn
It gives vast produce in the shape of roots.

Thus are the farmers blest against their will ;
They lose one way to prosper in another,
And cannot be persuaded they are happy,
Because not happy in the way they want.
    The farmers at an Agricultural Show
Come forth in all their territorial greatness ;
Their cheeks are ruddy as a rosy apple ;
Their persons jolly, braced by country air,
Favoured no doubt as well by country living.
Their dress is in the very tip of fashion.
Ah ! how unlike their plodding ancestors !
Their chief ambition is to ride good horses,
Adapted doubtless for the hunting-field ;
And show their tastes in various breeds of dogs.
They have the confidence and self-possession
Of gentlemen of independent fortune,
Without the easy air and the politeness
Of well-bred men who mix with well-bred men.
Their features seldom are symmetrical,
Although their persons may be well-proportioned ;
They are men of shrewdness rather than of reading,
Fond of a joke, as are true Englishmen,
And view the engines, and the implements,
The cattle, and the various animals,
With sober, thoughtful earnestness of purpose,
And a keen eye to monetary profit.
How different from their stolid forefathers,
Ignorant, obstinate, and intractable,
Fond of hot potions and of long clay pipes,
With minds as narrow as their tastes were low !

The dearest crony that I ever had
Was a plain farmer—an old bachelor—
A rough, original, and unpolished diamond,
Kind, simple, social, natural, and out-spoken,
Beloved by young and old, and rich and poor ;
An absent-minded man, who blurted forth
His thoughts, without much heed to time or place ;
He seldom seemed to listen to another,
And interrupted anybody else,
Absorbed by passing fancies of his own ;
Poetry he loved, and also loved to quote it,
But broke down mostly ere he reached the point ;
Burns was to him almost a " vera brither ;"
His favourite study, and his frequent topic,
Was womanhood—that unsolved mystery ;
He was a hearty champion of the sex,
But only ventured to the brink of marriage.
I loved him almost as one loves a woman,
His very presence gave a sense of pleasure ;
He died, as he had lived, a bachelor—
Died, ere I even knew that he was ill ;
I lost him, as through life has been my lot
To lose too soon the dearest of my friends.
    The world rolls faster than it used to do ;
A life-time has beheld a wondrous change.
My good old father, born in the dark ages,
In the year Seventeen hundred seventy-four,
Survived to travel in a railway train !
How many grand events in history
Happened within his lengthened term of life !

Born ere the proud and prosperous Confederacy
Across the Atlantic, feeling their young strength,
Declared their independence of Old England,
And so set up in business for themselves,
Fighting against great odds for liberty,
And rearing for themselves a grand Republic—
My father lived through the French Revolution,
That bloody earthquake of our modern times,
Which both upheaved and rudely overturned
The old, decayed, corrupt foundation stones,
On which the social edifice was built,
Clearing the ground for a more popular structure.
My father saw Napoleon's proud career,
His humble origin as corporal,
His bloody battles over frightened Europe,
His elevation to Imperial rule,
Uplifted on the carcases of millions,
And then his downfall, and, at last, his death—
A lone caged eagle biting his bars in vain.
My father lived through all the forty years
Of peace that followed the great Emperor's fall,
Witnessed the slow improvement of our laws,
Shared in the work of slave emancipation,
The long and arduous contest for Reform,
And the great struggle to repeal the Corn Laws ;
Saw the unsheathing of the sword again,
When France and England went to war with Russia
To save the Moslem Empire from its doom,
And conquered Russia at Sebastopol
With countless cost of human life and treasure,

The good whereof remains to be revealed;
But which, just like the letting out of waters,
Has been succeeded by fresh floods of blood,
Both in old Europe and in young America.
But other changes my poor father witnessed—
The change from dim oil lamps to flaring gas;
The change from old stage coaches and slow travelling
To railway trains and rapid locomotion;
The change from dear and scanty newspapers
To penny papers always full of news;
The change from costly and vexatious postage,
Crossed letters, and contracted correspondence,
To penny postage and its countless blessings;
The change from taxes upon everything
To those on incomes and on luxuries;
The change from what we call the good old times—
The good old times were very bad old times—
To modern usages, electric telegraphs,
Photography with all its many pleasures,
Science and arts unknown in days of old,—
All this my poor old father lived to see,
And died, without a wrinkle in his face,
Happily, at the great age of ninety-one,
On the eleventh day of January,
In the year Eighteen hundred sixty-six.

    He was a man who had his little faults;
He had a little spark of vanity;
He was a little head-strong in his ways;
And had a little self-love in his nature;
But these were nothing to his sterling merits.

He was a man of great sincerity;
One of the tip-top virtues of our manhood;
A man of strong religious principle;
Of kindliness and true benevolence—
Perhaps a little narrow in his creed.
He took a little pride in being humble—
Surely a man deserves a little praise
Who blames himself with meek disparagement—
He was a man of true originality,
One who impressed all strangers with his worth,
And with his homely sense and sympathies;
His loud clear voice and dignity of manner
Made everything he had to say impressive,
Soothing in sorrow, terrible in rebuke.
He had a noble scorn of being in debt;
Having in early life been long a debtor,
He never liked to trust, nor to be trusted,
Nor would eat butchers' meat, nor bakers' bread;
Nothing but what was paid for would he use.
As village shopkeeper he was a doctor,
And had three grand specifics for diseases—
Diachylon salve, to draw out thorns or needles;
Flour to stanch wounds and keep them from the air,
And thus allay inflammatory action;
And a mild pill, to be taken every day,
To keep the bodily organs gently oiled,
And help the action of defective nature:
A theory of medicine wiser, he maintained,
Than violent remedies tried at intervals.
He took his pills himself, and died of old age.

Yes, how the strong man sank to second childhood,
Weak and bed-ridden, deaf, and dim of sight,
Not only weak in body, but in mind,
Though strong as ever in his resolute will—
The will is our last faculty which dies,
It does not weaken with all other weakness—
But conscious of his great infirmities,
In weariness of body and of spirit,
How earnestly he prayed to be released,
And taken from this troublous mortal state
To join his long-lost loved ones up in heaven !
Poor human life ! O may I die a man,
And not live on to be a child again,
Without the promise and the charm of childhood !
   The drought of Eighteen hundred sixty-eight
Will be remembered in long years to come—
A summer to be famed in history,
When hundreds of poor labourers in the country
Were stricken by the ardent sun and died,
And the broad fields, for many months together,
Were parched and dusty as the Queen's highway—
No showers between the haysel and the harvest
Having refreshed the hot and panting earth—
When the leaves dropped from many trees for dryness,
As if the autumn had already come,
And the poor flocks and herds suffered from thirst,
So as before this time was not remembered
By the most ancient and oracular people ;
While from the poet's brow, who wrote these lines,
The drops of perspiration chased each other

T

Adown his cheeks while penning "deathless verse"—
The perspiration and the poetry
Flowing together with congenial freedom.
So once I saw the dwellers in " Parnasse "
In their shirt-sleeves, regardless of the heat,
Elbowing with might and main, their fiddle-bows !
   With not less stern devotedness of purpose,·
Our legislators in the House of Commons,
Kept up their hammering on the great State anvil,
Feverish with heated air and hard hot work,
Till Parliament was happily prorogued,
And the poor jaded members, like young school-rogues,
Scampered off gladly to their country homes,
Or sought the moors, sea-side, or Continent.
   The country now is calming down again,
O'erpowered with heat, and surfeited with speeches.
The disestablishment of Ireland's Church
Has been the bone of all this fierce contention.
The present House has passed its sentence on it ;
Parliament soon will therefore be dissolved,
That the whole nation may record its verdict
Through a decisive General Election.
   If State support alone sustains the Church,
The Irish Church is tottering to its fall ;
The greatest public fraud upon a people
That modern times have witnessed on this earth—
An alien Church thrust on a free community !
With what vitality do ill weeds grow,
And how long time it takes to root them out !
But wholesale robbery is not all profit.

Nations, like men, when they do wickedly,
Have to pay dearly for it in the end.
Ireland is England's haunting skeleton—
At once her shame, her danger, and disgrace.
Ireland, the loveliest and the wretchedest
Of Christian lands that I have ever traversed,
Won by the sword and governed by the sword,
The battle-ground of angry hostile creeds,
The very nest of rankling bigotry,
Will soon rejoice in justice and in freedom,
Which her illustrious liberator—O'Connell—
Toiled hard, so many years, to win for her.
Erin's green isle, her mountains, and her valleys,
And sweet Killarney's hills and glittering waters,
Shall waken to a new and gladsome life,
And every son of Erin, now in exile
In distant lands of freedom and of plenty,
Or clinging still to her luxuriant bosom,
Shall kiss the shamrock with a new devotion,
And feel his heart rebound with holy joy
That, equal with her twin-born sister—England—
She takes her proper rank amongst the nations
In freedom, wealth, and strength, and beauty's dower.
  I love the fine old church-towers of our country,
Perhaps half-covered over with dark ivy,
That stand like rocks against the flow of ages,
Unaltered by the change of times or tastes,
The silent revolutions of opinion,
The light of science, and the spread of knowledge.
These grand old churches and rich parsonages

May be compared to snug and cozy birds' nests,
From which the greedy cuckoos of Episcopacy
Have shouldered out the sparrows of old Rome.
    When Mister State was married to Mistress Popery
They made a very shocking mess of it.
It was a match of interest on both sides ;
In truth, a very ill-assorted match ;
No real love was lost on either part.
The wife was not a bit too good before,
And Mister State was always a regular brute.
It needed no great prophet to foretell
What the result of such a match would be.
Wife went on dreadful, shocking, desperate ;
For ever trying to get the upper hand.
Then Mister State set to and beat his wife ;
He was not going to be ruled by her,
And make himself a general laughing-stock,
Not he ! or he would know the reason why.
And thus these two kept up a terrible row.
At last old Mister State rose in a fury,
And said he would not bear it any longer,
And so at once divorced his scolding wife,
Stripping her first of all her goods and money,
Which he bestowed on Mistress Episcopacy,
And then was fool enough to marry her.
She looked demure and very good at first,
But had a nasty temper of her own,
And soon revealed the stuff that she was made of.
She proved as jealous as an old she tiger,
And stuck her nails into the former wife,

And scratched her face and arms maliciously,
Quarrelled with poor old Mister State about her,
And made a very dreadful piece of work,
Saying his former wife was slyly trying
To get once more into his house again,
And turn her out of doors into the streets ;
Professed to love her husband very fondly,
And coaxed him to do many foolish things ;
And with her jealousy and horrid temper,
Threatened to pull the venerable house down
About his ears, half-frightening him to death.
This is the present state of their affairs,
And what the end will be nobody knows !
 The odious union of Church and State
Is only potent for unhallowed ends.
Does it not warp the Bishops of the Church,
Not to say anything of meaner men,
To do the bidding of the Ministry,
Whatever slough they wish to drag them through ?
Have not the bench of Bishops always voted
For every cruel, every unjust law,
Until repentance ceased to be a virtue ?
Have they not basely voted for the slave trade ?
Have they not voted heart and soul for slavery ?
Opposed the amelioration of all laws
That bore oppressively upon the people—
The Criminal Law, that strangled men by hundreds ;
The Corn Law, which most surely starved its thou
Yes, every law that stained the Statute Book ?
Have they not always stood in opposition

To Parliamentary Reform, which sought
To rectify the clumsy old machinery
By which the laws of England were enacted?
The Bishops have done this, and more than this,
And drawn their tens of thousands from the land,
Living in princely luxury and state;
Not like the bishops of the early ages—
Plain fishermen, who fished for souls, not mitres.
    The Established Church is in its agony.
She came dishonestly by her possessions,
And now they are the baits for birds of prey
To peck, and hungry wolves to raven for.
Her dignitaries alarmed rush to and fro,
And yelp and howl with un-dissembled terror.
The swollen priests, who trampled over us,
Who lived upon the fatness of the land,
And drained the South to satisfy their thirst,
Are stricken with bewilderment of soul:
Like some doomed vessel in the Arctic Seas,
The vessel of the Church is in the pack,
And drifts—who can foretell where she may drift?
    I have no love for the Establishment;
It leans upon the State, and not on God.
It is itself both founded on injustice,
And is unjust to its own ministers.
The strutting turkey-gobblers of the Church
Are crammed and over-fatted with good things—
These are the bishops, down to deans and rectors:
The lean and hungry barn-door fowls of the Church
That live on stones and chaff, and scrap to get them,

These are the hard-worked, hunger-bitten curates.
The Establishment enjoys its domination ;
It loves to stickle for its legal rights,
And wield the whip over Dissenting Pograms,
Claiming its clerical dues by force of law,
Not for the value of the paltry shillings ;
But to enable it to domineer,
And set its haughty foot upon our necks,
Demanding shillings, and, by law-expenses,
Swelling the shillings often into pounds ;
Seizing the tables, chairs, and looking-glasses
Of the poor tradesman, or hard-stinted widow,
Who conscientiously declines to pay.
    No shriek of fear has been more often raised
Than this, " The Church of England is in danger !"
Is one Church more in danger than another?
They do not mean the Church then after all !
They mean the power of taxing everybody
For the behoof of their particular Church ;
Its wealth, its pride, its power they tremble for.
They fear to be despoiled of all the booty,
Of which King Harry robbed the Catholics,
By despot power, the faggot, and the block.
Is the receiver better than the thief ?
Can true religion thrive by means like these?
The assumption by the Church of special rights
Does violence to the nation's moral sense.
This is the Church that used to send its bailiffs
Into my father's house, year after year,
With warrants signed by legal functionaries,

To seize his goods and chattels by distraint,
And sell them at perhaps not half their value
To satisfy its miserable church-rates,
Which he had rather gone to goal than paid.
A parson never looks you in the face.
Can it be pride in such a holy man ?
Or rather is it not a sense of shame ?
Perhaps a twinge of conscience at his heart
Gives to his cheeks their usual ruby blush ;
Perhaps the memory of law-wrung gains
From poor Dissenters stings him to the quick,
And makes him always look another way.
   And does a blessing rest upon the Church ?
What is the matter with the Establishment ?
Is it not tortured with the spirit of schism
Without the power of purifying itself—
Curing its ancient taint of leprosy,
And exorcising its own evil spirits ?
Truly the Church of England is in danger,
But chiefly by disease within itself.
Can the Church live on merely empty forms ?
Does she fulfil her mission as a Church ?
Her greatest foes are those within her fold.
All systems, whether of the Church or State,
Must canter with the spirit of the age,
Ever advancing with the march of light.
To stagnate is to grow corrupt and perish.
The established Church of England stagnates thus
And therefore breeds within herself blind worms
And reptiles gendered of the seed of Rome ;

And here the secret lies of her decline.
She has abundance of fat dignitaries,
Archbishops, bishops, and the rest of them,
Rolling and choking in a slough of wealth—
In wealth almost as boundless as their greed ;
But she possesses in herself no power
Of self-correction and of self-amendment ;
Bound hand and foot as partner with the State,
And dragged through all the mire of politics.
  England, my country, what can have bewitched thee
To sell thy birthright for a mess of pottage ?
English roast beef for meagre Romish soup ?
Thy birthright is religious liberty,
Won from old Rome in many a sturdy contest,
And paid for by the priceless blood of martyrs.
How many a man, and many a woman, too,
Has perished at the stake for their religion—
Even in Smithfield, in the heart of London,
And even in the streets of Colchester !
And many a faggot of well-seasoned wood
Has been consumed in the absurd attempt
To burn the living principle of truth,
And make men leave the doctrines of the Bible
For priestly fables and for pompous shows.
England, my country ! what has bewitched thy clergy
That they return, like sows that have been washed,
To wallow in the loathsome mire of Rome—
Her absolutions and indulgences,
Her senseless rights and gaudy ceremonies—
Descending to the mummeries of the Papists,

Who worship God as though he were a baby
To be amused with tinkling bells and pictures,
And dresses worthy of a mountebank,
With censers, candles, flowers, and golden cups,
And every sort and kind of pretty plaything !
Heart-worship is the worship God requires,
Not pomps, processions, ceremonies and forms :
The plough-boy poet of the Scottish hills
Left us the grandest line of modern song—
" The Power incensed, the pageant will desert ! "
    The Christian Church never more bravely flourished
Than when it leaned not on an arm of flesh,
Before the time of the great Constantine ;
It may have grown in wealth, and pomp, and state,
But not in holy life, and truth, and purity ;
And when the arm of flesh shall be withdrawn,
And in the place of this unsafe support
The Everlasting arms be underneath,
Then will it flourish as in days of old.
    Nature is just and balances her accounts.
After a drought she gives us floods of rain.
How welcome is a shower after a drought !
The sun-burnt earth gasping with feverish heat,
Eager and faint with long-continued thirst,
Like a poor baby seizing its mother's breast,
Drinks in the rain with ravenous enjoyment.
The precious drops rattling and pelting down
Make pleasant music on the window panes ;
A fresh and grateful fragrance fills the air ;
All nature welcomes the reviving shower ;

Each tremulous leaf grows greener in the rain ;
The earth appears to throb with conscious pleasure ;
The birds hop chirruping from bough to bough ;
The very earth-worms deep beneath the soil
Hear, in their dark and dreary dwelling-places,
The cheerful patter of the falling shower,
And share unseen the general joyfulness ;
There is not anywhere a living thing,
From the faint flocks and herds amidst the fields
To the most tiny insect in its cell,
But what rejoices in the bounteous gift
Of rain, the harbinger of boundless good.
The hearts of men dilate with satisfaction,
Each one, with warmth, congratulates his neighbour,
And hopes for four-and-twenty hours of it,
And joyful gratitude in incense rises
To God, the fountain of beneficence.
  I am a member of the Sect of Friends.
A sect reviled and ridiculed and flouted,
With quirks and quibbles of the penny-a-liners,
And even learned men who should know better,
Men who know little of the things they talk of.
Sects dimly read each other's inner life,
And so through ignorance misjudge each other ;
The best things in the world are most abused ;
So has it happened with the Sect of Friends ;
And yet its members individually
Are mostly treated with respect and praise.
A sect in numbers inconsiderable,
Diminished to a very few in England

By rigid rules and unwise regulations,
And over-prudence in contracting marriage,
But growing rapidly across the Atlantic:
A sect whose doctrines being little known,
And nothing popular, are therefore freely
Misrepresented by the outside world;
And yet a noble sect, who boldly stood
For liberty of conscience and for truth
In the dark days of bigot persecution;
Who, when more numerous sects slunk cowardly
Into safe garrets, or down into dark cellars,
To worship God by stealth, in fear and trembling,
Assembled boldly in their meeting-houses,
And, when expelled by brutal soldiery,
Stood in the open streets to worship God;
Yes, even in the streets of Colchester!
Till hurried off with blows and violence,
Inflicted equally on men and women,
To dungeons dismal as the times were dark!
Thousands were thus imprisoned wrongfully,
And hundreds perished in most loathsome cells
By cruel usage and by prison fevers.
Such dungeons now are happily unknown,
Thanks to John Howard and the advance of light;
Yet neither mockings, buffetings nor scourgings,
Nor fines, nor long imprisonments, nor tortures,
Could drive them from the solid rock of Truth;
The storms of persecution only made them
Cling closer to the doctrines which they held,
The ancient principles of Christianity,

Of Christ's atoning sacrifice for all,
And the free gift of vital saving grace
Implanted in the heart of every one.
Whoever wish to understand the matter,
Let them read " Bates's Doctrines of the Friends,"
Or, if they want unanswerable logic,
" Barclay's Apology" will serve their turn.
Friends were the real and valiant Protestants ;
They took their stand for liberty of conscience,
And perfect fredom in the forms of worship ;
Protested against hireling ministry ;
Protested against human interference
Between the soul of man and his Creator ;
Protested against empty forms and ceremonies,
And outward ordinances employed in worship,
As superseded by the coming of Christ,
And non-essential to the soul's salvation ;
Believing that the saving grace of God
Is freely offered to the human family ;
Protested against war in all its forms ;
Protested against oaths and imprecations ;
Protested against human slavery,
And capital punishment for any crimes ;
Protested, on the other hand, in favour
Of peace, and progress, and humanity ;
Of justice, godliness, and temperance ;
Of woman's mission to proclaim the gospel,
And relative equality with man ;
The free diffusion of the Holy Scriptures ;
And of the education of the people.

To this small sect was given a lofty mission,
Not to make proselytes by sea and land,
But to uphold a standard to the world
Of pure and simple Christianity,
Untrammelled by the State, and uncorrupted
By the cunning craftiness of selfish men.
Our mode of worship is most primitive,
Simple and natural and reasonable,
Needing no interference of a priest
Between the worshipper and his Creator.
It is to sit in reverential silence
Before the awful majesty of God,
And seek to draw in spirit near to Him,
Through Christ, who is the alone appointed way;
Who promised to draw nigh to us in spirit;
Who is not far from any one of us;
Who is Himself a Spirit, and who seeks
The one true worship, that, in spirit and truth,
So that His holy presence may be felt
In sweet communion of the life divine.
When the most blessed Jesus was on earth
He broke five loaves amongst five thousand men,
And gave them to His fainting followers,
By which the multitude were all sufficed,
And so, in His illimitable power,
Where two or three are gathered in His name,
He can reverse the mighty miracle
Out of the rich abundance of His goodness,
And break five thousand loaves of spiritual bread,
Amongst the few who truly hunger for Him,

And nourish their souls to everlasting life.
The heart, the heart, the heart is everything !
  Is not this mode of worship reasonable,
Wiser and better and more profitable,
Than to be lulled to sleep by drowsy sermons ?
Or dinned to death by noisy platitudes,
Which may be called a weariness to the flesh,
And are not worship, but an interruption
To solemn thoughts and spiritual communion ?
Our mode of worship has the special effect
Of prompting in the soul the deepest reverence,
For the most perfect holiness of that Being,
Omnipotent, omniscient, omnipresent,
The triune Deity whom we adore,
Whose very name we almost shrink to utter ;
Wherein we differ much from other people,
Who deem religion a mere matter of forms,
Gestures, and ordinances, and vain observances :
Too oft the hireling preachers of the gospel,
Making a market of their sacred things,
Bring down the Deity to their own low level,
And name His name just as familiarly
As if he were the mayor of Colchester.
  All merely human systems of religion
Inevitably lead to One-man-ism.
The setting up of a mere man as priest,
And only go-between 'twixt God and man,
Instead of Christ, the High Priest of our profession,
The only priest of the new Covenant,
So that a congregation cannot worship

Without the assistance of a minister
To do the business for the helpless people ;
And thus the minister assumes a lordship
Over the feeble heritage of God,
And calls the people under him "my people,"
And makes himself a kind of sponsor for them ;
And thus mistaken notions of true worship
Come to be held by those who should know better,
Who fancy they are really worshipping
When they are only listening to a preacher,
Not understanding that availing worship
Must be communion 'twixt the soul and God,
And holy works accordant to His will;
It is an easy way of worshipping
When we can have it done by deputy;
Such worship ends in mere formality.
Listening to music and to prayers and sermons
May lull the carnal mind to a false rest;
This is not drawing nigh to God in spirit,
Who must be worshipped in spirit and in truth !
　　True ministry is not allied to priestcraft ;
'Tis humble service to the best of Masters.
Priestcraft is lordship over things divine,
Remorseless, bigoted, selfish, and despotic,
Turning the screw of the confessional
On tender consciences and feeble minds ;
And priests are governed by one policy—
Aiming to keep a toll-gate into heaven,
To constitute themselves heaven's doorkeepers,
And shut or open at their own discretion,

Letting none pass but those who buy their tickets.
They love to clap a padlock on the mind,
And keep the key of knowledge to themselves.
  Goodness depends not wholly upon creed ;
Each creed can boast of its undoubted saints.
Mine is the only sect that never persecuted
When it possessed the power to persecute—
A power it once possessed in Pennsylvania—
Giving fair play to men of every creed ;
Not like the persecuted Independents,
Who fled from England to America
To escape from suffering and enjoy repose,
And there became the hottest persecutors.
Their magistrates cut off the ears of Friends,
And had them stripped and flogged at the cart-tail
From town to town, women as well as men,
In frost and snow, and pain, and weariness,
And hung a number of them on the gallows—
Among the rest, the noble Mary Dyar——
Trying to strangle tender consciences
By strangling human beings by the neck,
Thus tarnishing the name of Independents
With the eternal stain of persecution,
A name which they have tried to change away.
  Whenever sects or parties change their names
They do it for the very best of reasons ;
They do it to improve appearances ;
They do it as a man leaves off a coat
When he has worn an ugly hole in it—
The man looks better but remains the same,

But power has a corrupting influence,
And, intermingled with religious zeal,
Too easily becomes severe and cruel,
Though modern ways of thinking and of doing
May throw a gloss upon life's outer aspect ;
For there are fashions even in religion,
And fashions ever have been given to change.
Our ancestors, austere and knuckle-headed,
Loved their religion as they loved their ale—
Strong, hard, and sour, and griping to the stomach ;
In modern times we like it mild and heady.

The sect of Friends, perhaps, has done its work,
Fulfilled its mission, and is dying out.
It has descended sadly from its watch-tower ;
But as it has approached the outer world,
The outer world has slowly gathered towards it,
Adopting many of its principles,
And being all the better for the change ;
It seems a pity that a sect so useful
Should perish from the land that gave it birth ;
But human imperfection largely enters
Not only into every institution,
But even the framework of religious sects.
Principles ever tend to singularities,
For men of principle are always singular
To those who have no principle themselves.
These are too oft the few and those the many.
Principles are the timbers of the oak,
And singularities are but the leaves.
The elders of the sect, not given to change,

Were left behind in fashion's onward race,
And so became uncouth in their appearance,
And in their manners, to the world around them.
These singularities were non-essentials,
Which soon became essentials through tradition.
And so usurped the place of principles,
Making consistency with ancient usage
Of more importance than with gospel truth;
And as the sect declined in vital strength,
Its inward discipline was made more rigid
To supplement its ancient principles,
Hedge it around from contact with the world,
And save it from its proneness to decay;
Thus overlaying Bible principles
By disciplinary rules and regulations,
Good in their aim, but bad in their result,
And narrowing the basis of the sect.
O had our predecessors been content
To cleave to gospel principles alone,
And let them do their work in every soul,
Working diversely in each different nature,
But blending all in harmony and love,
How had our sect stood strong through all assaults,
And sent forth living branches o'er the land!
Broken and peeled and humbled as it is,
The tree must still be judged of by its fruit,
And where can I discover finer samples
Of conscientious humble piety,
Of purity and holiness of life,
And of benevolence that knows no limits,

Than such as still are found in this small sect ?
I need not travel fifty miles from Colchester
To find a good and worthy specimen,—
An ancient man beloved by high and low,
And personally known to everybody,
Whose daily life is one delightful sermon,
With heavenly sweetness in his countenance,
And sweetness in his words to rich and poor,
And in his pockets sweets for babes and sucklings :
A man to folks, of every sect and station
Alike on friendly and familiar terms ;
A man of pleasantry in conversation,
Yet wisely chastened with divine instruction ;
His mind is richly stored with holy truths
That fall in loving fervour from his lips,
Evincing that his thoughts are oft in heaven
In sweet communion with his dearest Lord.
The many good deeds of his daily life
He only wishes to be known to God,
And yet the fragrance that ascends from them,
Like that from lilies of the vale, reveals them.
He is a preacher of the sect of Friends,
Whose only pay is peace, not sordid gold ;
He can perceive the needle's eye of truth,
And thread it skilfully as if at random :
Rebuke the sin yet not offend the sinner.
Of such men are the salt of this gross earth ;
And yet the myrmidons of our State Church
Have yearly seized the goods of this good man
To pay their mean inexorable claims !

Man is himself the temple of his God
Wherein He dwells and in whose courts He walks;
Happy the man whose spirit finds Him there;
Who learns with Him to walk, with Him to talk,
From day to day, and even from hour to hour,
Breathing the atmosphere of prayer and praise.
This is the secret of true happiness!
If a man's spirit talks but to himself
He finds too oft unprofitable company,
No peace, no rest, no joy, no staff to lean on.
If a man talks to his own covetousness,
It hardens and it closes up his heart;
If a man talks to his imagination
It leads him on into a labyrinth;
If he prefers to talk to his ambition
It makes him reckless and unscrupulous;
If a man talks to his conceit and pride,
These are the certain preludes of a fall;
And if he talks to his desire of pleasure,
He finds too oft the end is disappointment;
So is it with the round of all our passions.
But he who talks with God lives above earth,
Above its toils, and pains, and joys, and sorrows,
He leans upon an Arm that never fails—
He rests in sweet assurance of the future,
The foretaste of those joys that know no end!
    My sect is not so narrow in its nature
As not to bring forth men of eminence.
West, the original historic painter;
Dalton, the author of the Atomic theory;

Young, who deciphered the Rosetta Stone ;
Luke Howard, who found out the law of clouds ;
My uncle, Bracy Clark, dear kind old man,
The father of the Veterinary art :
All these were members of the sect of Friends ;
And living still amongst us we possess
A noble architect in Waterhouse ;
Whittier, the stirring poet of the West,
And John Bright, foremost statesman of the age.
     The members of this sect were leading men
In introducing the great railway system—
Most powerful of revolutionists.
That strong-built man, good, generous Edward Pease,
Whose voice was soft and gentle as a woman's,
Supplied the capital and enterprise,
As Stephenson the genius, to construct
The fiery courser of mechanic art.
Young Fox it was who drove the famous "Rocket,"
Which gained the first prize as a railway engine.
The earliest board of railway potentates
Were half of them connected with this sect ;
And Bradshaw is the universal Guide ;
Whilst Edmondson contrived the railway ticket
Which is adopted now on every line.
     One Sabbath day, some twenty years ago,
I saw a stranger in our congregation,
Appearing to belong to nobody.
I asked him to come home with me to dine,
And he assented to my invitation.
He seemed a serious care-worn sort of man,

Of middle age and moderate intellect,
Who might have had to struggle for a living.
We dined, and had some chat which I forget,
Save that he told me he had just invented
A kind of ticket for the use of railways,
Which he was trying then to introduce;
And so we parted never more to meet.
I in my time have met with many inventors,
Whose grand inventions never came to anything :
Great poets also who have died unknown.
I thought but slightingly of his invention,
And I discovered nothing in the man
That gave a token of his genius.
This man was Edmondson, whose little tickets
Are perfect specimens of ingenuity,
Neither to be excelled nor superseded,
Used everywhere where railways are in use,
And bought by tens of thousands every day,
Earning a fortune for the skilled inventor.

    Fiercely throughout the land the uproar rages
Of " Disestablishment," and " Church in danger ! "
The uproar that broke out at Ephesus,
Amongst the noisy craftsmen of Diana,
Breaks out afresh, even in a Christian church,
When you lay hands upon the temporalities.
Prophets, with eyes inflamed, and hands outspread,
Make piteous moan, and beat their ample breasts,
Frightened themselves, and frightening other people,
With dreadful prophecies of coming ruin.

    Men love to peer into the golden future,

Safe on the gilded battlements of Hope ;
But there are mournful prophets who can see
Nothing but trouble, danger, and disaster :
No ray of sunshine in a world of gloom !
I have known many men in my long life,
Who, though they laid no claim to inspiration,
Were very fond of uttering prophecies.
It is a delicate way of claiming wisdom,
And far more often used by moral cowards,
Who have a nervous fear of coming changes,
Than by redoubtable men that seek reform.
These prophecies are very safe investments.
If they come true they earn the credit of them ;
If they prove false 'tis easy to forget them.
I have read scores of prophecies that England
Was trembling on the very verge of ruin,
Delivered in the senate of our country,
Where wisdom sits enthroned in solemn wigs,
And holiness expands in sleeves of lawn—
That Roman Catholics would swallow England
If they should ever obtain Emancipation—
That Parliament would be unchristianised
If Jews were eligible to sit as members—
That the Established Church would be uprooted,
And trail its sacred glories in the dust,
If ever low Dissenters were allowed
To share its honours and its privileges—
That land would soon go out of cultivation,
And landlords be inevitably ruined,
And everybody else be ruined with them,

If the starvation Corn Laws were repealed—
That Free Trade would enrich the foreigner,
And beggar us by freeing us of trade—
That the cheap labour of the serfs of Tambof
Would lower the wages of our working men,
And swamp our markets with a flood of corn—
That parliamentary reform was something
So very dreadful, that our Constitution
In Church and State—our glorious Constitution—
Must tumble headlong, and be swept away
By an inundation of the working classes,
If ever reform in Parliament were granted !
I wonder very much how many times
They have told us that the sun of England's glory
Was on the point of setting—to rise no more !
   These prophecies spring up like morning mush-
     rooms
From the pestiferous soil that suits them best,
And die as quickly in the glare of day ;
Are they not chronicled for endless laughter
In the grave pages of the Quarterly ?
And yet in spite of all these prophecies,
Old England never held her head so high ;
Never was richer and more prosperous ;
Never more honoured by surrounding nations ;
Never more dreaded by her enemies.
Under the rule of Queen Victoria
No nation ever was more freely governed ;
No government was ever more secure.
The people love the throne right heartily,

And never were so merry and so happy.
'Tis true the good old vessel of the State
Is constantly in need of small repairs
To keep her properly in sailing trim,
And find employment for her idle hands ;
Yet her old timbers are as sound as ever.
She has abundant wealth of stores on board,
And bunting for another thousand years ;
And if her company are loyal and true,
And pull together as men ought to pull,
The good old ship will always hold her own,
And still remain the mistress of the seas !

Here endeth Book the Sixth of this my Poem.
The fervid sun sinks slowly, proudly, down
From the clear face of the resplendent sky,
Burying himself behind a bank of clouds,
Gloomy and dense, impervious to his rays,
Save that his ardent glory gilds the edge
Of the long mountain range of clouds which stand
Before him in their rugged majesty,
With an insufferable line of fire,
Appearing like a dazzling flash of lightning,
Arrested in the moment of its course ;
But fading, as all bright things fade, away.

BOOK VII.

BOOK VII.

RAPIDLY roll the irrevocable years !
Men cannot half keep pace with galloping Time.
History pours forth her never-ending story
Faster than mortal man can take it in—
The web so infinite, and the threads so mixed !
This year is waning, and the days grow short,
And I must bring my poem to an end ;
Say what I have to say, and then retire.
It has extended far beyond my prospect,
And I must set a limit to my fancies.
I am resolved to end it with the year,
And bring into a final farewell book
The scattered utterances I fain would speak.
A happy brevity is sometimes telling.
  I have a passionate love of poetry ;
Yet have I read but little for long years,
Fearing that, like a fond canary bird,
My muse should catch another songster's note.
Poetry furnishes men with useful texts,
And prose expands them into handsome sermons.
The poet's brain is a condensing engine,
Turning out texts for other men to preach from.
The orator's brain is more of a spinning jenny ;
He makes the most of what he has to say ;

A pound of wool will make a mile of yarn.
A poet puts the world into a nutshell ;
The orator, out of a nutshell, brings a world ;
But modern poets toil at disadvantage.
Our predecessors harvested the swath,
And left us nothing but the scanty gleaning ;
But Nature happily is inexhaustible,
And yields an after-growth to those who seek.
    The poet's lot is eminently happy.
He dwells within an Eden of his own,
Of glades, and mossy rocks, and flowing streams,
Midst flowers of richest hues and sweetest fragrance,
Trees laden with all kinds of golden fruits,
Fair to the eye and tempting to the palate.
His ears are soothed by songs of joyous birds,
The lullaby of brooks and fluttering leaves.
His mind, which knows no yoke, no galling chain,
Soars free above all worlds, all fears, all shadows.
The Will-o'-the-Wisp of his imagination
Goes dancing o'er the dewy meads of fancy ;
Who does not envy him his glorious raptures !
He dwells secluded from the busy world ;
And probably the world knows nothing of him.
I would much rather be a true-born poet
Than I would be a royally-born prince ;
Princes are plentiful compared to poets ;
While they are living they are far too public,
And stand too much exposed to common talk ;
And when they die they quickly are forgotten,
Leaving no works to be remembered by.

The poet has the empire of all time !
But least of all things would I be a poet
If I were forced to earn my bread by it,
And be compelled to live by writing verse,
Spinning my very brains for daily bread.
A man may live on air as soon as poetry,
Unless he happens to possess a name.
Poetry is a thing about as saleable
As warming-pans in Abyssinia.
Thin meagre diet is the poet's food.
I should have died, and turned to dust and ashes,
Long years ago if I had lived on poetry.
I have been one of the fraternity
Some five-and-forty precious years at least,
And written epic, elegy, and ode,
At a considerable cost of time,
And the expenditure of reams of paper,
But never earned five shillings by my poems.
No, not a crown in money or in bays,
Only one half-a-crown my sister Ann
Once gave me, for some verses writ to order,
In the scant-pocket-money-days of boyhood.
She was the only patron I have had.
Beautiful, fair, and fiery was she ;
But her I lost, and lost nigh all in her.
So much for money profit ; as for bays,
All I possess are growing in my garden.
With that most potent talisman of gold
I bought my house, my garden, and my bay-tree.
    Always throughout my life it has been my maxim

To try to do whatever I have to do
In the best way in which it can be done.
When I brewed beer I strove to brew the best
In all the thirsty town of Colchester,
Which is the dryest corner of old England;
It was my honest pride to excel all others;
And so, likewise, in writing poetry,
I aimed to write on steadfast principles,
And so produce quite a "superior article,"
Such as might merit to live after me,
Regardless of expense of time, or trouble,
And without hope of any money profit.
The worthy business folks of Colchester,
Intent upon the two great aims of life—
The men for gain, the women for sweet dresses—
Know just about as much of poetry
As I of Sanscrit or of Arabic;
And have more taste for fine fat beef and mutton,
Than for the whole of the fine arts together.
Unless my beer had been far more appreciated
By a "discerning public" than my poems,
I had been laid long since in my cold grave.
    Blessed with a very hopeful disposition,
I sometimes ponder on my poem's fate,
Whether it will be read and be admired
Wherever England's language has been pushed;
Or whether from the press it will drop still-born,
And serve to line the trunks of servant maids—
Whether it will enrapture the whole nation,
Or go to the grocer's to enwrap his butter.

Since I became a man, a thousand poems,
With far more learned lading than my own,
Have floated out of dock, and put to sea,
And never have been heard of afterwards;
A very melancholy fact to think of;
How can I hope that my poor bark will live?
Perhaps its lightness will ensure its safety.
I have perused, for five-and-thirty years,
That standard journal, called the *Athenæum*,
And seen the launch of many ponderous poems,
Laden with learning to the water's edge,
And full of mystical philosophy:
Some have been rather sharply criticised—
Because that journal loves to wield the scalpel,
(It snubbed me in my outset for ambition);
And some of them have been immensely praised,
As having the clear veritable ring,
The passion and the power of genius,
And yet a man may count upon his fingers
The few stray poems that have shot the rapids,
Borne the rude blasts of all the magazines,
Escaped the rocks and shoals where hundreds perish,
And reached the bourne of popularity.
How then can I expect that my poor bark
Should be more fortunate than all these wrecks?
Hope, the last comforter of drowning men,
Sustains and cheers me in my venturous course.
  This blessed year of Eighteen sixty-eight
Will be made memorable by strange events;
Not only by the agitations of men's minds,

X

But by the feverish agonies of Nature.
Volcanoes have belched forth black clouds and flames,
Spit red-hot stones into the face of heaven,
And poured down rivers of fierce burning lava ;
While terrible earthquakes in both hemispheres
Have rudely shaken this thick-crusted globe.
How terrible, beyond imagination,
Must be the bubbling of the ground beneath us,
As if a mighty cauldron, so to speak,
Boiled violently, urged by subterraneous fires;
When a whole region, like a feather bed,
Is shaken to and fro, and up and down,
By some internal and mysterious force,
Stronger than of the Titans in old time,
And with the thunder, as of iron chariots,
Thousands on thousands, rushing into battle,
Tumbling whole cities suddenly to the ground,
And burying half their doomed inhabitants,
Amidst the horrible outcries of the living ;
Driving the ocean backward from the shore,
And then returning it in an enormous wave,
Drowning with its recoil the drunken earth,
And casting mighty ships high on the land,
And thus completing the dread devastation.
Such was the earthquake in Peru, this autumn,
Which cost the lives of forty thousand people,
And wasted a vast region of the globe—
A wonderful convulsion of earth's bowels
More terrible than any ever known,
Recorded in the chronicles of history !

Thrice happy England, to stand firm and strong,
Amidst the shakings of less favoured countries !
Blest island of the circumambient seas,
Upheld as by the hand of the Eternal,
The ark of truth, and faith, and righteousness,
Amidst the heaving billows of the world !
What ardour filled my soul in my young days
For truth, for justice, and for liberty;
And how my spirit groaned beneath oppression
When George the Fourth, that mass of vice, was King ;
And Eldon, that old ogre, crushed all hearts.
I was a humble struggler for reform ;
Wrote letters in the local newspaper
That were attributed to some great man,
And threw my heart and soul into a poem,
A book of doggrel Hudibrasic verse,
Full of the grey-haired wisdom of a boy,
On which I spent hard labour and long time,
When I might well have been a learner still ;
And when at last I had completed it,
By stealth in sweet delicious secresy,
And thought to rouse the very heart of England
In favour of reform in Parliament,
I could not find a publisher to print it,
Though I tried hard and schemed abundant schemes.
There was a knock-down blow for youthful hopes !
The blockheads little knew the gem they flouted.
Ere long King George the Fourth gave up the ghost,
William the Fourth assumed the crown of England,
And Charles the Tenth of France, ruling too tightly,

Was overthrown, and driven from his realm.
In that great crisis of our country's history
The iron Duke of Wellington stood up
Among his peers, Prime Minister of England,
And uttered his immortal fulmination,
Refusing all reform in Parliament.
Then all the floodgates of the popular wrath
Were opened wide against the Ministry.
They fell—and then Earl Grey arose to power,
In the year Eighteen hundred thirty-one,
And with his friends carried the Whig Reform Bill,
Borne onward by the nation's ardent zeal,
Spite of enormous Tory opposition,
Pushed to the very verge of civil war.
The thing was done without my thunder-bolt,
And done as well as if it had been fired:
A very mortifying fact indeed;
Nothing was left for me but to retire
Into the worm-hole out of which I came;
Yet not quite crushed.   I tried in after years
With other song to win myself a hearing,
But tried in vain, yet never lost all hope.
Thus I went plodding on in secresy
Some five-and-thirty years of dull existence;
Long weary years of darkness and of silence,
Uncheered by man's applause or woman's smiles,
Not comprehending what could be my mission,
Or what would be the upshot of my life,
Yet felt that there were precious gifts in me—
A living spring within a fountain sealed—

A wonder and a mystery to myself;
Bound to a little round of homely duties;
Living through life without a bosom friend,
Cut off from happy social intercourse,
A humble servant in my father's house,
Rocking the cradle of declining age;
But now at length the clouds are all dispersed,
For in the evening time it shall be light;
The dreary past has passed away for ever;
The sun bursts forth upon my future track,
Gladness and brightness cheer my onward course,
Domestic love crowns me with happiness,
And this outburst of song, which has been lying
Hidden within my soul so many years,
Yet never would take outward form before,
Though many times I sought to call it forth,
I now perceive to be my pleasant mission,
Destined, I trust, to work the good of men.

　I have abounding cause for thankfulness,
For very many blessings heaped upon me—
Abundant as the billows of the sea—
And not the least of these, a happy temperament,
Which neither time nor troubles could destroy;
Not only daily bread but daily breath,
Good health, no head-ache, stomach-ache, or heart-
　　ache;
A comfortable home and loving wife,
With means to live on in a homely way,
Without the losses, cares, and toils of business.

　The worn-out shoes and slippers which, for luck,

When we departed on our wedding tour
Were showered upon our carriage with rude force,
By our well-wishers, were not thrown in vain !
　'Tis said that when a man arrives at forty
He either is a fool or a physician ;
I being sixty now am something more.
A bad digestion acts upon the conscience,
And many a man believes himself a sinner,
And even thinks that other men are sinners,
When he is suffering from redundant bile.
My rules of health are few and very simple—
To drink my tea and coffee hot and sweet,
Avoid all pickles ; and take care to eat
Plenty of pastry, rather than too much meat,
And not work hard with head, or hands, or feet.
　How much I owe my father and my mother !
It brings a blessing to have praying parents.
From them I have derived a constitution
Healthy and sound in body and in mind.
They broke me in when I was but a child,
And taught me the great lesson of submission,
By the true family law, the law of love,
And fitted me to bear the yoke of life.
They daily put up prayers to God for me,
And ever set before me an example
Of truthfulness and staunch integrity,
And strove to fill my breast with true religion ;
They made me well acquainted in my childhood
With high examples of long-suffering saints,
And thus infused their spirit into me,

And fortified my soul against foul wrong—
George Fox, the boldest of the sons of men,
Enamoured only with the spirit of truth,
Whom no imprisonments or stripes could daunt,
Or cause to shirk the stern commands of duty;
Penn, the refined and courtly gentleman,
The model of a Christian and a patriot,
The founder of a justly-governed State;
And Thomas Story, strong in argument,
The Lord High Chancellor of Pennsylvania,
Whose ponderous journal is a mine of logic;
Ellwood, the friend and confidante of Milton,
Whose charming memoirs fascinate the young;
Woolman, the pure and conscientious Christian;
Chalkley, the meek adventurous traveller;
John Roberts, the hard-hitter for the truth;
And good Job Scott, a genius little known,
Whose fervid eloquence is unsurpassed.
What infinitely better pabulum
For youthful minds than heathen Greek and Latin
And knowledge unavailable in life !
　　Though I was broken in when I was young,
The yoke of life was hard as I could bear;
But now I can rejoice that I have borne it.
The secret of success in life is simple :
We are wild colts by natural temperament,
And must be broken in to go in harness ;
Without it, youngsters seldom come to good,
But kick, and plunge, and rear, or run away,
When 'tis good luck if all goes not to smash.

If I have any solid stuff in me,
I owe it to the training of my youth.
Sooner or later troubles come upon us,
Both high and low and rich and poor together ;
No rank however lofty can escape ;
But years of suffering or of sacrifice,
If patiently endured for Christ's dear sake,
Doubtless win for us our good Father's favour,
And will be recompensed a thousand fold
In that eternal life for which we long.
We are beset in life with many trials.
Some men are tried by long adversity,
And some are tried by great prosperity;
The last we often find the worst to bear.
Some enjoy happiness when they are young,
And have their troubles in declining years,
When they are weak and cannot bear the burden,
And being spoilt in youth break down in age.
Others are forced to bear the yoke in youth,
When they are strong and able to sustain it,
Proving good discipline for after life.
These have a peaceful and serene decline,
Enjoying all the golden fruits of autumn.
Thus am I happy in my latter years.
I seem to have reached at length the Promised Land
After my weary wilderness probation—
Blest with good health, with strength, and competence,
And a good home over my snow-white head,
And having a little ring-dove by my elbow
To coo to me, and keep me company,

And wean me from the noisy world outside.
   Sweet is the calm repose of matrimony.
The sailor tossed upon the restless sea,
Driven by the wind and drifted by the tide,
Seeing no land, but ever craving for it,
Lonely, and comfortless, and buffeted,
Biding all weathers on his dreary watch,
Hoping and longing for the happy day
When he shall reach the haven of his rest—
Such is the weather-beaten bachelor;
But marriage is the harbour of sweet love,
The symbol of a higher and better life,
A quiet settlement of the affections,
With nothing better in the world to care for;
The gladsome interchange of mutual love;
Not the slow wasting wish for happiness,
But its serene and undisturbed enjoyment;
The charm of fond select companionship,
Of mutual interests, objects, and engagements;
The bliss of having one's enjoyments doubled,
And life's inevitable sorrows shared;
The happy exception to the general rule,
Which sternly censures and condemns monopoly;
Its sweet monopoly is half its charm.
Bachelorship is utter selfishness.
And selfishness is sure to be revenged
With loneliness and misery and contempt.
But matrimony is self-sacrifice;
It blesseth by bestowing happiness,
And it receiveth blessing by bestowing.

There is which scattereth and yet increaseth.
It gives a sense of homeness to the feelings,
Communion instead of isolation,
And happiness instead of misery.

   Spain, the most abject of the States of Europe,
Although the richest in the gifts of Nature,
Ruined by Popery and priestly sway,
Has made September, Eighteen sixty-eight,
A glorious epoch in her history,
And driven the wretched Bourbons from her throne.
The race most loyal amongst Europeans,
Unable longer to endure the rule
Of Isabella and her bloated priests—
The iron rule of old-world bigotry
And stone-blind soul-enslaving superstition—
Has risen as one man spontaneously,
And swept the hateful dynasty away :
The bitterest satire on the craft of kings,
Written upon the silent page of history !
A Bourbon now no longer fills a throne !
France, Italy, and Spain have each cast out
These senseless monarchs, who assumed to rule
By right divine, scorning all human rights.
The last of them has met her just reward ;
A woman infamous to after ages.
Hardly a woman—something more than a woman—
Resembling strongly Mary Magdalen
Before the seven devils went out of her,
But worse, because unwilling to repent !
Well may the downfall of these stubborn despots

Act as a solemn warning to all rulers,
Teaching that governments are made for men,
Not men for governments to trample on,
And that the true foundation of a throne
Is liberty, secured by righteous laws.
  No easy thing it is to build a throne
Out of the rotten rubbish of past times;
A throne requires not only sound materials,
But length of time to gain solidity:
A government is a very ticklish thing;
Ignorant fools may sometimes throw one down,
But it requires wise men to build one up.
An edifice must have a good foundation,
Solid and broad proportioned to its greatness.
So must the fabric of a noble state,
And knowledge is the stuff to build it with;
Practical knowledge of familiar things;
Knowledge of human rights and obligations,
With kindly training in the social duties,
And culture of the spiritual life—
These form the solid basis of a people.
Ignorance is the dull dead weight of nations,
Chief source of danger, crime, and pauperism.
It is as much the duty of a State
To teach the ignorant to read the laws,
As to avenge the laws on those who break them.
Men's souls are hide-bound by their ignorance.
An Education-Law to sweep our kennels
Of youthful ignorance and profligacy,
Is just as needful as a general Poor Law.

The pauper must be taught as well as fed.
A little knowledge with a little kindness,
A little fatherly and motherly care,
Would rescue thousands from a life of crime.
The surest way to do away with vice
Is to suppress it in its early germ.
The darnel and the charlock of society
Must not grow up to blossom and to seed.
Stamp out the sparks while they are only sparks,
For any spark may burst into a flame !
   As Education is the grand concern
In the promotion of a people's greatness,
The teacher's office is a noble mission,
Requiring high and generous endowments.
He should have knowledge in all useful things,
Yet be himself a humble learner still :
He should be kind and gentle in his manners,
And yet possess inborn authority,
With ready tact to win and to control,
Ruling by the all-conquering power of love.
Mastering the spirit of his inner self,
He feels the dignity of his position,
And somewhat of its high responsibilities.
A teacher of unvarying truthfulness,
Of Christian morals in their widest scope,
He well may magnify his noble calling,
Yet feel he dare not magnify himself,
Daily relying upon help Divine.
As on the one hand he lifts up the low
To the exalted standard of a man,

So he deserves a liberal recompence,
Commensurate with the greatness of his task;
And as, upon the other hand, he stoops
In humble condescension to the weakness
Of the unlettered and the ignorant,
So he deserves a full reward of honour.
Enthusiastic in his occupation,
He looks on nothing as contemptible
That ministers to his exalted object,
And disciplines the minds of future men;
But, bearing that one object full in view,
Seeks with unflagging assiduity
To mould the minds and manners as they grow,
To cheer the timid and the indolent,
Rebuke the wayward and intractable,
Win the affections and respect of all,
And kindly help the dull of comprehension,—
Appraise the characters of every one,
With careful judgment and discrimination,
And so adapt the influence to be used
According to the nature to be governed.
  And what is chiefly needed to be taught?
To read and write and cipher readily,
And comprehend the maps of different countries.
A scholar who can read and write and cipher,
Has all the ropes of learning in his hands,
And if he loves the beautiful in language,
And learns the few chief laws of English grammar,
The haven of renown lies straight before him;
The field of letters is a level racecourse:

A pen, an ink-pot, and a ream of paper—
Thus furnished, the most potent peer of **England**,
And his own barber, stand on equal terms.
  But knowledge is a boundless continent,
A sort of universal rabbit warren,
A pleasant labyrinth of runs and burrows,
Where scholars may disport themselves for ever,
And education is an endless work ;
For, after all that other men can teach us,
If we would give a finish to our learning
We must pursue the work and teach ourselves.
I was not taught by others, but I learned.
I learned in the same school that Shakespeare
    learned—
The school of Nature and the minds of men.
Alas, how very little have I learned !
How infinitely more have I forgot !—
Perhaps it may come back to me in heaven.
We must continue learning till we die,
Just as continually as we keep forgetting ;
The commonest things are best worth learning well ;—
To discipline the eye to see and judge ;
The hand to draw the likenesses of things ;
The voice to charm the educated ear ;
The ear to test the harmonies of sound ;
The man to show the gracefulness of manners.
How odious are all sorts of affectation !
Religion, taught us in the tones of cant,
Or poetry mouthed forth in strains of rant,
Disgust the ear, and alienate the heart.

What is worth doing is worth doing well.
The human voice deserves especial culture
In talking, reading, and in recitation,
In concert to the subject of discourse,
In tones impressive, natural, and clear,
Refined by taste, exaggerating nothing.
How many people, dressed in the tip of fashion,
Deceive the eye until they ope their lips,
And so reveal their untaught origin ?
How many a lady, beautiful and blooming,
Who seems a very angel without wings,
Like a poll parrot in its gaudy plumes,
Speaks but one word, and loses all her charms
　　One of the striking features of this age
Is the great work, progressing round about us,
Of carrying into every nook and corner
The glorious tidings of mankind's Redemption—
The great revival of religious life.
The mission-ship speeds forth across the sea,
To every region underneath the sun,
With prayers and blessings filling all her sails ;
While zealous and devoted missionaries
Seek out waste places of the heathen world,
Bible in hand, and love of souls at heart,
Midst perils of the sea, and of the land,
Midst pestilence, and savage persecution,
In weariness, and painfulness and hardships,
In hunger and in thirst, in cold and heat,
And, with great self-denial, and much labour,
Learn the unlettered tongues of savage nations

To preach to them the words of truth and life,
Making the wilderness in many places
To blossom as the rose and sing for joy.
And not alone abroad, but here at home,
Amidst the courts and alleys of our cities,
Where ignorance and vice are prone to nestle,
And wretches dwell who have no faith or hope—
Outcasts who shrink from entering church or chapel—
The humble preacher tells of Jesus' love,
And strives to win the lost to truth and virtue ;
Schools are established to reclaim the children,
And lay a good foundation for the future ;
While everywhere the eager Bible-woman,
In simple confidence, and love unfeigned,
Enters the dwellings of the sick and sinful,
And reads to them the precious words of Truth,
And prays with them as simple children pray,
So that from many a low and wretched bed,
In poverty, and dirt, and desolation,
Lips that perhaps have been long years polluted,
Are joyfully enabled to breathe prayer,
And sing the wonders of redeeming love !
　Great is the work, for evil is the world.
When one looks round it makes one's heart to sink,
In contemplation of the field of labour.
The field is wide, and yellow unto harvest,
But, sad to say, the labourers are few,
Considered in proportion to the labour.
What can one person do in this great work ?
Look here ! faint-hearted one, into my hand ;

Upon its palm I hold a grain of wheat.
How insignificant it seems in size,
How inappreciable its weight appears,
How powerless for any kind of good ;
Yet of such kernels are our millions fed !
These kernels form the very staff of life.
See how I solve at once this knotty problem :
Let every one throw in his grain of help,
And then the work will easily be done,
And the great harvest of the world be reaped !
   The Tea-kettle, with its grand high-pressure power
Of irresistible yet submissive steam,
Has turned the old world wholly topsy turvy ;
And so the Tea-pot, in a gentler way,
Wields at its will the modern moral world,
Warms and inspires and fashions it anew,
And elevates it into nobler forms.
Every good cause and every generous object
Gains strength, and fervour, and determination
When it is heated over a cup of tea !
Blest leaf ! the product of the Flowery Land,
Invested with a fragrance, and a flavour,
A delicacy, a charm, an animation,
Caught from the sun and soil of far Cathay,
How are thy potent influences diffused
Through every rank of life ! whether thou art sipped
From the gold burnished porcelain of proud halls,
Or the coarse earthen cups of the thatched cottage—
Whether by jewelled duchesses and nobles,
Or the lone, weary, widowed washerwoman—

All find in thee an innocent inspiration,
Which leaves behind no baneful Nemesis.
Thou art the small, cheap, luxury of millions !
Life is made up of trifles multiplied,
Moments compose the tissue of our years,
Small grains of wheat form the chief food of nations,
And tiny leaves, from the Celestial Empire,
Gladden the hearts of world-wide Christendom,
And help to civilise the human race.
Let us do honour to the immortal Teapot,
The true palladium of our happy country !
Talk of the Lion and the Unicorn—
They are the emblems only of the past;
The Tea-kettle and the Tea-pot are become
The symbols of our national strength and virtue !
    Civilisation has but one true basis,
And that is Bible Christianity.
The Bible is the first and best of books,
Fitted for every scale of intellect,
Suited for every mood and state of mind,
Full of the loftiest wisdom and instruction,
And overflowing with faith, hope, and charity,
And truth, and light, and life, and love divine.
Some men affect to disbelieve the Bible,
And try to shake its authenticity,
Seek to pick holes in the rock-wall of truth,
And thereby damage their own reputations.
Some men err strangely on the other hand,
And absolutely deify the Bible,
Styling it blasphemously the Word of God ;

When the same Bible tells us that the Word
Was in the beginning ere the world was made;
It was with God, in truth the Word was God;
It was, we read, the Word that made the world;
Hence that which made the world was not the Bible.
How strange that Doctors of Divinity,
Men who are taught at Oxford or at Cambridge,
Should say the Bible is the Word of God!
And yet these men presume to set us right,
With much display of learning and conceit,
On subjects which were meant to be obscure,
And mislead people in the plainest matters.
Scholars split hairs and find out clear distinctions
Where common people see no difference;
Or, if the difference be discoverable,
The importance of the difference is all moon-shine.
The world, our rolling ship, some people think,
Will hold together but a little longer:
So much the greater reason to stand ready,
And on the watch, for what may quickly come.
Men bind themselves to systems and to creeds,
As mariners bind themselves to masts and spars,
To carry them in safety to the shore.
There is safe standing-room for every one,
A solid rock never to be o'erthrown;
The rock of Truth, firm-fixed as adamant,
Amidst the heavings of the earth and sea,
Even when all doors are thrown from off their hinges,
And every builded wall shall quake and fall.
  The great and all-important Bible truths

Are plain enough to childlike comprehensions ;
It is the spirit of critical research,
And the vain love of building theories,
That lead men into dreary scepticism;
And even sin, the Unpardonable Sin.
How dare men sin against the Holy Ghost !
For this is the unpardonable sin.
Good men with over-conscientious minds
Are apt to fear that they have sinned this sin.
Oxford and Cambridge and the learned doctors
Cannot relieve them from the dread idea.
All men have sinned ; they know that **they have**
     sinned :
Yet, knowing not the nature of this sin
Of blasphemy against the Holy Ghost,
They, trembling, fear they have committed it.
What then is this unpardonable sin—
This blasphemy which shall not be forgiven ?
It is, to attribute to the power of Satan
The miracles wrought by the power of the Holy Ghost.
    The mind of man oft, like the eagle, soars
Into the dazzling precincts of the sun,
The very presence of the source of light,
And then sinks down to earth to prey on carrion,
And swallow the flinty stones of unbelief.
Some men of narrow and dogmatic minds
Content themselves with a convenient creed,
Which helps them over every difficulty,
Without more trouble than to jump a kennel.
Their creed consists in total·unbelief

Of everything they cannot understand—
These people, having slender understandings,
Are thus relieved from understanding much.
All that is contrary to human reason,
Is contrary to their dogmatic creed,
And therefore quietly is disbelieved ;
An easy way of jumping over difficulties.
This creed of theirs is like a child's toy-waggon,
Which breaks down twenty times or more a day,
The crazy wheels for ever coming off,
And yet they serve their purpose just as well,
And please the child as though they were all right.
These people cannot tell the why and wherefore
Of scores of things, and yet believe them fully—
How the will acts upon their hourly movements ;
How the eye mirrors objects at a distance ;
How the nerves take the picture to the brain ;
How the brain prints the picture on the mind ;
How the mind stores away its varied knowledge ;
How the earth brings forth different coloured flowers;
How different kinds of fruits have different flavours ;
How men of reason, reason without reason.

    Here is a reasoner of this knowing class,
And I will put a few plain questions to him.
Thou hast a watch-chain, hast thou got a watch ?
Sometimes there is no watch when there's a chain ;
Appearances are oftentimes deceptive ;
Does this agree with thy experience ?
Thou hast a watch : well, and who made thy watch ?—
Thou mayest have heard that it was made in London,

But dost thou know the man that made thy watch?—
Art thou quite sure that it was made by man?
Perhaps it was not made by man at all;
Perhaps it came spontaneously by nature;
In other words by Natural Selection.
Is it not safe and reasonable to conclude
It came into existence of itself?
Thou own'st with all thy skill thou didst not make it.
Knowest thou a man who ever made a watch?
Thou dost not know a man able to make it.
Canst thou believe that it was made by man?
Does not experience go against this notion?
Thou see'st 'tis made, but dost not know the maker;
But how canst thou believe in its existence,
And comprehendest not its origin?
It ticks, the hands move round as if alive,
Is it alive, and has it got a soul?
Can it not reason quite as well as thou canst?
Wherein consists the difference between
Life within man and life within a watch?
Is not a watch alive, or what is life?
Canst thou explain? Dost thou believe in life?
Hast thou a soul more than a ticking watch?
Hence, fool! would'st thou be wise, go, watch thyself!
    To human reason life is an enigma.
We see but dimly what is best for us.
To our short-sighted vision it would seem
That life is governed by the rule of contrary;
The physical clock of the world goes right enough;
The moral clock seems oftentimes bewitched;

Yet he who framed the one arranged the other.
. But what strange contradictions do we see !
Beauty and youth struck prematurely down,
While tottering age keeps on its aching pace ;
Manhood restrained by irksome poverty,
And womanhood condemned to loneliness,
While age lacks strength to profit by its riches.
Vice, in august attire, rides in a coach,
While virtue, thinly clad, trudges on foot.
The race we often see is not to the swift,
Nor is the battle always to the strong.
A melancholy thing it is to mark
That wealth and wisdom often come too late—
Wealth when the power to use its treasures ceases,
And wisdom when the trembling utterance fails.
And why is this?   How solve we the enigma?
Nothing in life is taxed so high as faith,
But nothing pays so large an interest !
Doubtless our life is the great school of faith ;
And without faith we cannot please our Maker.
Can these things be, and we believe them right?
This is the lesson that we have to learn.
Yes, if we be not faithless, but believing,
We thus shall learn to trust in Providence,
And so become the graduates of heaven.
There is another life beyond our life,
Where we shall know the mysteries of our being :
Shall stand behind the marvellous clock of life,
And comprehend its complex mechanism.

The Frost-king has come slyly in the night,

From his Ice Palace in the mystic North,
To play his pretty gambols in the South,
And with his shivery sceptre crisped the fields.
Autumn, responsive to his brisk salute,
Has donned the gayest mantle in her wardrobe ;
The forest oaks, and elms, and graceful beeches,
Mingled with evergreens of various shades,
Are glorious in the richness of their tints.
The sun, well pleased to view the phantasy,
Smiles on the landscape with a balmy softness.
All nature looks as in a fairy dream.
The beauteous world would almost seem like heaven.
O world, world, world ! Bright world, beautiful world !
How loath we are to leave thee, loveable world,
And all the favourite scenes we know so well !
Trees which we planted, paths we daily trod,
The shady lane, the moss-encrusted gate,
The brook, the cowslip mead, the golden woods ;
Bright world, beautiful world, loveable world,
How the heart cleaves to thee even to the last,
Too often with increased intensity !
We need the aches of age to wean us hence,
Loosen our hold of this endeared existence,
Teach us that earth is not our final rest,
And lead us to aspire to heavenly joys,
Glory that never fades, and life eternal.
    Mysterious are the links of our attachment
That bind us sweetly to our native scenes.
Our birthplace is inextricably associated
With all our early vivid memories.

The parlour, where I sported with my toys;
The shop—for I was born behind the counter—
Which had a drawer where Shrewsbury cakes were
    kept;
The bed-room, where I slept so peacefully,
And dreamed the calm and innocent dreams of child-
    hood;
The garden, where I ran delightful races
With my poor long-lost brother and sweet sisters,
And watched from day to day the growth of flowers,
And feasted on the gooseberries and apples—
These fruits have now no more their ancient relish—
The green, where threatening geese alarmed my boy-
    hood,
The nibbled meadows and the whispering brook;
The ever-flowing spout of limpid water,
Where idle children loved to splash themselves;
The grand old church-tower just across the road,
Whose peal of bells enthralled my childish ears;
And the old church itself, beneath whose roof
Repose the harmless broken effigies
Of two of England's proudest ancient earls;
The small yet thickly-populated churchyard,
Adorned and scented by umbrageous limes,
Where bees, attracted by the blossoming boughs,
Kept up a soothing murmur in the air,
Sucking rich honey for their winter store—
How do I dote on these sweet scenes of childhood!
And when I take my way to London town,
Along the iron road that cuts in twain

My native hamlet—dear secluded Boreham—
And catch a glimpse of the old church-tower's summit,
It seems to take me back to those old times.

Old Guy Fawkes' Day once more comes round again,
The fifth day of November. Remember! Remember!
The boys of England, always on the alert
For bonfires, mischief, fun, and fizzing fireworks,
Are sure to jog our slumbering memories,
And warn all England of her dreadful danger,
When bloody Papists craftily conspired
With gunpowder to "blow her quite away."
Who can restrain a smile to see the Guys
Besiege our doors on this notorious morning,
Surrounded by a group of noisy boys,
Shouting their well-known doggrel in our ears !—
Some dressed, and stuffed, and masked like harlequins,
With hedge-stakes, lanterns, and such accessories,
Outrageous in their gross absurdities ;—
Some merely effigies of straw and rags ;
Others alive, and perched on patient donkeys ;
While others, humbler still, proceed on foot.
When I was young one Guy sufficed the parish.
The cunning leaders pocketed the doles,
Enjoying thus a snug monopoly.
But in these modern times of competition,
Freedom of trade, and social independence,
A dozen different aspirants of fortune,
With a few humble followers of their own,
Start each their Guy upon their own account,
Anxious to do some business for themselves,

Collecting half-pence in obsequious wise,
To purchase fireworks for the evening fun ;
When a huge bonfire, formed, alas, too often
Of stolen sticks, and straw, and broken palings,
Completes the obstreperous frolic of the day ;
Round it the urchins crowd, armed with their hedge-
        stakes,
And beat and stir the fire to make it blaze ;
While the red glow upon their forms and faces,
And their wild antics moving to and fro,
Give them the look of demons upon earth.
  After the mummery of Guy Fawkes' Day
The British nation buckles on its armour
Sternly, yet cheerfully, for earnest deeds.
Parliament is dissolved by Queen Victoria.
The last of Whig-Reform-Bill Parliaments
Has done its work, and is worn out and dead.
The first of Household-Suffrage Parliaments
Is summoned by the Queen's supreme command,
And the whole nation ardently responds.
From east, from west, from north, from south, the cry
Of stubborn battle rings in England's ears.
The Tory leader is the strange Disraeli—
A Liberal once, but now a renegade—
Allured by hopes of power and worldly glory :
Disliked, despised, distrusted by his followers,
But yet impossible to be dispensed with,
He bows his head—the bending reed of party.
The leader of the Liberal host is Gladstone,
A Tory both by birth and education ;

But moulded by his judgment and experience,
And the ambition to bring peace and plenty,
He stands the champion of the Liberal ranks.
That man is good for naught who grows no wiser,
Who never advances with advancing knowledge,
And never changes his old-world opinions,
Bound hand and foot to his original go-cart.
When a man turns from good to bad, 'tis odious,
But he who turns from bad to good is noble.
The name of Gladstone is a tower of strength,
The ringing watchword of expectant England.
Honest, unbending, zealous for the right,
For justice, for retrenchment and reform ;
Truthful, straightforward, masterful, far-seeing,
A scholar with all knowledge in his grasp,
And gifted with the lips of eloquence,
Persuasive beyond those of other men—
Such is the victor in the coming fight.

    And now the candidates for Parliament,
On either side in party politics,
Rush into print, divulgent of their creeds,
Seeking to win the electors' suffrages.
A rallying cry is almost half the battle !
Newspaper scribes by thousands upon thousands
Bend low their brows over vast fields of paper,
Penning with force their pungent editories.
The *Times*, the soaring eagle of the press,
Which always scents the field of coming battle,
And takes with prescient eye the winning side,
Screams out the keynote of the wordy war.

The *Daily News*, like a sagacious hound,
Noses the track, and fiercely follows suit
With patient earnestness of argument.
The *Daily Telegraph*, with ready wit,
Darts like a swallow o'er the field of strife,
With playful wing making a sport of work—
The *Morning Star*, like the new risen lark,
Utters its piercing notes in the keen air.
The *Standard*, like the African hyena,
Both laughs and howls in savage waywardness.
The *Herald*, like the wild boar of the wilderness,
Foams in its coverts dark and paws the ground.
Hundreds of chirping sparrows of the press
Keep up a deafening clatter of their own.
A strange unusual ferment stirs the country;
The mail-bags swell with tons of politics;
The very trains drag heavy with their weight;
Committees muster in snug private rooms
To scrutinise the lists of the electors,
And hosts of canvassers o'erspread the land
To win the suffrages of doubtful people.
   And now immense assemblages collect
In halls, in theatres, or open air
To listen to their favourite candidates;
While local orators give tongue and wind
To their pent-up vociferous eloquence,
Stirring the passions of their auditors,
With fervid utterances of party opinion,
And clamorous cock-crows ring from hill to hill:
A mighty earnestness pervades the land.

Each party is most sanguine of success,
And boldly prophecies its coming triumph.
　　After long agony of expectation,
And din of popular strife on either side,
The eventful time arrives for the elections.
First march the cities and the borough towns
In the fore-front of the contending armies.
London begins the game—Guildhall grows warm ;
Our friends make head against the artful foe,
But Rothschild falls beneath a Tory spear.
O wayward fortune of uncertain battle,
To see a Rothschild fall by the hand of Twells !
Old Westminster comes boldly to the front,
But our great Stuart Mill is overthrown !
The ancient crypts re-echo at his fall,
And the great heart of England heaves a sigh.
Lambeth sends forth her true and valiant knights ;
The foremost is the proud Lord Mayor of London :
Two knights in arms rush forth from London Tower;
Two more advance from sturdy Marylebone ;
Old Southwark also sends her champions forth,
By Layard led, the chief of Nineveh—
Henceforth the human-headed bull of Southwark.
Young Chelsea gives good proof of stalwart strength ;
Young Greenwich, with a keen shrewd eye to glory,
Resolves to make an excellent beginning,
And sends the best of knights to fight her cause.
Fair Finsbury fulfils her promises,
And furnishes her heroes for the fight.
Young Hackney thinks it scorn to fall behind ;

Sweet Edinboro' town upholds her glory,
Puts forth her sinewy strength and proudly wins;
Glasgow is bonny in the good old cause,
And lovely Dublin rings with victory.
Bold Birmingham maintains her high renown:
John Bright, the tribune of the British people,
Stands like a rock amidst a sea of waves,
That break upon him harmlessly in foam.
Manchester trembles in the shock of war,
And Ernest Jones, her third great champion,
Yields to the foe and tumbles in mid fight;
But Liverpool wakes up and plays her part,
And wins a Rathbone for her pride of place.
York stands stock still, having a wooden leg,
And cannot scale the wall to meet the foe;
Bristol maintains her rank and wonted honour,
And sends two champions forth to bear her name;
Beautiful Bath follows her bright example;
Chester, and Worcester, and old Nottingham,
Blunder, and lose each one a gallant knight.
At Nottingham the gallant Osborne fell,
And fell, like Holofernes in old time,
By the fair hand of an enslaving woman—
The treacherous hand he had so gaily kissed.
Darlington my Darling wins a Backhouse;
Young Exeter excels old Exeter,
And hurls the Attorney-General from his seat;
Hereford answers blithely to the challenge,
And sends the Solicitor-General to the dogs.
On Ashton field we lose a gallant knight

In Milner Gibson, who had done good service;
Who stood by Cobden in the Corn-law struggle,
And untaxed knowledge through the penny press.
Sharp Sheffield whets her sword and rights herself,
And sends the recreant Roebuck to his doom;
Bradford is true to Liberal principles,
But turns her back upon the eminent man
Who would have added honour to her name—
Miall, who through long years of earnest toil
Has sought to free religion from State thraldom:
Bradford, like many a spoilt and foolish beauty,
Goes through the market and picks up a sheep's-head!
Durham does noble service in our cause;
Bedford wins double honours in the field,
Having the best of implements to fight with;
Plymouth maintains her honourable rank,
And need not be ashamed to see her face
Reflected in her lovely looking-glass;
Devonport does great deeds for truth and right,
And rolls the bellowing Ferrand in the dust;
Brighton sustains her name and fair renown;
Hastings beats off the Tories from her soil,
As her proud rocks beat back the surging sea;
Names will not do alone to conjure by;
With her, a man is better than a name.
Hull, with her hearts of oak, maintains the right;
Ipswich fails not for lack of enterprise,
And drives her ploughshare o'er Corruption's grave:
Leeds lets a foe creep slyly into camp;
Gloucester steps proudly out into the field,

And her good champions win the spoils of war.
Stout was the fight at noble Macclesfield,
But Macclesfield is not the town to yield.
Leicester is staunch and true, and toes the front ;
Maidstone, amidst the smiling fields of Kent,
Sets down her foot resolved to do or die ;
Lincoln's great heart is sound as her great bell ;
Old Newcastle-on-Tyne is built of bricks,
And will not yield to fawning flatteries ;
Reading maintains the credit of her biscuits ;
Northampton gallops forward gallantly,
With Gilpin at her head to win the race ;
Oldham is equal to her honest self ;
Rochdale, the famous birthplace of John Bright,
Nobly co-operates for the general good ;
Old Norwich waddles slowly to the field,
Like a lame duck across her market square ;
Poor Yarmouth, who had held her head so high,
Having lost caste and honourable name,
Sits with her face buried between her hands
By the sea-beaten shore, shedding salt tears
Of vain repentance at her hopeless ruin—
Slighted, despised, forgotten, and unnamed,
She has no invitation to the ball.
Blackburn and Bolton, Preston, Salford, Coventry—
All these turn recreant in the shock of war ;
Bridgwater boldly takes the field and wins ;
Sandwich will not be worsted in the fight ;
Carlisle does all that Englishmen can do ;
Oxford, though old and crusty to the eye,

z

Is full of young and warm and generous blood;
Cambridge shoots forward in a line with Oxford—
Cambridge will never be content to follow;
Old Peterborough stands like her cathedral
Upright and strong, and with unbending back;
Wigan gives proof enough of stubborn stuff;
Tamworth sustains the potent name of Peel;
Derby is faithful to the People's cause,
Her hardy ranks move forward as one man;
Newark is staunch as the original ark;
Old Rochester stands firm as her old castle;
The men of Grantham are the men to win;
Stoke-upon-Trent is stout upon the foe;
Beautiful Salisbury sets a proud example,
Upright and lofty as her famous spire;
Windsor flaunts high in the air the Liberal flag;
Stroud battles nobly for the nation's cause,
And Horsman flies the field before the fight;
The men of Halifax can wield the axe;
The town of Sunderland sees through the smoke,
And charges manfully the trembling foe;
Tiverton mourns the gay Lord Palmerston,
But arms two stauncher heroes for the battle;
Scarborough is as steadfast as her rocks;
While Wolverhampton arms her trusty champion,
Great Villiers, bravest of the moral brave,
Who, long before the Free-Trade League was formed,
Bearded the haughty Landlords' Parliament,
Denounced their Corn-laws and stood firm for truth.
    And how did Colchester perform her part?

Firmly and gallantly and honourably;
She organised her ranks by daily drill;
Put forth her strength upon pure water principles;
Baked four-and-twenty blackbirds in a pie,
And fell upon the foe with stunning force.
In vain St. Peter's vicar—parson Caddell—
Pounded his pulpit and poured forth his twaddle;
The pulpit is no place for politics.
Our champions were the knight of Wyvenhoe Park,
And a State doctor down from London town.
The foe was led by two vain mountebanks,
The one a soldier—that was enough for him,—
The other a lawyer—that was enough for him,—
The brother of the Tory Attorney-General,
Who just before was slain at Exeter:
These flaunting champions both were fairly worsted,
And will be hard to find another day.
Colchester gave them native oyster shells.
The Tory ranks were terribly chagrined,
And skulked for very shame to the back streets.
The Liberals knew no bounds to their rejoicing,
And grasped each other's hands in ecstacy;
Down-trodden long, they now held up their heads,
And breathed the invigorating air of freedom.
The " Old Blue Pig " is now the " Yellow Cock."

And now the heavy Counties marched to battle,
The gallant mounted yeomanry of England,
In all the pomp and chivalry of war;
And many of our gallant gentlemen
Were felled disastrously upon the field.

The enemy brought forth their new 12-pounders,
And most ingenious engineries of combat,
Such as base men are fain to fight withal ;
These were breech-loading pulpit blunderbusses,
Which did tremendous mischief to our ranks—
Crushing-machines devised by landlord skill,
The fire and faggot of intimidation,
The quart-pot of intemperate cajolery,
Thumbscrews to terrify the little tradesmen,
And bribery to win the waverers ;
But, nevertheless, our troops fought valiantly.
South Essex won her spurs without a scratch ;
East Surrey rolled the Tories in the dust ;
The men of Cornwall won immortal laurels,
And East and West carried the day with ease ;
East Staffordshire achieved a victory ;
West Gloucestershire rode headlong on the foe ;
South Durham made a glorious rush at last,
And swept the foe in terror from the field ;
East Derbyshire covered herself with glory ;
Yorkshire maintained the honour of her name,
And added to her laurels in the fight.
Elsewhere defeat or partial victory
Marked the grand contests of the English Counties,
Which need the weapons of a new Reform Bill.
Buckinghamshire, as erst, stood by Disraeli,
The many-gifted Tory Champion,
And faithfully sustained him in the saddle.
The mess in Middlesex was enough to vex
  The patience of the meekest Liberal chief ;

Cumberland lost her venerable Marshall :
But Lancashire the worst betrayed her trust.
Frailty, thy present name is Lancashire !
Who could believe that Lancashire, which fought
Erewhile the glorious battle of Free Trade,
Puffed up with pride of wealth and vain gentility,
And led by the nose by mischievous church bigots,
Should give occasion to most keen reproach ?
North Lancashire rushed firmly to the contest ;
Knowsley and Chatsworth put forth all their strength ;
Stanley and Cavendish led their rival legions :
Sore was the fight and fatal was the day.
Lord Hartington was fain to kiss the dust :
But South East Lancashire beheld the worst,
The basest and the direst overthrow,
For there the Liberal chief, immortal Gladstone,
In his own native county was defeated.
Such honour doth a prophet find at home !
" Too venturous chief ! ah, whither didst thou run,"
Seeking to win, against tremendous odds,
With chivalry that reached to the sublime !
Gladstone was crushed by his own countrymen,
And would have fallen headlong to the ground,
Had not Minerva, in the shape of Greenwich,
Caught in her friendly arms the Liberal chieftain.
    Meanwhile, all Scotland brought her powers to
        bear
In the great contest for the truth and right,
And mowed the Tories down rank after rank ;
E'en Keir of Keir himself was doomed to yield.

Ireland excelled herself in the great cause,
And dealt hard blows to Tory bigotry
With the shillelah of well-seasoned zeal ;
Ulster and Munster, Leinster and Connaught, each
Resolved to crush the galling usurpation
Of a tyrannical and alien Church,
Which long had gored the sides of Ireland,
And kept alive the bitterness of creeds.

And Wales was not behind-hand in the fight,
But bravely played her honourable part,
Contributing her not ignoble share
In the one nation's glorious victory.
Carnarvonshire and proud Carmarthenshire
Rivalled each other in the righteous contest,
Carnarvonshire will ever be Carnarvonshire—
Carmarthenshire will never be outdone.
Old Merthyr more than most did nobly well,
And sent her Richard forth as champion,
A man of peace, a champion still for good,
A man to stand before the face of kings.
" Peace hath her victories," as Milton says,
" Not less renowned than war." Yes, better and nobler !
War's victories are victories of evil :
The victories of peace are sung in heaven !

The battle being won, the victors stood
Stunned and bewildered with their own success,
Or silent with a sudden throb of joy.
The vanquished groaned and sullenly submitted ;
All waiting stood to see what next would happen :
It came, and came before it was expected.

The Tory chieftain saw the field was lost,
And bowed his head before impending fate.'
Feeling that flight were better than surrender,
Under the cover of mysterious darkness
The beaten Tory government retired !
   Like as a noble ship with all sails set,
Stun-sails, top-gallant-sails, sky-scrapers, flying-jib,
Suddenly strikes upon a sunken rock,
Heels over, and goes down without a warning,
With captain and with every soul on board—
So did Disraeli's government go down !
   Gladstone, the Liberal chief, summoned by the
        Queen,
Now took the abandoned helm of government,
Who, gathering round him his devoted friends,—
Foremost of whom stood forth the great John Bright—
Formed in short space of time a Liberal cabinet ;
A glorious triumph for the just and true,
A glorious triumph for the sect of Friends ;
For when John Bright, in virtue of his office,
Became, beyond all mean dispute "right honourable,"
And kissed our gracious Queen's extended hand,
He did not take the common oath of office,
But took instead his honest affirmation.
This was the triumph of a principle !
How many of his suffering predecessors,
The members of his persecuted sect,
In ancient times were thrust into foul dungeons,
Rather than take a Heaven-forbidden oath,
And sealed their sturdy testimony by death ;

And now a member of this very sect
Becomes an honoured Minister of the Crown ;
Excused the oath, he takes his affirmation.
This is indeed the triumph of a principle—
A victory worth waiting long to witness !
   Great is the work before our Government
To clean the reeking stable of the State ;
The labour of a modern Hercules.
Reform is needed upon every side :
Land-law and Poor-law, Bankrupt-law and **Church-law.**
We need a change of legal principles ;
A change of customs and of usages ;
A change in our overts with other nations ;
A change from secret war to open peace ;
A change, in short, from barbarous old-worldism
To government on Christian principles.
And, not the least of all, our Courts of Law
Require a wise and sound re-modelment ;
They savour of the dreary olden times,
When racks and thumbscrews were familiar things.
Ostensibly they stand to give us justice ;
But torture is the element they deal in.
Their mode of work is lordly, like the eagle's,
They pounce down suddenly upon their victim,
And with remorseless bills tear out his eyes ;
With talons strong as iron callipers,
Rend off the flesh from his poor worthless bones,
Leaving alone a whitened skeleton,
A moral warning to the thoughtless world
Who hope for justice from the beaks of Law !

My song is nearly ended, like the year :
Begun in loneliness and desolation,
As a resource from gnawing misery,
And ending now in tranquil happiness,
Domestic quietude, and heartfelt joy.
Within the temple of the human heart
There is a sacred secret inner court,
A cabinet of curious workmanship,
Full of old shelves, and drawers, and pigeon-holes,
In which the soul stores up its joys and sorrows,
Its dearest hopes, its projects, and ambitions.
'Tis well to keep them under lock and key.
And yet sometimes it is a sweet relief,
When we foregather with a kindred soul,
Knit to ourselves by secret sympathies,
To turn the key and half reveal our treasures.
As we grow old we grow less chary of them.
The hold they had of us is gently loosened,
As we draw nearer to a better world.
I have my memories, which are agonies;
Yet many secrets, which were sacred once,
I now care very little to preserve.
Few men remain whose praise or blame I heed :
And so I write about myself with freedom.
My friends and neighbours may throw scorn upon me,
And say that I am too communicative ;
But, if my poem should live after me,
Those who survive me will not blame me for it.
What will my readers care for me and mine
Unless I take them to my confidence ?

There is a wondrous charm in mystery ;
We love to pry into the unknown future,
As well as puggle in the grimey past.
Who was the author of the Letters of Junius ?
Who was the man that wore the Iron Mask ?
The teeming novels which pour forth each month
Owe nearly all their charm to mystery.
The mystery solved, the interest ceases quickly ;
The book is closed and never opened again.
Shakespeare, although transcendant in his genius,
Owes half his interest to the mystery
Spread o'er his life and every page he wrote.
The medicine men of the Red Indian tribes
Derive their power from being mystery men.
Like them, we make a craft of our Professions—
Clothe science in a Latin nomenclature
And old-world unintelligible gibberish,
As if our beautiful elastic English
Were not adapted to all sorts of science.
The selfishness, perhaps, of men of learning,
May make them wish to cast a hedge around
The little rotten boroughs of their knowledge.
How robberies and murders hold us breathless,
With an intense absorbing interest,
Until the hidden mystery is solved.
Soon as the villainous perpetrators are hanged,
We care no more about them, and forget them.
Awhile ago a wedding guest was missing;
The gentleman was lost from London streets.
He was a simple country clergyman,

Known to his friends, and his parishioners,
But quite unheard of by the outer world,
And, therefore, just as little cared about.
A man of no more note or consequence
Than any other village clergyman,
Being, it should be said, a bachelor;
And yet because this gentleman was missing,
He grew at once into celebrity;
All England set to work to solve the mystery,
They put suspicion on the faintest scent,
Trying to hunt him, like a pack of hounds.
All sorts of theories were contrived about him,
And some of them by no means to his credit.
Letters were written to the daily papers—
Each editor wrote his clever editory—
If all the printed matter issued about him
Were gathered from the papers into a heap,
No doubt 'twould be as large as any haystack.
After some weeks the missing man was found
Roaming about mysteriously in Cornwall,
But could afford no satisfactory reason
For suddenly becoming "a lost man;"
And curiosity, by being satisfied,
Revenged herself by soon forgetting him.

But I have told a plain unvarnished story;
My moods may change, but I am still the same.
I deal in truths of everlasting interest,
And principles that time can never stale.
The truth, though old, is also ever new;
It is a well of ever-flowing springs;

The well is old, the water ever new.
The critics, like a flock of hungry vultures,
May fall upon my poem with their beaks
And rend it limb from limb unmercifully,
Gloating on all its faults and peccant humours,
And may be justified in what they do.
In every ear of wheat there must be chaff;
Some things I may have said to pique these critics:
I have fair confidence in my performance,
But small reliance on the world's good judgment;
I deem but slightingly of modern taste.
Yet am I willing frankly to confess
The mind of man is weak and fallible,
And oft mistaken in its estimates;
We cannot see so clearly in ourselves
What we can easily perceive in others;
And even Judges differ in their judgments;
Their wigs may be alike but not their brains.
I have depicted with a pen and ink
A likeness of the age in which I live—
Too bold a likeness for these mincing times—
And also sketched some likenesses of people,
And in so doing have portrayed myself.
I care not for punctilious correctness,
So that I gain in vigour and in spirit.
How wearisome is faultless namby pamby!
I write to please myself, not other people,
And am content to satisfy myself;
I never was the man to square my notions,
By other people's notions of the proper;

I choose to think and write in my own way,
And would be followed rather than be a follower.
I have not written for the great and learned,
Nor do I wish my poem to be petted,
Handsomely bound in gold and red morocco,
By ladies kind in scented drawing-rooms :
Nor illustrated in a sumptuous manner
By showy prints ungermane to the text,
The figures borrowed from the theatre :
I wish my poem to be read and prized
By common unsophisticated people,
And find a home on every cottage shelf.
A book which any man may sit and read
In his arm-chair, and, when he lays it down,
Rise up a cheerfuller and better man.
I do not write a book of idle fiction,
About imaginary knights and ladies,
And strange events that never could have happened,
Or dreamy legends of the " Table Round,"
In slipshod verse, sung by the Laureate flat :
I write of facts that everybody knows of,
And of myself, a 'man without a name—
A man of truths more than a man of facts,—
The inspirations of poetic instinct,
And not the dull deductions of pure reason.
  The Christmas season has come round again ;
The air is mild, the days are fine and cheery ;
But mighty rains have deluged all the land,
And blustering gales made sport of chimney-pots ;
While many a gallant ship has come to grief,

And many a sailor perished in the waves ;
But nought can mar the joyousness of Christmas.
This is the festival of man's redemption ;
At this glad season all are of one mind ;
One sentiment pervades all hearts alike ;
The joy of sweet, though brief, re-union.
The railway trains drag heavily with their loads ;
The engines pant with shoals of passengers ;
Children and parents, brothers and sisters meet ;
Cousins by dozens throng the Christmas fire ;
Lovers rush madly to each other's arms ;
Far-separated friends are brought together,
Drawn by a universal magnetism ;
Nor cold nor frost can chill youth's eagerness,
Nor rain nor fog can damp the general ardour ;
Good wishes, smiling faces, kindly greetings,
Kisses and shakings of the hand abound ;
Good cheer, if ever, now is to be seen
In every English home, or ought to be.
Roast beef, which is the pride of Englishmen ;
Plum-pudding, one of England's institutions ;
Mince-pies, the regular patties of the period ;
Nuts, oranges, apples, almonds and raisins, figs,
Sweet-meats and bon-bons, snap-dragons and kisses,
Gladden the palates of both old and young ;
And merry Christmas games enliven them,
Riddles and romps, charades and madrigals ;
Everywhere gleams the emblem of the season,
Green holly, with its clusters of red beads,
Slyly entwined with sacred mistletoe ;

The Christmas-tree holds out its tempting baits;
Enjoyment is the order of the day ;
So England celebrates, with heart and hope,
The birth of the holy Babe of Bethlehem,
Laid in a manger on sweet-scented hay,
And lulled to sleep by songs of heavenly angels.
   Farewell old Eighteen hundred sixty-eight !—
A year of memorable agitations,
Both of the earth and of the minds of men.
Vast regions have been rudely tossed and shaken,
And populous cities levelled with the dust ;
While burning mountains rolled down rivers of fire.
All human passions have been greatly stirred :
Even within this happy isle of England
Events of vast concernment have occurred.
The year will leave us better than it found us.
To me it has been one of happiness :
A year of deep and heartfelt gratulation,
To see the triumph of the right and just—
A year of peaceful, sweet, domestic joy,
With the fond mate whom Heaven has given to me—
A year of pleasant literary labour.
I have achieved the work I set myself,
Written at various times, in various moods,
Touching on many human interests,
Linked to events of deathless history,
To names of men of permanent renown,
To spots associated with great events,
And scenes whose beauty will for ever charm.
This song, which I designed in my lone lot

To be the picture of my " setting sun,"
Has changed into a kind of happy sunrise,
And yet may prove the dayspring of my fame.
The matter has come freely to my pen,
Distilling often with the dews of night ;
The garden of my brain has brought forth freely
After the fallow of so many years,
The simple fruits and flowers I love the best.
Seeds sown long years ago have sprung to life.
The poem which I long desired to write,
And often tried, but never could begin,
Failing from over-pitching of the key,
At length has sprung spontaneously to light :
Events, and not my will, have shaped its substance.
And if this offspring of the intellect
Which the great Giver has bestowed on me
May but survive while our brave language lasts,—
A favourite book of healthy-minded people—
I want no child of mine to bear my name,
No lawyer, soldier, priest or simpleton.
    This is the last day of the fading year !
Though keen the winter's morn with sparkling frost,
The cloudless sun shines forth rejoicingly,
Opening a glorious prospect of the future ;
Winter gives timely promise of the summer,
And spring delightful hope of golden autumn.
The trees are leafless, but the swelling uplands
Are tinted with the sweetest blush of green ;
The prelude of another bounteous harvest.
The well-drilled army of green-coated soldiers

Stand in close ranks armed with their pointed spears,
Millions of these bright spears are lifted up
For man's behoof, each in its little rank ;
These are the innocent spears that shed no blood
At bad men's bidding, nor make desolate
The widow's bosom, and the orphan's home ;
Not the sharp spears of all-destroying war,
Which drive back nations into barbarism,
And blast the brightest prospects óf a people,
But the green spears of wheat, which hold out promise
Of peace and plenty in the coming year—
Abundant food to bless the heart of man :
These are the trusty spears to save our country !
But, as for me, I tremble for the future ;
Not at the spears of wheat, or spears of war ;
There are more terrible spears than these for me ;
I tremble at the spears of the keen critics.
I am about to face the heartless world,
Bearing my little volume in my hand.
I shall go forth blindfolded to be shot at ;
The Philistines will quickly be upon me.
A host of dreadful critics hem me round ;
Grimacing monkeys stand behind my back !
No avenue is open for escape,
Except by base retreat, and that I scorn.

Here endeth Book the Seventh, which is the last
Of this my long, and strange, yet truthful poem.
My work is finished with the closing year.
The hollow-sounding and deep-toned church-bells

That soon will grimly toll the old year out,
Will ring the new year in to-morrow morning,
With noisy peals of heartless merriment.
The Setting Sun declines in lowering clouds,
With a few beams of glory breaking through,
But spreading a thick curtain o'er the future,
With not a peep-hole to reveal its story,
Nought to assure us of its certainties,
Only a glimmer of its probabilities;
Not even giving, to the inquisitive public,
The slightest indication or forewarning
That this, my little book, will soon come forth
Into the bleak cold world, with the spring lambs,
Tremblingly, timidly, innocently, playfully,
An English poem, unlike any other.

F. B. KITTO, PRINTER, BISHOPSGATE WITHOUT, LONDON.

Now ready, second edition, corrected and enlarged, price 5s.

THE SETTING SUN,

A Poem in Seven Books.

By JAMES HURNARD.

LONDON: F. B. KITTO, 5, BISHOPSGATE STREET WITHOUT, E.C.

Opinions of the Press.

THIS is no common book. Its title is indicative, not of the
subject, but of the age of the author. This record of commonplace events is made the vehicle for conveying opinions and
observations by no means commonplace. Lord Chesterfield
advised his son to read no books he could not quote. He might
have studied this with advantage, since it abounds with terse
and epigrammatic lines, and similes as original as forcible.
Here and there the author communicates great truths, and we
come upon them unawares, led up by details so trivial they
would else be worthless the recounting. " The Setting Sun "
runs out of the common category. It contains gems of thought
which are true poetry whatever be the setting. To end where
we might have begun, the poet opens with the question—

"What can I do to benefit mankind?
    *   *   *   *   *   *   *
'Tis little one can do, yet not a zephyr
Goes sighing softly through the forest leaves
But helps the mighty processes of nature ;
And not a wavelet curls on the seashore

But serves to form the bounds of earth and ocean ;
And thus the poet, dropping here and there
The seeds of truth and beauty, must do good."
Can we find anything finer in Cowper or Thomson ?—*Durham Chronicle.*

It has a claim to almost unapproachable originality—in rhythm, metre and unique composition, it has we believe, no parallel in modern English literature. . . The author has steered a bold and untrodden course, eschewing all ordinary rules of composition, and forming a school of his own like other master minds. . . The book is evidently the production of a man of good natural education and ability.—*Aberystwyth Observer.*

"The Setting Sun" is amusing and readable, the lines flow evenly, and there is much that will interest the cultivated and thoughtful, the author being a man of great observation and much experience of life.—*Church Opinion.*

Hurnard wrote this poem to combat false tastes, false styles, and false opinions. It is in the main narrative and descriptive, varied by refined sentiment, philosophical reflection, and stinging satires.—*Rotherham and Masbr'' Advertiser.*

The ear detects in a moment the ring of the true poetic metal. —*Ibid.*

It is a personal poem, or, as a grandiloquent poet would call it, "a Life-drama," and details much of Hurnard's history and experience. As it emanates from the ripe wisdom of age, it may be read with profit by the greatest minds.—*Ibid.*

His feelings are finely expressed in his poetry, which gushes with happiness, gratitude, and benevolence.—*Ibid.*

Unlike all other blank verse, the endings of many lines consist of double syllables. Where the subject is truly poetical in its essence, the language seems naturally to assume the choicest poetic garb. Examples are so numerous that the difficulty is what to choose, and what to leave unnoticed.—*Barnsley Chronicle.*

This remarkable work.—*Ibid.*

He is most poetical in descriptions of external nature. Beauties of this kind are so abundant that we have an excess of poetic wealth to choose from.—*Ibid.*

A poem in blank verse containing much quaint originality of idea, and many passages of great beauty. Many passages throughout the volume will be found to have the true poetic ring. Notwithstanding the strange crotchets which abound, there is much sound sense in the poem, and it will doubtless have many appreciative readers.—*Buckingham Advertiser.*

We cannot refrain from presenting our readers with a few choice extracts from this poetical bouquet.—*Somerset and Wilts Journal.*

The poem, though in a great measure personal, refers to a variety of subjects, all of which are treated in a most happy style, and cannot fail, we think, to interest the public. We think the book cannot fail to have a benefit upon the community at large morally, socially, and politically.—*Yarmouth Independent.*

The author of this poem claims for his work the merit of originality, which it certainly possesses in an eminent degree. He attacks political and social abuses vigorously, and is an uncompromising foe to clerical domination. His numbers appear to combine the simplicity of Wordsworth's earlier ballads with the graphic minuteness of Crabbe's "Tales of the Hall" or "Borough." Though "The Setting Sun" can scarcely rank as a work of first-rate merit, it is replete with high thoughts flowing from a heart of courtesy.—*Guernsey Mail and Telegraph.*

A singular title to a poem and yet an appropriate one when explained. The poem is written in a conversational style, and treats of a great variety of subjects ; the opinions are expressed forcibly, but pleasantly and charitably, as becomes a man whose sun of life is " setting." It is divided into seven books, a startling length for a poem, but there is no heaviness about it. The author's life has evidently been a roving one. His power of description of ocean scenery is a speciality, and he dwells with fond affection on the scenery of Colchester, its ancient ruins and picturesque walks. The circumstances under which Lucas and Lisle, the conquered Royalist·chiefs, were executed after the siege of Colchester, are graphically and feelingly written.— *Essex Telegraph.*

Certainly in the 350 pages we are introduced to a great variety of subjects. None of them are tediously harped upon, the author excites our sympathy as well as interest ; he tells us freely of his childhood, his early love, his joys, his sorrows, his disappointments, his bereavements, and for the most part this is well worked up. When he commenced his books he was a bachelor, and he concluded it amid the joys of wedded life, yet he always appears to have approved of early marriages. Some parts of the poem must have especial charm for the ladies. There is enough of variety to amuse the most fastidious. There are the items of a lawyer's bill (a curiosity, and probably the very first that has ever been rendered into verse), and there are places and events and people shown as in a picture, drawn too with skill though by an enthusiastic and rather daring artist. The poem is with its digressions the true history of the life of its author. He is an Essex man. In his work there is evidence of true poetic sentiment, and this is frequently, concisely and forcibly expressed. There are in the poem some exquisite and beautiful ideas, and good may result from its perusal. It must be satisfactory to observe the unaffected and pious gratitude with which the poet acknowledges his improved circumstances. —*Essex Weekly News.*

LONDON: F. B. KITTO, 5, BISHOPSGATE STREET WITHOUT, E.C.

99 — morals

34
38   1
39,
————
64-68 2 ✓
————
99 ✱   ⌐₃   leave till the end

                              350-1 Christmas
111-12

140-6 B.R.   330 Guy Fawkes
          —⌐₄ Colchester
               rvl.   Elections
191

Literature, Arts, Music
Architecture, Politics, ⌐₅
Physicians, Lawyers
    D + Gladstone
                                    304
                            ⌐₇ (poetry)
          ⌐₆   313
                                matrimony
    setting up
                    283-4

religion

CPSIA information can be obtained at www.ICGtesting.com
Printed in the USA
LVOW10s1617190716

496926LV00022B/864/P

9 781165 122141